Opera in the Viennese Home from Mozart to Rossini

Domestic musical arrangements of opera provide a unique window on the world of nineteenth-century amateur music-making. These arrangements flourished in especially rich variety in early nineteenth-century Vienna. This study reveals ways in which the Viennese culture of musical arrangements opened up opportunities – especially for women – for connoisseurship, education, and sociability in the home, and extended the meanings and reach of public concert life. It takes a novel stance for musicology, prioritising musical arrangements over original compositions and female amateurs' perspectives over those of composers, and asks: what cultural, musical, and social functions did opera arrangements serve in Vienna *c.*1790–1830? Multivalent musical analyses explore ways in which Viennese arrangers tailored large-scale operatic works to the demands and values of domestic consumers. Documentary analysis, using little-studied evidence of private and semi-private music-making, investigates the agency of musical amateurs and reinstates the central importance of women's roles.

NANCY NOVEMBER is a professor of musicology at the University of Auckland. Combining interdisciplinarity and cultural history, her research centres on chamber music around 1800, probing questions of historiography, canonisation, and genre. She is the recipient of a Humboldt Fellowship and three Marsden Grants from the Royal Society of New Zealand Te Apārangi.

Opera in the Viennese Home from Mozart to Rossini

NANCY NOVEMBER
University of Auckland

Shaftesbury Road, Cambridge CB2 8EA, United Kingdom

One Liberty Plaza, 20th Floor, New York, NY 10006, USA

477 Williamstown Road, Port Melbourne, VIC 3207, Australia

314–321, 3rd Floor, Plot 3, Splendor Forum, Jasola District Centre,
New Delhi – 110025, India

103 Penang Road, #05–06/07, Visioncrest Commercial, Singapore 238467

Cambridge University Press is part of Cambridge University Press & Assessment, a department of the University of Cambridge.

We share the University's mission to contribute to society through the pursuit of education, learning and research at the highest international levels of excellence.

www.cambridge.org
Information on this title: www.cambridge.org/9781009409803

DOI: 10.1017/9781009409797

© Nancy November 2024

This publication is in copyright. Subject to statutory exception and to the provisions of relevant collective licensing agreements, no reproduction of any part may take place without the written permission of Cambridge University Press & Assessment.

First published 2024

A catalogue record for this publication is available from the British Library

Library of Congress Cataloging-in-Publication Data
Names: November, Nancy, author.
Title: Opera in the Viennese home from Mozart to Rossini / Nancy November.
Description: [1.] | Cambridge, United Kingdom ; New York, NY : Cambridge University Press, 2023. | Includes bibliographical references and index.
Identifiers: LCCN 2023031390 (print) | LCCN 2023031391 (ebook) | ISBN 9781009409803 (hardback) | ISBN 9781009409827 (paperback) | ISBN 9781009409797 (ebook)
Subjects: LCSH: Music – 18th century – Austria – Vienna – History and criticism. | Music – 19th century – Austria – Vienna – History and criticism. | Music – Social aspects – Austria – Vienna – History – 18th century. | Music – Social aspects – Austria – Vienna – History – 19th century. | Operas – Instrumental settings – History and criticism. | Salons – Austria – Vienna – History. | Women musicians – Austria – Vienna. | Hausmusik – History and criticism. | Opera – 18th century. | Opera – 19th century.
Classification: LCC ML246.8.V6 N68 2023 (print) | LCC ML246.8.V6 (ebook) | DDC 780.9436–dc23/eng/20230707
LC record available at https://lccn.loc.gov/2023031390
LC ebook record available at https://lccn.loc.gov/2023031391

ISBN 978-1-009-40980-3 Hardback

Cambridge University Press & Assessment has no responsibility for the persistence or accuracy of URLs for external or third-party internet websites referred to in this publication and does not guarantee that any content on such websites is, or will remain, accurate or appropriate.

Contents

List of Figures [*page* vi]
List of Tables [viii]
List of Musical Examples [x]
Acknowledgements [xii]

Introduction [1]

1 Opera in the 'Fruitful Age of Musical Translations' [11]

2 *Kenner und Liebhaber*: Meeting the Domestic Market [39]

3 Female Agency in the Early Nineteenth-Century Viennese Musical Salon [73]

4 Canon Formation, Domestication, and Opera [103]

5 Rossini 'As the Viennese Liked It' [137]

6 Industry, Agency, and Opera Arrangements in Czerny's Vienna [182]

Bibliography [231]
Index [247]

Figures

0.1 *Chamber Music*, colour etching by Clemens Kohl after Johann Sollerer, Vienna 1793. Courtesy of Archiv, Bibliothek und Sammlungen der Gesellschaft der Musikfreunde in Wien, shelf mark Bi 1815   [*page* 1]

4.1 *A Schubert Evening in a Vienna Salon* by Julius Schmid (1897). Centralised women (next to Franz Schubert, at the piano) from left to right: Katharina Fröhlich; the actor and singer Sophie Müller (standing); Anna Fröhlich (partly hidden); Barbara Fröhlich; Schubert; Josephine Fröhlich (with music in her hands). Courtesy of Alamy Images   [110]

4.2 Handwritten programme for a private evening entertainment in the home of the Viennese lawyer Ignaz von Sonnleithner on 1 December 1820. Courtesy of Archiv, Bibliothek und Sammlungen der Gesellschaft der Musikfreunde in Wien, shelf mark 10520/133   [114]

4.3 Set design by Maler Militz for *Fernand Cortez* by Gaspare Spontini, staged at the Vienna State Opera in 1893. Historisches Museum der Stadt Wien. Courtesy of Di Agostini Editore/agefotostock   [130]

5.1 Bar graph showing repertoire performed at the Kärntnertortheater, 1811–30, by genre   [141]

5.2 Title-page engraving of a solo piano arrangement of excerpts from *Il barbiere di Seviglia* (Vienna: Sauer & Leidesdorf, 1823). Courtesy of Österreichische Nationalbibliothek Musiksammlung, shelf mark MS8875-qu.4°/4   [147]

5.3 Leidesdorf & Sauer's 'Collection of Complete Operas' series title page (Collection des Operas completes de Rossini, 1820s). Courtesy of Österreichische Nationalbibliothek Musiksammlung, shelf mark MS70339-qu.4°/4   [152]

5.4 Title page of *Euterpe: eine Reihe moderner und vorzüglich beliebter Tonstücke zur Erheiterung in Stunden der Musse* (Anton Diabelli & Comp., 1818–45). Courtesy of Österreichische Nationalbibliothek Musiksammlung, shelf mark MS1117-qu.4°/10   [159]

5.5 Title page from *Trifles: Arranged for Piano-Forte with Consideration of Small Hands* (*Kleinigkeiten für Piano-Forte mit Berücksichtigung kleiner Hände eingerichtet*), vol. 2 (Vienna: Diabelli, 1830). Courtesy of

List of Figures vii

Österreichische Nationalbibliothek Musiksammlung, shelf mark
MS48.296–4° [166]

6.1 Title page from *Die musikalische Biene: Ein Unterhaltungs Blatt für das Piano Forte* (1819–20), volume 3 (Vienna: K. K. Hoftheater, 1819), with close-ups showing the names of composers on flowers and leaves (left to right: (a) Paër, Haydn, Mozart; (b) Spontini, Rossini, Salieri, Paisiello, Weigl, Cherubini, Boieldieu). Courtesy of Österreichische Nationalbibliothek Musiksammlung, shelf mark MS9687-qu.4°/3 [183]

6.2 Title page from Carl Czerny's *Dix grandes fantasies concertantes pour deux pianos sur des motifs choisis des opéras classiques et modernes*, Op. 797 (Hamburg: Cranz, c.1840), Courtesy of Österreichische Nationalbibliothek Musiksammlung, shelf mark MS 15.481–4°/1 [186]

6.3 The contents of the first fifty volumes of the weekly *Wiener musikalisches Pfennig-Magazin für das Piano-Forte allein*, edited by Czerny, series 2 (Vienna: Haslinger, 1835), dedicated to broadening the repertoire of amateur pianists. Courtesy of Österreichische Nationalbibliothek Musiksammlung, shelf mark MS26.641–4°/1 [199]

6.4 Title page of a collection of operas arranged for piano 'mit Hinweglassung der Worte', published by Haslinger and advertised in Czerny's *Pfennig-Magazin*, series 2 (1835). Courtesy of Österreichische Nationalbibliothek Musiksammlung, shelf mark MS26.641–4°/1A [201]

6.5 Title page, *Le goût moderne: Nouveau recueil de rondeaux, variations et impromptus sur les thêmes les plus élégants des nouveaux opéras*, for piano four hands, Op. 398 (a periodical publication from Diabelli, 1830s). Courtesy of Österreichische Nationalbibliothek Musiksammlung, shelf mark L18. Kaldeck 42051–4°/1 [215]

6.6 Sebastian Gutzwiller's *Basler Familienkonzert* (1849). Courtesy of Alamy Images [224]

6.7 Moritz von Schwind, Wilhelm August Rieder, and Anna Hönig (left, right, below), shown in a circle of Schubert friends at a 'Schubertiade'. Sketch by Moritz von Schwind (1868), from memory. Courtesy of Alamy Images [225]

Tables

1.1 John Platoff's list of the most popular operas in Vienna, 1783–92 (with my annotations)   [*page* 14]

1.2 List of Mozart's compositions in the year 1786 (opera-related compositions are shown in bold)   [17]

1.3 Numbers of opera arrangements of the top fourteen composers represented in Viennese opera performances in Johann Traeg's 1799 catalogue   [23]

1.4 Numbers of opera arrangements of the top eight operas represented in Viennese opera performances in 1783–92 in Traeg's 1799 catalogue   [24]

1.5 Arrangements for string quartet of operas and ballets ('Quartetti aus Opern und Ballets für 2 Violini, Viola e Vllo. arrangirt') in Traeg's 1799 music catalogue; 'g/G' indicates a manuscript; 'M' indicates a publication from Mainz   [28]

1.6 Wind ensembles of eight parts ('Harmonie-Stücke zu 8 Stimmen') in Traeg's 1799 music catalogue; 'g/G' indicates a manuscript   [29]

1.7 Mozart's *Figaro* arranged, published by Artaria & Comp., Vienna, 1798–1806   [34]

1.8 List of Mozart opera arrangements published by Traeg & Son, in ascending order of plate number   [35]

2.1 *Figaro* arrangements available in Traeg's 1799 catalogue, annotated according to the possible gender of performers   [43]

2.2 Ignaz von Mosel's list of the best male and female singers in Vienna (in order of importance) c.1800, categorised as artists and professors (*Künstler und Professoren*)   [54]

2.3 (a) Opera arrangements advertised by the forerunner to Diabelli and Cappi's Viennese firm, 1817; (b) Opera arrangements advertised by the forerunner to Diabelli and Cappi's Viennese firm, 1816–18   [56]

2.4 *Le nozze di Figaro* numbers included in Artaria's 1806 arrangement, listing both the scene number in the respective act and the song number. Bracketed tempo indications in the first column are indicative only   [66]

4.1 Michele Clark's list of the total number of pieces arranged from Rossini's operas and advertised as available for sale from 1815 to 1830 from Viennese publishers   [134]
5.1 *Journal für Quartetten Liebhaber*, published by Chemische Druckerei, opera arrangements in the first three volumes, 1807   [139]
5.2 Most popular opera composers at the Kärntnertortheater, 1811–30   [142]
5.3 Most popular operas at the Kärntnertortheater, 1811–30   [142]
5.4 Manuscript arrangement by Franz Alexander Pössinger of Rossini's *Tancredi*, compared to the original score (Österreichische Nationalbibliothek Musiksammlung shelf mark Mus.Hs.2991)   [154]
5.5 *Euterpe für das Pianoforte*, first volumes (Vienna: Cappi & Diabelli, 1819)   [162]
5.6 Advertisement for *Euterpe*, translating 'Viennese currency' (*Wiener Wahrung* or W. W.) into the new coins (*Conventions Münzen* or C. M.)   [163]
5.7 Other series from Diabelli in the 1820s, featuring opera arrangements   [165]
6.1 Mozart-opera-related publications that appeared in the publishing catalogue of Senefelder, Steiner, and Haslinger in the 1830s and 1840s   [191]
6.2 Excerpt from Anton Ziegler's *Addressen-Buch*, showing the Clary family pianists (and one singer) in Vienna in 1823   [194]
6.3 A selection of Czerny's arrangements by publication date, showing the range of genres he covered in his career   [207]

Musical Examples

2.1 *Der Tiroler Wastel*, by Jakob Haibel, arranged for *Harmonie* by Franz Joseph Rosinack Schörtzel (fl. 1800), bars 1–9   [*page* 58]

2.2 Papageno's aria 'Der Vogelfänger bin ich ja', bars 1–14 (bar 14 is missing in the original), from an early nineteenth-century quartet arrangement (anonymous) of Mozart's *Die Zauberflöte* (Paris: Sieber, n.d.)   [60]

2.3 'Porgi amor' from Mozart's *Le nozze di Figaro* (Cavatina, No. 11), arranged for string quartet in Artaria's complete arrangement of *Figaro* (Vienna: Artaria, 1806), bars 1–25 (editorial slurs are shown with dotted lines)   [61]

2.4 Excerpt from the Finale in Mollo's string-quartet arrangement of Mozart's *Don Giovanni*, Act 2 Scene 15, bars 1–21 (editorial dynamics are shown in parentheses)   [64]

2.5 String-quartet arrangement of 'Non più andrai' from Mozart's *Le nozze di Figaro* (Vienna: Artaria, 1806), bars 57–9   [67]

2.6 Belmont's first aria in Mollo's piano reduction of *Die Entführung aus dem Serail* (Vienna, n.d.), bars 20–36   [70]

2.7 Orchestral introduction to 'Marten aller Arten' in Mollo's piano reduction of *Die Entführung aus dem Serail*, bars 1–28   [71]

4.1 From Spontini's *Fernand Cortez*, in *Anthologie musicale ou Recueil périodique pour le Forte-Piano / Musikalischer-Sammler für das Forte-Piano* (Vienna: Artaria & Co., n.d.): (a) Introduction, bars 1–24; (b) Allegro vivace, bars 1–22   [127]

4.2 Anton Wranitzky's string-quartet arrangement of Spontini's *Fernand Cortez* (Vienna: Bureau de Musique des Theatre, n.d.), Overture, bars 1–22   [129]

5.1 Cavatina 'Di tanti palpiti' from Rossini's *Tancredi*, arranged by Diabelli for voice and guitar in *Philomele: eine Sammlung der beliebtesten Gesänge mit Begleitung der Guitare* [sic] (Vienna: Diabelli, 1819), bars 1–10   [149]

5.2 Joseph Mayseder, *Variations Concertantes pour le Piano-Forte et Violon: Sur la Cavatine 'Di tanti palpiti'*, Op. 16 (Vienna: Artaria, c.1820), variation six, bars 1–24   [158]

5.3   Mauro Giuliani, variations for two guitars on 'Di tanti palpiti' from *Tancredi* (Vienna: Weigl, n.d.), opening of third variation, guitar 1, bars 1–7   [159]

5.4   Excerpts from Rossini's *Otello* for piano four hands, in *Euterpe: eine Reihe moderner und vorzüglich beliebter Tonstücke zur Erheiterung in Stunden der Musse* (Vienna: Cappi and Diabelli, 1819): (a) Andante sostenuto; (b) Vivace marziale (bars 1–9), Österreichische Nationalbibliothek shelf mark MS1117-qu.4°/10   [160]

5.5   (a) Trio, No. 2 from *Le siège de Corinthe* in Franz Schoberlechner (Vienna: Artaria and Haslinger, 1826) piano reduction, bars 1–19; (b) Trio, No. 2 in Haslinger and Artaria's *Le siège de Corinthe, zweckmässig bearbeitet für die Jugend*, bars 1–35   [167]

5.6   (a) Preghiera finale in Haslinger and Artaria's *Le siège de Corinthe, zweckmässig bearbeitet für die Jugend* (Vienna: Artaria and Haslinger, 1827); (b) Finale based on the Preghiera in Thalberg's Op. 3, *Impromptu pour le piano-forte sur les thêmes favoris de l'opéra: Le siège de Corinthe* (Vienna: Artaria, c.1828), bars 1–22 and 144–9   [170]

5.7   Ignaz Moscheles' piano parody on 'Di tanti palpiti' from *Tancredi* (Vienna: Steiner, 1817), bars 1–64   [175]

6.1   Introduction, Leopold Jansa, *Hommage à Mozart: Introduction et Variations sur un thême de Mozart* (Vienna: Senefelder, Steiner, and Haslinger, 1842), bars 1–6 and 21–3   [192]

6.2   Excerpts from Bellini's *La Sonnambula* showing 'browsing' from the score: (a) Czerny's *Fantaisie 3ième sur les motifs favoris de l'op[é]ra Sonnambula de Bellini* for solo piano, bars 1–32 (Vienna: Diabelli, 1833); (b) full orchestral score, bars 1–7 and 55–62   [209]

6.3   Czerny Op. 196 for solo piano: *Introduction, Variations et Rondo für piano forte über die beliebte Cavatine v. Giuseppe Nicolini (Or che son vicino a te) gesungen von Mad. Pasta in Wien bei Vorstellung der Oper: Tancred* (Vienna: Diabelli, 1829), showing end of Introduction, with the singer's ornamental embellishments; and Allegretto grazioso, bars 1–18   [214]

6.4   Czerny's four-hand piano arrangements of the *Variations Brillant* on *Il crociato in Egitto* by Meyerbeer, Op. 125 (Vienna: Haslinger, 1826), bars 1–16   [217]

6.5   From Czerny's *Souvenir théâtral*, Fantaisie (No. 1) on Meyerbeer's *Robert le diable* (Vienna: Diabelli, 1832), bars 1–32   [219]

6.6   Opening of Czerny's arrangements of Bellini's *Norma* in: (a) *Bibliothek für die Jugend* (Vienna: Haslinger, c.1835) bars 1-21; (b) *Souvenir théâtral* (Vienna: Diabelli, 1833), bars 1–21   [220]

6.7   Overture to *Alphonse and Estrella* for piano four hands, created for and dedicated to Anna Hönig by Franz Schubert, Op. 52 (Vienna: Sauer and Leidesdorf, 1826), bars 1–23   [228]

Acknowledgements

I recall the time well. It was the spring of 2001 and I sat nervously in the ground-floor seminar room of Lincoln Hall, Cornell University, being grilled by my dissertation advisors during the 'A' exam (Admission to PhD Candidacy). One question threw me right off target: 'Nancy, you study instrumental chamber music from the period around 1800, with a focus on Vienna: what do you think people generally enjoyed listening to back then?' My mind raced over all the material I had studied. String quartets ... Haydn, Mozart, Beethoven ... and thankfully alighted on Schubert. I knew that part of the answer was vocal music – and not so much the original chamber music I had studied. And yet I also knew that vocal ideas and aesthetic penetrated that 'instrumental' music through and through.

I passed. Got the degree. Water under the bridge. But the niggling question would not go away. So, my treasured dissertation committee, please find attached, in the following pages, my belated answer to your question. This book is dedicated to you, Neal Zaslaw, James Webster, Neil Saccamano, and Annette Richards (who posed the question).

Numerous other people have helped me formulate this answer. Key among these were librarians at the Austrian National Library; colleagues speaking at the conference 'Women's Agency in Schubert's Vienna', notably Andrea Lindmayr-Brandl; colleagues and librarians at Beethoven-Haus, Bonn, especially Christine Siegert; and expert readers, particularly Edward Klorman. My thanks also go to my research students, several of whom worked on related topics or offered considerable support as research assistants: Modi Deng, Sam Girling, Imogen Morris, Aleisha Ward, and Denise Hayes. Janet Hughes and Janet November offered numerous useful editorial comments.

This project was made possible by generous support from the Marsden Fund of the Royal Society of New Zealand Te Apārangi.

Introduction

At first glance, Figure 0.1 might be taken for a performance of original chamber music, not opera; and today we might be inclined to see male dominance rather than female leadership. But the facts behind it are almost certainly quite otherwise. Johann Sollerer's depiction of private-sphere music-making in Vienna in 1793 shows a sextet of five male musicians around a woman seated at a fortepiano, almost certainly playing an arrangement of Papageno's aria from Wolfgang Amadeus Mozart's *Die Zauberflöte*, 'Der Vogelfänger bin ich ja', led from the fortepiano played by a woman. Not only the instrumentation, especially the flute, but also the larger context points to this.

Figure 0.1 *Chamber Music*, colour etching by Clemens Kohl after Johann Sollerer, Vienna 1793. Courtesy of Archiv, Bibliothek und Sammlungen der Gesellschaft der Musikfreunde in Wien, shelf mark Bi 1815

In 1802, Ludwig van Beethoven called his era a 'fruitful age of translations', referring to the vogue for arrangements of public music for performance in the home.[1] Of all the many arrangements of various types of music produced in Vienna in his era, opera arrangements enjoyed the greatest popularity and were arguably the most 'fruitful' in terms of their variety, utility, and dissemination. So, for example, in Johann Traeg's Viennese music catalogue of 1799, opera arrangements in their various forms more or less take over the chamber music section. And *Die Zauberflöte*, which was particularly popular at this time, appeared thirty-five times in the catalogue, in nineteen different kinds of musical arrangement.[2]

The musical arrangements discussed in this book are mainly translations of operas into chamber music for small-scale ensembles, which was the most common type in Vienna around 1800. These opera arrangements include many without text and many more with text, the latter mainly for piano. The final chapter refers to the increasingly heavy emphasis on piano as the preferred medium for arrangement in the early to mid-nineteenth century; and to the increasingly loose relation between the original work and music derived from it, like the then tremendously popular variations, potpourris, paraphrases, and fantasies based on operas.

Scholars have often ignored these opera arrangements or dismissed them as second-rate. But they offer a unique window on a mostly hidden world of richly diverse amateur music-making, and especially on women's roles. This study takes a novel approach, privileging opera arrangements over original operatic compositions, and the perspectives of amateur performers (defined more closely in Chapter 2) over those of composers. Several studies of opera arrangements from the era in question have already been published, focusing on particular composers or particular arrangement forms; in these, the interest lies in arrangements' function as

---

[1] Ludwig van Beethoven, *Wiener Zeitung* 87 (30 October 1802), p. 3916. Translations from German are my own unless noted. On 'translation' as applied to arrangements see Stephen Davies, 'Versions of Musical Works and Literary Translations', in *Musical Understandings and Other Essays on the Philosophy of Music* (Oxford: Oxford University Press, 2011), pp. 177–87; Jonathan Kregor, *Liszt as Transcriber* (New York, NY: Cambridge University Press, 2010); and Peter Szendy, *Arrangements, dérangements: La transcription musicale aujourd'hui* (Paris: Ircam L'Harmattan, 2000). On 'cultural translation' *c.*1800 see Philip V. Bohlman, 'Translating Herder Translating: Cultural Translation and the Making of Modernity', in Jane F. Fulcher (ed.), *The Oxford Handbook of the New Cultural History of Music* (Oxford: Oxford University Press, 2011), pp. 501–22.

[2] Alexander Weinmann (ed.), *Johann Traeg: Die Musikalienverzeichnisse von 1799 und 1804* (Vienna: Universal Edition, 1973).

reception documents.[3] This book differs in that it considers arrangements' multiple functions, and 'end users' – *salonnières* and performers, rather than the original composers. Two questions drive the study: what were the cultural, musical, and social functions of opera arrangements in Vienna *c*.1790–1830? And what does this culture of musical arrangements tell us about musical and social ideals and agency in this period, particularly as they concern women?

This book explores the performance and functions of opera arrangements in Vienna over fifty years around 1800, roughly from 1781 (when Mozart arrived in Vienna) to 1827–8 (when Schubert and Beethoven died). The final chapter considers the period immediately thereafter. Vienna around 1800 is nowadays mainly seen as the seat of high-Classical culture, and the start of the Romantic era in music. The idea that musical works demand fidelity to the original, in performance and study, is part of a package of modern assumptions.[4] But this dominant understanding of Viennese music in fact emerged gradually,[5] eclipsing other approaches to musical works and musicality which are explored in detail in this book. Although a reviewer from 1829 decried musical arrangements as 'derangements' and an 'epidemic addiction', he also recognised them as a productive, transformative part of musical culture.[6] Opera arrangements fed into key developments in Viennese music culture at this time, including

---

[3] In particular Andrea Klitzing, *Don Giovanni unter Druck: Die Verbreitung der Mozart-Oper als instrumentale Kammermusik im deutschsprachigen Raum bis 1850* (Göttingen: V & R Unipress, 2020); Silke Leopold, 'Von Pasteten und Don Giovanni's Requiem: Opernbearbeitungen', in Silke Leopold (ed.), *Musikalische Metamorphosen: Formen und Geschichte der Bearbeitung* (Kassel: Bärenreiter, 2000), pp. 86–93; Herbert Schneider, 'L'arrangement d'opéras pour quatuor à cordes: Le cas de Guillaume Tell de Rossini', in Joann Élert, Etienne Jardin, and Patrick Taïeb (eds.), *Quatre siècles d'édition musicale: Mélanges offerts à Jean Gribenski* (Brussels: Peter Lang, 2014), pp. 229–40; and the essays in Hans-Joachim Hinrichsen and Klaus Pietschmann (eds.), *Jenseits der Bühne: Bearbeitungs- und Rezeptionsformen der Oper im 19. und 20. Jahrhundert* (Kassel: Bärenreiter, 2011).

[4] See especially Lydia Goehr, *The Imaginary Museum of Musical Works: An Essay in the Philosophy of Music*, rev. ed. (Oxford: Oxford University Press, 2007). For relevant critique see: Raymond Erickson (ed.), *Schubert's Vienna* (New Haven, CT: Yale University Press, 1997); and Robert Pichl, Clifford A. Bernd, and Margarete Wagner (eds.), *The Other Vienna: The Culture of Biedermeier Austria* (Vienna: Lehner, 2002).

[5] See Keith Chapin, 'The Visual Traces of a Discourse of Ineffability: Late Eighteenth-Century German Published Writing on Music', in Cliff Eisen and Alan Davison (eds.), *Late Eighteenth-Century Music and Visual Culture* (Turnhout: Brepols, 2017), pp. 123–53; and Martha Woodmansee, *The Author, Art, and the Market: Rereading the History of Aesthetics* (New York, NY: Columbia University Press, 1994).

[6] Ignaz R. von Seyfried, 'Louis van Beethoven: Troisième grande Sinfonie en *ut* mineur, (c-moll) Oeuvre 67; arrangée pour Pianoforte, avec accompagnement de Flûte, Violon, et Violoncelle, part J. N. Hummel ...', *Caecilia: Eine Zeitschrift für die musikalische Welt* 10/39 (1829), pp. 174–8.

musical institutions, concert life, the role of women in music-making, and emerging ideologies, such as serious listening and the concept of the musical work. Opera arrangements destined for private performance by amateurs helped keep operas in performance and in listeners' minds; in these ways they also contributed to canon formation.

Amateur music-making has remained hidden to us because music historians since the mid-nineteenth century have concentrated largely on public-sphere musical phenomena: the formation of the classical canon of music and the emergence of concert life.[7] This emphasis on the public sphere became central to Western music histories, and persists. But it is particularly unrepresentative of Vienna *c.*1800, where large public assemblies, including symphony concerts, were often forbidden. Instead, Viennese music-making flourished in the home both before and after the Napoleonic Wars, in the social isolation caused by invasion, surveillance, censorship, and a cholera epidemic. And much of this Viennese domestic music consisted of arrangements – especially of operas, but also of ballets, concertos, symphonies, and so on – although scholars of chamber music focus almost exclusively on original compositions.[8] Even researchers focusing on nineteenth-century arrangements have missed the critical potential of arrangement studies by generally maintaining the 'composer-and-masterworks' paradigm.[9] They

---

[7] On Vienna see Eduard Hanslick, *Geschichte des Concertwesens in Wien* (Vienna: Braumüller, 1869). See also Leon Botstein, 'The Patrons and Publics of the Quartets: Music, Culture, and Society in Beethoven's Vienna', in Robert Winter and Robert L. Martin (eds.), *The Beethoven Quartet Companion* (Berkeley, CA: University of California Press, 1994), pp. 77–109; Alice M. Hanson, *Musical Life in Biedermeier Vienna* (Cambridge: Cambridge University Press, 1985); David Wyn Jones, *Music in Vienna: 1700, 1800, 1900* (Woodbridge: Boydell & Brewer, 2016); Jones, *The Symphony in Beethoven's Vienna* (Cambridge: Cambridge University Press, 2006); William Weber, *Music and the Middle Class: The Social Structure of Concert Life in London, Paris and Vienna between 1830 and 1848*, 2nd ed. (Aldershot: Ashgate, 2004); and Mary S. Morrow, *Concert Life in Haydn's Vienna: Aspects of a Developing Musical and Social Institution* (Stuyvesant, NY: Pendragon, 1989).

[8] Briefly addressed in my *Cultivating String Quartets in Beethoven's Vienna* (Woodbridge: Boydell & Brewer, 2017), especially pp. 65–76 and 103–6.

[9] Christopher Hogwood, 'In Praise of Arrangements: the "Symphony Quintetto"', in Otto Biba and David Wyn Jones (eds.), *Studies in Music History Presented to H. C. Robbins Landon on His Seventieth Birthday* (London: Thames and Hudson, 1996), pp. 82–104; Hans Grüß, 'Bearbeitung – Arrangement – Instrumentation als Form der Aneignung musikalischer Werke von Beethoven bis Schubert', in Andreas Michel (ed.), *Ansichtssachen: Notate, Aufsätze, Collagen* (Altenburg: Kamprad, 1999), pp. 387–92; Walter Koller and Helmut Hell, *Aus der Werkstatt der Wiener Klassiker: Bearbeitungen Haydns, Mozarts und Beethovens* (Tutzing: Schneider, 1975); Michael Ladenburger, 'Aus der Not eine Tugend? Beethovens Symphonien in Übertragungen für kleinere Besetzungen', in *Von der Ersten bis zur Neunten: Beethovens Symphonien im Konzert und im Museum* (Bonn: Beethoven-Haus, 2008), pp. 17–29; Mark Kroll (ed.), *Twelve Select Overtures, Arranged for Pianoforte, Flute, Violin and Violoncello by J. N. Hummel*, Recent Researches in the Music of the 19th and Early 20th

emphasise canonical composers (Haydn, Mozart, and Beethoven) and genres (the symphony). And there is a focus in previous scholarship on arrangements from the later nineteenth century.[10]

This book offers critical insights into the complex interrelation of public concert life with private and semi-private music-making,[11] revising our understanding of these spheres, and reinstating the central importance of

---

Centuries, vol. 35 (Middleton, WI: A-R Editions, 2003); Kroll (ed.), *Mozart's* Haffner *and* Linz *Symphonies, Arranged for Pianoforte, Flute, Violin and Violoncello by J. N. Hummel*, Recent Researches in the Music of the 19th and Early 20th Centuries, vol. 29 (Madison, WI: A-R Editions, 2000); my *Beethoven's Symphonies Arranged for the Chamber: Sociability, Reception, and Canon Formation* (Cambridge: Cambridge University Press, 2021); Nancy November, 'Performing, Arranging, and Rearranging the Eroica: Then and Now', in November (ed.), *The Cambridge Companion to the* Eroica *Symphony* (Cambridge: Cambridge University Press, 2020), pp. 221–38; November (ed.), *Chamber Arrangements of Beethoven's Symphonies. Part 1: Symphonies Nos. 1, 3, and 5 Arranged for Quartet Ensemble*, Recent Researches in Nineteenth-Century Music, vol. 75 (Middleton, WI: A-R Editions, 2019); November (ed.), *Chamber Arrangements of Beethoven's Symphonies, Part 2:* Wellington's Victory *and Symphonies Nos. 7 and 8 Arranged for String Quintet*, Recent Researches in Nineteenth-Century Music, vol. 77 (Middleton, WI: A-R Editions, 2019); November (ed.), *Chamber Arrangements of Beethoven's Symphonies, Part 3: Symphonies Nos. 2, 4, and 6 Arranged for Large Ensembles*, Recent Researches in Nineteenth-Century Music, vol. 78 (Middleton, WI: A-R Editions, 2020); Matthew Oswin, 'Beethoven's "Kreutzer" Sonata: Nineteenth-Century Art of Arrangement – One Piece, Three Ways', MMus thesis (Victoria University of Wellington, 2013); Wiebke Thormählen, 'Playing with Art: Musical Arrangements as Educational Tools in van Swieten's Vienna', *Journal of Musicology* 27/3 (2010), pp. 342–76; and Uwe Grodd (ed.), *J. N. Hummel: Mozart's Six Grand Symphonies* (Wellington: Artaria Editions, 2015).

[10] See Thomas Christensen, 'Four-Hand Piano Transcription and Geographies of Nineteenth-Century Musical Reception', *Journal of the American Musicological Society* 52/2 (1999), pp. 255–98; Zsuzsanna Domokos, '"Orchestrationen des Pianoforte": Beethovens Symphonien in Transkriptionen von Franz Liszt und seinen Vorgängern', *Studia Musicologica Academiae Scientiarum Hungaricae* 37/2–4 (1996), pp. 249–341; Kara L. van Dine, 'Musical Arrangements and Questions of Genre: A Study of Liszt's Interpretive Approaches', PhD diss. (University of North Texas, 2010); Kregor, *Liszt as Transcriber*; and Mark Kroll, 'On a Pedestal and under the Microscope: The Arrangements of Beethoven Symphonies by Liszt and Hummel', in M. Štefková (ed.), *Franz Liszt und seine Bedeutung in der europäischen Musikkultur* (Bratislava: Ustav hudobnej vedy SAV, 2012), pp. 123–44.

[11] On this subject see also Otto Biba, 'Public and Semi-Public Concerts: Outlines of a Typical "Biedermeier" Phenomenon in Viennese Music History', in Pichl, Bernd and Wagner (eds.), *The Other Vienna*, pp. 257–70; Joachim Eibach, 'Die Schubertiade: Bürgerlichkeit, Hausmusik und das Öffentliche im Privaten', Themenportal Europäische Geschichte (2008), www.europa.clio-online.de/2008/Article=307; Erickson, *Schubert's Vienna*; Jürgen Habermas, *The Structural Transformation of the Public Sphere: An Inquiry into a Category of Bourgeois Society*, trans. Thomas Burger and Frederick Lawrence (Cambridge, MA: MIT Press, 1989); Gisela Mettele, 'Der private Raum als öffentlicher Ort: Geselligkeit im bürgerlichen Haus', in Dieter Hein and Andreas Schultz (eds.), *Bürgerkultur im 19. Jahrhundert: Bildung, Kunst und Lebenswelt* (Munich: Beck, 1996), pp. 155–69; Nicolai Petrat, *Hausmusik des Biedermeier im Blickpunkt der zeitgenössischen musikalischen Fachpresse (1815–1848)* (Hamburg: Wagner, 1986); and Heinrich W. Schwab, 'Kammer-Salon-Konzertsaal: Zu den Aufführungsorten der Kammermusik, insbesondere im 19. Jahrhundert', in Kristina Pfarr, Christoph-Helmut Mahling, and

the roles played by women.[12] Focusing on Viennese musical amateurs, such as the novelist Caroline Pichler and intellectuals like Fanny von Arnstein, I consider opera arrangements not as inferior versions of original operas but as cultural goods in their own right with important social functions, such as enhancing people's well-being through social interaction and fostering women's cultural ownership.[13] The book's emphasis is on middle-class music-making, allowing for the fact that this term is broad and nebulous, and that social mobility was prevalent among the Viennese who might be thought to belong to this group. Indeed the culture of arrangements might have helped in climbing the social ladder, as I discuss in Chapter 4. In Chapters 5 and 6, I make a distinction between the upper echelons of the middle class on the one hand – who had the time, money, and influence to put on relatively lavish musical salons – and, on the other hand, the considerably larger number of musical amateurs who could afford to engage in music-making in the home, but not on a large scale or via regular salons. Opera arrangements offered amateurs agency in respect of education, entertainment, and sociability in the home, and a bridge to public music-making. This was particularly valuable to female amateurs, who otherwise had little say or share in the public spheres of music composition, criticism, and orchestral performance, or indeed in public life more generally.[14]

Karl Böhmer (eds.), *Aspekte der Kammermusik vom 18. Jahrhundert bis zur Gegenwart* (Mainz: Villa Musica, 1998), pp. 9–29.

[12] See also David Ferris, 'Public Performance and Private Understanding: Clara Wieck's Concerts in Berlin', *Journal of the American Musicological Society* 56/2 (2003), pp. 351–408; and Wolfgang Fuhrmann, 'The Intimate Art of Listening: Music in the Private Sphere during the Nineteenth Century', in Christian Thorau and Hansjakob Ziemer (eds.), *The Oxford Handbook of Listening in the 19th and 20th Centuries* (Oxford: Oxford University Press, 2019), pp. 279–83.

[13] See David Gramit, 'Selling the Serious: The Commodification of Music and Resistance to it in Germany (circa 1800)', in William Weber (ed.), *The Musician as Entrepreneur, 1700–1914: Managers, Charlatans, and Idealists* (Bloomington, IN: Indiana University Press, 2004), pp. 81–101; Emily Green and Catherine Mayes (eds.), *Consuming Music: Individuals, Institutions, Communities, 1730–1830* (Rochester, NY: University of Rochester Press, 2017); Marie S. Lott, *The Social Worlds of Nineteenth-Century Chamber Music: Composers, Consumers, Communities* (Urbana-Champaign, IL: University of Illinois Press, 2015); and Bernd Sponheuer, *Musik als Kunst und Nicht-Kunst: Untersuchungen zur Dichotomie von "hoher" und "niederer" Musik im musikästhetischen Denken zwischen Kant und Hanslick*, Kieler Schriften zur Musikwissenschaft (Kassel: Bärenreiter, 1987). See also James Parakilas, 'The Power of Domestication in the Lives of Musical Canons', *Repercussions* 4/1 (1995), pp. 5–25; and Pierre Bourdieu, *Distinction: A Social Critique of the Judgement of Taste*, trans. Richard Nice (Cambridge, MA: Harvard University Press, 1984; original French ed., 1979).

[14] See in particular Gunilla-Friederike Budde, 'Harriet und ihre Schwestern: Frauen und Zivilgesellschaft im 19. Jahrhundert', in Ralph Jessen and Sven Reichardt (eds.), *Zivilgesellschaft als Geschichte: Studien zum 19. und 20. Jahrhundert* (Wiesbaden: VS Verlag für Sozialwissenschaften, 2004), pp. 327–43.

A focal point of the study is the performance of opera arrangements in the Viennese musical salons, where salons are defined as regular heterosocial gatherings of intellectuals, artists, patrons, and professionals, meeting primarily to pursue sociability, as well as knowledge, through music-making. This definition encompasses most of the private and semi-private gatherings that took place in Vienna around this time, although not the numerous, largely undocumented instances of family music-making and small gatherings of performers with no audience present.

Nineteenth-century salon culture in Berlin, England, Paris, and Weimar has been researched; but these studies have seldom extended to Vienna, or to the culture of arrangements.[15] Rebecca Cypess and Nancy Sinkoff look at musicians in Berlin, and Cypess takes account of arrangements. David Wyn Jones provides some suggestive insights on Viennese women's roles in musical culture.[16] And Freia Hoffmann discusses the effect of gender on the choice and meanings of instruments in the nineteenth century.[17] I extend these perspectives in a detailed account of amateurs' agency in Viennese musical culture in these years, through the vehicle of opera arrangements.

Vienna mirrored trends and developments in other important centres of salon culture around this time, including those in Berlin (particularly due to family connections between *salonnières*: Fanny von Arnstein and the Itzig family, for example), and in France. In Viennese society around 1800, salons developed in response to the rapidly changing sociopolitical situation, a process of change that was paralleled elsewhere at different times and in different ways. But in Vienna, a strand of continuity emerges among

---

[15] Especially relevant: Anja Bunzel and Natasha Loges (eds.), *Musical Salon Culture in the Long Nineteenth Century* (Woodbridge: Boydell & Brewer, 2019); Waltraud Heindl, 'People, Class Structure, and Society', in Erickson, *Schubert's Vienna*, pp. 36–54; Chung-Mei Liu, 'Die Rolle der Musik im Wiener Salon bis ca. 1830', master's thesis (University of Vienna, 2013); Helga Peham, *Die Salonièren und die Salons in Wien: 200 Jahre Geschichte einer besonderen Institution* (Vienna: Styria Premium, 2013); Wiebke Thormählen, Jeanice Brooks, and Katrina Faulds, 'Music, Home and Heritage' project, www.rcm.ac.uk/research/projects/musichomeandheritage/; and Phyllis Weliver, *Mary Gladstone and the Victorian Salon: Music, Literature, Liberalism* (Cambridge: Cambridge University Press, 2017).

[16] Rebecca Cypess and Nancy Sinkoff (eds.), *Sara Levy's World: Gender, Judaism, and the Bach Tradition in Enlightenment Berlin* (Rochester, NY: University of Rochester Press, 2018), especially chapter 8, pp. 181–204; and Cypess, *Women and Musical Salons in the Enlightenment* (Chicago, IL: University of Chicago Press, 2022).

[17] Freia Hoffmann, *Instrument und Körper: Die musizierende Frau in der bürgerlichen Kultur* (Frankfurt am Main: Insel Verlag, 1991); Freia Hoffmann, 'Klang und Geschlecht: Instrumentalpraxis von Frauen in der Ideologie des frühen Bürgertums', *Neue Zeitschrift für Musik* 145/12 (1984), pp. 11–16.

changes and differences: there was an abiding taste for performing opera 'in private', and in many and various arrangements.

To understand why this sort of performance took place, and how typical it was, evidence needs be triangulated. I establish key people and situations to clarify the agency exercised by amateurs, and the function performed by arrangements in Viennese society c.1790–1830. In the foreground of this picture are the consumers: influential Viennese musical amateurs like Arnstein and Pichler, and also middle-class men like Leopold von Sonnleithner and Raphael Kiesewetter. I explore these amateurs' dealings with non-human vehicles of agency – the arrangements themselves – and with other key agents in this culture: composers, publishers, reviewers, and arrangers. I compare men's roles with those of women, considering how the network and dynamics of relationships change in this era.

Thus the evidence I analyse includes not only musical works, but a broad array of documents, attesting to manifold actions, intentions, and interactions. Little-studied sources such as iconography, instruments, letters, memoirs, music-instruction manuals, and music collections afford insight into the identities, musical involvements, and tastes of amateurs. I discuss music catalogues as evidence of opera in the home, and then consider salons for which particular repertoire is documented. There are very few salons (or any other kinds of venue for musical performances in the home) for which specific arrangements are mentioned. Most of the specific information as to repertoire relates to the later period covered by this book: the 1810s and 1820s.

Pulling back the curtain on this evidence reveals an extensive part of social and musical life that is highly significant, but probably quite new to the modern reader. To obtain a rounded picture, the book circles around this evidence, looking at it from different perspectives, while moving forward in a broadly chronological fashion. Chapter 1 focuses on the perspective of composers, and starts to build up a sense of the operas that were most popular in various arrangements around 1800. Chapters 2 and 3 centre the musical amateurs, with particular attention to women in Chapter 3. The emphasis shifts to publishers in Chapter 4, with a consideration of the role of domestic arrangements in establishing the systems of opera canon formation. Chapter 5 then returns to the amateurs, now considered as 'the market', exploring the forces that led to the Rossini vogue in 1820s Vienna. Finally, the perspective of arrangers comes to the fore in Chapter 6, Czerny's in particular. The overall effect of this approach is to recentre the home in Viennese music history in the crucial years when public concert life was developing, and to see its inhabitants as key agents and influencers in musical life at this time.

This book concerns cultural history, but analysis of the opera arrangements themselves is central. These arrangements are the main lines of evidence of what was played, by whom, and with what degree of skill. The arrangements reveal the priorities and needs of people of the time. Studying them helps us to answer cultural and sociological questions about Vienna around 1800, building on the work of Jones, Alice Hanson, Mary Sue Morrow, and Tia De Nora.[18] The focus of the musical analysis is on illuminating aspects of agency using representative Viennese opera arrangements from the period. Arrangements studied in detail represent both canonical and lesser-known works, and both well-known and anonymous arrangers. I compare the chosen arrangements with their original versions, and investigate the ways in which arrangers translated large-scale, public works to accord with the wishes and values of amateurs who made music in domestic contexts.

This research complements the work of Edward Klorman on 'multiple agency' in chamber music. He considers how chamber musicians conceived of their musical actions and agency as they played.[19] Workshops with performers formed part of the research for this book, allowing me to take account of the authority of performers as creative agents by considering where the arrangements left room for the performers' own interpretations – of such aspects as instrumentation, technique, performance style, the addition of sung or spoken text, and even staging.

The book offers an 'alternative' history of opera, to balance a history that to date has been centred on public performance, when it considers performance at all. It is a counterpart to the studies of Mary Hunter, James Webster, and several others, who wrote seminal books in the 1990s elevating the importance of *opera buffa* in late eighteenth-century Viennese musical life.[20] This book puts more emphasis on opera performance and functions in cultural life than the 1990s scholarship did; its context opens up the repertoire, including *opera seria*, to a fuller exploration of its meanings. Finally, I open the drawing-room door onto a major space for

---

[18] See n. 7; together with Tia DeNora, 'Musical Patronage and Social Change in Beethoven's Vienna', *American Journal of Sociology* 97/2 (1991), pp. 310–46.

[19] Edward Klorman, *Mozart's Music of Friends: Social Interplay in the Chamber Works* (Cambridge: Cambridge University Press, 2016), especially Chapter 4, pp. 111–55.

[20] Mary Hunter, *The Culture of Opera Buffa in Mozart's Vienna: A Poetics of Entertainment* (Princeton, NJ: Princeton University Press, 1999); James Webster and Mary Hunter (eds.), *Opera Buffa in Mozart's Vienna* (Cambridge: Cambridge University Press, 1997).

opera around 1800 – we start to see not only who was listening to and performing opera, and how widely, but also how and why. Exploring the domestic cultural space allows us to glimpse the motivations and agency of women and of amateurs, especially since the Viennese salons were a primary site for their performance and afforded pathways to leadership roles in the musical public sphere.

1 | Opera in the 'Fruitful Age of Musical Translations'

> If only there were a theatre there that deserved the name – for that is the sole source of my entertainment here.
>
> (Mozart writing about Salzburg, from Vienna[1])

When Mozart arrived in Vienna in June 1781, Europe was in the grip of a vogue for opera, and a more general enthusiasm for theatre. It was quelled somewhat in cities including Salzburg, where Joseph II was imposing reforms including theatre closures, and other limitations on musical life, evidently prompting Mozart to move permanently to Vienna. There the theatres (four of them by 1800) kept the middle- and upper-class Viennese well supplied with their favourite forms of entertainment, except during summer and Lent. The revolutionary and sentimental plots that were fashionable in literature were taken up by librettists and composers, contributing greatly to the popularity of opera, which elaborated these themes and entertained a broad audience. Mozart and his colleagues were well aware of the demand for opera, both on the stage and in the home, and strove to meet it with their compositional and career choices. So the idea of the late eighteenth century as an age of 'Viennese Classicism' dominated by 'pure' instrumental music, as proposed in traditional histories of music, is wrong-headed. Not only was opera what many people wanted to perform, attend, and discuss in late eighteenth-century Vienna; also, the instrumental music composed at this time was often informed by the aesthetics, drama, and even specifically musical elements of opera and theatre.[2]

Moreover, much of the instrumental chamber music that was played in Vienna around 1800 comprised 'chamber' arrangements of opera – that is,

---

[1] Mozart to his father, 26 May 1781; see Wilhelm A. Bauer et al. (eds.), *Mozart: Briefe und Aufzeichnungen; Gesamtausgabe*, 8 vols. (Kassel: Bärenreiter, 1962–2005), vol. 3, *1780–1786* (1962), p. 121.

[2] As I have argued in the case of Beethoven's middle-period quartets: *Beethoven's Theatrical Quartets: Opp. 59, 74 and 95* (Cambridge: Cambridge University Press, 2013); and as Simon P. Keefe has argued in the case of Mozart's piano concertos: *Mozart's Piano Concertos: Dramatic Dialogue in the Age of Enlightenment* (Woodbridge: Boydell & Brewer, 2001).

translations of these large-scale vocal works for performance by a much smaller group of instrumentalists and vocalists than that originally intended, and often in domestic contexts. The period (*c*.1780–*c*.1830) covered by this book was a high point in the 'fruitful age of musical translations'.[3] This trend was driven partly by the social and political circumstances, which made private and semi-private music-making particularly feasible and appealing, creating a demand for chamber music that was within the reach of the enthusiastic amateur. But the vogue for arrangements was also a function of the music-publishing trade and its governance (or lack of it) around 1800.

This chapter explores the vogue for opera in Vienna from the perspectives of composers, and then, through the lens of publishers' catalogues, considers which types of opera and which composers were most liked, and how opera (in various 'musical translations') infiltrated into Viennese homes around 1800.

The Rage for Opera in Late Eighteenth-Century Vienna

When Mozart arrived in Vienna, he was not the pre-eminent figure he would later become. He was just one of a number of composers striving for success in the competitive world of Josephine Vienna.[4] There were no full-time professional orchestras, chamber groups, or regular concert series; these came about only slowly in the early to mid-nineteenth century. Public concerts were rare. They mainly took the form of composers' benefit concerts, held in Lent, when the theatres were not occupied with their usual fare of operas and plays. When Mozart settled in Vienna, he held a number of benefit concerts, at which he performed his piano concertos in particular, and he played piano in the homes of the nobility; but he was drawn to the opera, which he heard at the principal court theatre, the Burgtheater.

The Burgtheater was a focal point in Viennese musical life, and Mozart sought entry into its institutional ranks. In 1778, Joseph II had founded a National Singspiel company, which performed at the Burgtheater. Ignaz Umlauf was appointed Kapellmeister. Umlauf's *Die Bergknappen* was staged and the performance, featuring soprano Caterina Cavalieri, was highly acclaimed. This was the first *Singspiel* by an Austrian composer performed

---

[3] See Introduction, n. 1, Beethoven, *Wiener Zeitung*.
[4] See John Platoff, 'Mozart and His Rivals: Opera in Vienna in Mozart's Time', *Current Musicology* 51 (1993), pp. 105–11, Trinity College Digital Repository, https://digitalrepository.trincoll.edu/facpub/302.

in Vienna. It captured the audience's imagination, with its engaging plot, characterisation, and exceptional singers. Popular was the down-to-earth portrayal of the old miner Walcher (bass), who opposes the suit of the young miner Fritz (tenor) for the hand of his ward Sophie (soprano), whom he himself secretly wishes to marry. It also pleased the audience with the brilliance of Sophie's part and the graphic depiction of the collapsing mine, from which Fritz saves Walcher, ensuring a happy end. In 1781, Antonio Salieri was prevailed upon to write a work (*Die Rauchfangkehrer*) for the National Singspiel. And on arriving in Vienna Mozart found it expedient to set about writing *Die Entführung aus dem Serail* (1782) for the company, which became one of its most successful works. However, the majority of the Singspiel's repertory was drawn from foreign imports, including works of Christoph Willibald Gluck, André Grétry, Pietro Alessandro Guglielmi, and Pasquale Anfossi, performed in German translation.

Ultimately, though, Italian *opera buffa* was what the Viennese audiences most wanted to hear, and what the Emperor ordered. Joseph II gave up his project of building a national theatre in 1783 and ordered an Italian opera company to perform at the Burgtheater. Lorenzo Da Ponte was appointed as librettist, Antonio Salieri as director, and Umlauf became Salieri's substitute. The new company was a success. John Platoff traces the most popular opera composers and works in Vienna from 1783 to 1792, reckoned by numbers of performances, finding a strong preference for Italian composers of *opera buffa*.[5] Although some of the operatic hits were composed in and for Vienna, most were imports. The most successful opera composer of the day was Giovanni Paisiello (1740–1816), who visited Vienna only occasionally. Mozart and other non-Italians, like Englishman Stephen Storace and the Viennese Joseph Weigl, figure well down Platoff's list. But Vicente Martín y Soler (1754–1806), a Spanish composer who lived in Vienna from 1785 to 1788, takes third place, although his works are seldom heard today. Salieri (1750–1825), in second place, was the only Italian composer of operas popular in Vienna who actually lived there. The others passed through, at most: Domenico Cimarosa (1749–1801); Guglielmi (1728–1804); Giuseppe Sarti (1728–1802); Anfossi (1727–97); Giuseppe Gazzaniga (1743–1818); Felice Alessandri (1747–98); and Vincenzo Righini (1756–1812).

Although many of these composers' operas were not written specifically for Vienna, their characteristics clearly spoke to the Viennese: especially the plot types, character archetypes, and certain musical traits. Platoff's list of the most popular operas in Vienna from 1783 to 1792 appears in

---

[5] Ibid., p. 107.

Table 1.1 John Platoff's list of the most popular operas in Vienna, 1783–92 (with my annotations)

1. Martín y Soler, *L'arbore di Diana* (*dramma giocoso* in two acts with libretto by Lorenzo Da Ponte; through-composed conversations and encounters, punctuated by brief songs and ariettas; pastoral plot)

2. Paisiello, *Il barbiere di Siviglia* (*dramma giocoso*; libretto by Giuseppe Petrosellini; prequel to *Le nozze di Figaro*, 'rags-to-riches' plot in which Rosina rises to the position of Countess due to her virtue)

3. Paisiello, *Il re Teodoro in Venezia* (*dramma eroi-comico*; libretto by Giovanni Battista Casti; a king finds himself in a debtors' prison)

4. Sarti, *Fra i due litigant* (*dramma giocoso* in two acts; libretto after Carlo Goldoni's *Le nozze di Figaro*)

5. Martín y Soler, *Una cosa rara* (*dramma giocoso* in two acts with libretto by Da Ponte; mountain peasants with romantic relationship problems; prince and queen intervene)

6. Salieri, *Axur re d'Ormus* (*dramma tragicomico* in five acts; libretto by Da Ponte; buffo elements given prominent place; a king loses the trust of his people and commits suicide)

7. Mozart, *Le nozze di Figaro* (*opera buffa* in four acts; libretto by Da Ponte; sequel to *Il barbiere di Siviglia*, following the fate of Rosina, and featuring her misbehaving aristocratic husband)

8. Pietro Alessandro Guglielmi, *La pastorella nobile* (*commedia per musica* in two acts to a libretto by Francesco Saverio Zini; pastoral plot, involving a marquis in love with a shepherdess, who turns out to be noble)

9. Paisiello, *La molinara* (*commedia per musica* in three acts; libretto by Giuseppe Palomba; gentlefolk marry for money while the lower classes choose true love)

10. Storace, *Gli sposi malcontenti* (*opera buffa* in two acts; libretto by Gaetano Brunati, drawing on elements from Beaumarchais' *Le Mariage de Figaro*)

Table 1.1, with brief summaries. This list of hits reveals much depiction of 'real people' (middle class or servant class), and a preference for light, comic, or pastoral plots, typically involving a love triangle. There was clear preference for lightly moralising plots, with virtuous servants, and nobles who are shown to be dishonourable (or sometimes magnanimous) and who get their just deserts. In other words, class itself becomes a theme, and class mobility is depicted time and again as a real possibility. A culture of prequels and sequels – similar characters, similar situations – is also apparent, generating a 'family-tree' effect (for example, when *Il barbiere di Siviglia* leads to *Figaro*), or a series of rearrangements of a familiar idea. This trend responds to an appetite for representation of 'real life': as in a modern sitcom, the audience understands that plots are still 'open' at the end. The believable characters and situations can be developed in further iterations.

Performance and performative elements were crucial to engaging the Viennese audiences with these works. Paisiello's *La molinara* was typically popular, not just for its plot elements but also for its careful attention to musical characterisation, and its brilliant realisation by a cast of excellent singers. Mary Hunter notes that opera scores of this time show great attention to aspects of music that are readily accessible, immediately effective, and simply pleasurable: dynamic markings are comprehensive and change often, and articulation is detailed and varied, drawing attention to the sonorous surface. Hunter suggests that in the opera theatre the repetitive nature of the music would ensure that audiences, who might be only half paying attention, would at least partly follow the plot, and also pick up on characterisation and character development.[6] This repetition also made for successful arrangements for performance in the home. Performers could take pleasure in 'playing out' the various roles while realising textures and timbres that helped delineate characters. These operas translated well into arrangements for private or semi-private performance, in musical and dramatic terms: listeners and amateur performers could relax and enjoy the interaction between parts, since the drama unfolded at a leisurely pace.

The popularity of Paisiello's *La molinara*, like the others in this list, is also evident in the number and variety of arrangements of its music. *La molinara* appeared quickly in editions from Simrock (Bonn) for two clarinets, two horns, and two bassoons; and one printed by Schott (Mainz) for a flute, violin, viola, and cello quartet. A number of composers wrote variations on popular arias. The Act 2 duet 'Nel cor più non mi sento' from *La molinara* was used as a basis for variations by a number of composers, including Johann Nepomuk Hummel and Beethoven (WoO 70). Beethoven also composed a set of nine variations for piano (WoO 69) on 'Quant'è più bello', an aria (not, however, by Paisiello) added for the revival of the opera in Vienna in 1795, which Beethoven probably heard. *La molinara* was also performed in German as *Die schöne Müllerin* and *Die streitig gemachte Liebschaft*, and in 1789 it was performed in Paris as *La molinarella*, with nine arias by Cherubini, another composer whose operas enjoyed great success in Vienna around 1800. This example illustrates the general point that arrangement and rearrangement were integral to late eighteenth-century opera.

Composers across Europe – and especially in and around Vienna – in the era of Haydn, Mozart, and Beethoven were arguably governed more by the special character of opera – its popularity and hence effect on the composers' job security, its aesthetics, and its ontology (including arrangement and

---

[6] Hunter, *The Culture of Opera Buffa in Mozart's Vienna*, pp. 19–20.

rearrangement) – than by anything else in musical culture at the time. There is strong evidence to this effect regarding each of these three composers, and also regarding Schubert. In the case of Haydn, as Jessica Waldoff and James Webster have argued, vocal music and vocally based aesthetics were a matter of personal and professional identity and pride to the composer throughout his career.[7] He consistently placed his vocal works ahead of instrumental works in his public statements about his *oeuvre*, and Griesinger reported that he recognised his own skill in vocal music and lamented that he had not written more: 'Now and then Haydn said that instead of so many quartets, sonatas and symphonies, he should have written more vocal music, for he could have become one of the leading opera composers.'[8] His contemporaries agreed that Haydn had a great aptitude for vocal music, but also tended to see his instrumental music as 'vocal'. Johann Karl Ferdinand Triest, for instance, found that it was precisely Haydn's aptitude for song and skill at singing that underlay the music's 'meaningful, powerful simplicity'; its communicative power transcended the specifics of style, genre, and form.[9] Around 1770–6 Haydn was extensively engaged with composing and directing opera, but these works, largely written for the court of Prince Esterházy, did not have such widespread success as the operas of Mozart.

Mozart never managed to gain the coveted position of court opera composer, but he strove to be an opera composer from early in his career. Letters attest to this aspiration. In 1777, for example, he wrote to his father: 'I have an inexpressible longing to write another opera. . . . For I have only to hear an opera discussed, I have only to sit in a theatre, hear the orchestra tuning their instruments – oh, I am quite beside myself at once.'[10] And the following year he complained to his father: 'But there is one thing more I must settle about Salzburg and that is that I shall not be kept to the violin as I used to be. I will no longer be a fiddler. I want to conduct at the clavier

---

[7] Jessica Waldoff, 'Sentiment and Sensibility in *La vera costanza*', in W. Dean Sutcliffe (ed.), *Haydn Studies* (Cambridge: Cambridge University Press, 1998), pp. 70–1, 78; and James Webster, 'Haydn's Sacred Vocal Music and the Aesthetics of Salvation', in Sutcliffe (ed.), *Haydn Studies*, pp. 36–9.

[8] Georg August Griesinger, *Biographische Notizen über Joseph Haydn* (Leipzig: Breitkopf und Härtel, 1810), p. 118.

[9] Johann Karl Friedrich Triest, 'Bemerkungen über die Ausbildung der Tonkunst in Deutschland im achtzehnten Jahrhundert', *Allgemeine musikalische Zeitung* 3/24 (11 March 1801), cols. 406–7; trans. Susan Gillespie as 'Remarks on the Development of the Art of Music in Germany in the Eighteenth Century', in Elaine Sisman (ed.), *Haydn and His World* (Princeton, NJ: Princeton University Press, 1997), p. 372.

[10] Mozart to his father, 11 October 1777; see Bauer et al., *Mozart: Briefe und Aufzeichnungen*, vol. 2, *1777–1779* (1962), p. 45; trans. Emily Anderson (ed.), *The Letters of Mozart and His Family*, 3rd ed. (London: Macmillan, 1985), p. 305.

Table 1.2 List of Mozart's compositions in the year 1786 (opera-related compositions are shown in bold)

Rondo (for piano) in D, K. 485
Der Schauspieldirektor (*The Impresario*) K. 486
12 Duos (two horns), K. 487
Piano Concerto in A, K. 488
'Spiegarti non poss'io' (for *Idomeneo*) K. 489
'Non più, tutto ascoltai . . .' (for *Idomeneo*) K. 490
Piano Concerto in C minor, K. 491
***Le nozze di Figaro* (Opera buffa in four acts) K. 492**
Piano Quartet in E flat, K. 493
Rondo for piano in F, K. 494
Horn Concerto in E flat, K. 495
Piano Trio in G, K. 496
Trio for piano, clarinet, and viola in E flat, K. 498
String Quartet in D (the 'Hoffmeister'), K. 499
Variations for Piano in B flat, K. 500
Piano Trio in B flat, K. 502
Piano Concerto in C, K. 503
Symphony in D K. 504 ('Prague')
'Ch'io mi scordi di te . . . Non temer, amato bene' (text from *Idomeneo*), K. 505
Canons, K. 507–8

and accompany arias.'[11] He identified Vienna with the theatre and opera with satisfying composition and leadership roles; he saw it as an outlet for his creativity and for rewarding collaborations with others. His compositional activities on arriving in Vienna confirm that he was seeking a job in the field. In 1786, for example, the year that he composed *Figaro*, we find a typical emphasis on opera in his typically vast output, as Table 1.2 shows. *Der Schauspieldirektor* is even an opera about the opera house and the impresarios and divas who inhabit it. There is also a clear emphasis on chamber music in this list, another typical feature of Vienna in the era. This combination of opera fever and demand for chamber music drove the Viennese enthusiasm for arrangements of opera for the home.

In the case of Beethoven, the years that produced his middle-period quartets can be seen as a theatrical epoch in his career.[12] During this

---

[11] Mozart to his father from Paris, 11 September 1778; see Bauer et al., *Mozart: Briefe und Aufzeichnungen*, vol. 2, p. 473; trans. Anderson, *The Letters of Mozart and His Family*, pp. 612–13.
[12] See my *Beethoven's Theatrical Quartets*, pp. 5–7.

extended period he was particularly engaged with, and sought involvement with, theatrical works and theatrical concepts. The period stretches from around *Die Geschöpfe des Prometheus*, Op. 43 (1800–1) to *Leonore Prohaska*, WoO 96 (1815), and intensifies in 1804–6 and 1809–10 in his work on *Fidelio*, Op. 72, and *Egmont*, Op. 84. Attesting to the importance to Beethoven of his work for theatre, in the middle of this period he wrote a lengthy letter to the directorate of the Hoftheater in Vienna, some time before 4 December 1807. In it he makes a case for the Imperial Court Theatre to engage him as a salaried composer.[13] The proposed contract entails the annual composition of one opera and one smaller theatrical work, in return for a fee, and a concert for his benefit to be held in the theatre. A contract did not materialise, but not for lack of trying. This attempt can be understood as the culmination of Beethoven's concentrated period of career planning and compositional effort with respect to the theatre.

In Schubert's time, the rage for Italian opera continued unabated, with Rossini at the forefront, alongside a new and distinctly Viennese development in the popular theatrical tradition, which required a more sophisticated mode of attention. Popular elements included fairy tales, historical myths, and fantasy, all of which also incorporated social and political commentary.[14] Schubert, like Beethoven and Haydn, harboured unfulfilled hopes of becoming a successful opera composer.[15] Several of his operatic works were performed in the two opera houses of the time; but lasting success eluded him, although his theatrical songs like 'Gretchen am Spinnrade' (D. 118) were very popular. Perhaps because of Schubert's and Beethoven's unfulfilled hopes on the Viennese opera scene, these composers' late quartets are characterised by songfulness (especially Schubert's) and theatricality (especially Beethoven's).[16]

Why were these composers so keen on composing opera? This had to do not only with responding to popular demand but also with artistic dividends, as Mozart had found: he had the satisfaction of working with great poets of the time, like Lorenzo Da Ponte, and great singers like Cavalieri, Nancy Storace, Francesco Benucci, and Michael Kelly. There

---

[13] Sieghard Brandenburg (ed.), *Ludwig van Beethoven: Briefwechsel: Gesamtausgabe*, 8 vols. (Munich: Henle, 1996–8), vol. 1, *1783–1807* (1996), pp. 333–5.

[14] On this subject see Botstein, 'The Patrons and Publics of the Quartets', p. 97; for a more extensive discussion see Simon Williams, 'The Viennese Theater', in Erickson, *Schubert's Vienna*, pp. 214–45.

[15] See Botstein, 'The Patrons and Publics of the Quartets', p. 97; and Otto Biba, 'Schubert's Position in Viennese Musical Life', *19th Century Music* 3/2 (1979), pp. 111–12.

[16] See my *Cultivating String Quartets in Beethoven's Vienna*, pp. 205–21.

was also satisfaction in being able to choose texts that engaged more or less concretely with the world of ideas – for example with concepts of sentimentality, and ideas of heroism and freedom. Mozart, for instance, was enthralled by the possibilities of a comic plot, and, like Shakespeare, appreciated the variety of character types such a plot could accommodate.[17] But also, market demand was at an all-time high, so there were distinct career and financial rewards from opera and its spinoffs. In this time, when freelance musicians were seeking some kind of job security, the market factor should not be underestimated.

Other opera composers in Vienna in this era – lesser known today but extremely popular then – include Carl Ditters von Dittersdorf, Florian Leopold Gassmann, Paul Wranitzky (who also composed much chamber music), and Peter Winter (whose works became very popular after 1800). Also in vogue were the French operas of Gasparo Spontini (especially *La vestale*) and Luigi Cherubini (particularly *Les deux journées*). The operas and composers that were popular for domestic arrangements in Vienna at the time more or less matched those that Platoff identifies as favoured for public performance. But we will see that this emphasis changes.

The Rage for Opera Arrangements

At the time of Mozart's death in 1791, the enthusiasm for Italian opera was continuing unabated, despite – and perhaps partly because of – the political turmoil of the French Revolution. Writing about Vienna for the *Berlinische musikalische Zeitung*, Johann Gottlieb Carl Spazier observed: 'It is apparent from some recently received news about the state of theatre in Vienna how much taste there is for musical, and particularly Italian musical plays. Within a year (from November 1791, until December 1792), Italian opera was performed 180 times. A single opera seria was performed 24 times. Ballets were seen 163 times.'[18] In general, periodicals that reported on concerts elsewhere tended to turn to opera when they reported on Vienna.[19] Another Viennese correspondent, this one from Munich, observed a similar pitch of enthusiasm for opera eight years later: 'That the public's well-known love for the enjoyments of the stage has not decreased even during the horrors of war, but has probably risen still more, can be seen daily in the crowd at the

---

[17] Letter of 7 May 1783; see Bauer et al., *Mozart: Briefe und Aufzeichnungen*, vol. 3, p. 268; trans. Anderson, *The Letters of Mozart and His Family*, pp. 847–8.
[18] Anon., 'Über Wiener Theaterwesen', *Berlinische musikalische Zeitung* 13 (4 May 1793), p. 51.
[19] Morrow, *Concert Life in Haydn's Vienna*, p. 36.

entrances to the three favourite theatres.'[20] How might one explain such a turn to opera 'during the horrors of war'? Not only did opera afford viewers with entertainment to provide relief from the turmoil of daily life; 'rescue opera' and the like also afforded them a chance to understand wartime experiences and imagine possibilities of resolution.

However, the public's voracious appetite for opera did not translate readily into jobs for Viennese composers who sought stable employment in opera: that particular career path was open to very few. Indeed, in general, composers found it difficult to make a living from composing large-scale musical works. This was not just because of the paucity of coveted positions such as that of court composer. Public concert life was not yet established as it was in other European centres like London and Paris. At this stage, concerts largely took place in private or semi-private salons of the nobility. But in late eighteenth-century Vienna it had become increasingly difficult to mount large-scale performances in such settings, for sociopolitical and economic reasons. Following Hanslick's history of concert life in Vienna (*Geschichte des Concertwesens in Wien*, 1869), scholars have generally accepted that the Viennese nobility maintained their own orchestras in the late eighteenth century. But as Dorothea Link has shown, the main examples from this era come from outside Vienna.[21] And by 1800 courtly music-making and large-scale *Kapellen* (ensembles) were generally on the wane. In his *Yearbook of Musical Art in Vienna and Prague*, 1796, Johann Ferdinand Ritter von Schönfeld noted this decline:

Whether it is a cooling of the love of art, or a lack of taste, or domesticity, or other causes, in short, to the detriment of art, this praiseworthy custom has been lost and one orchestra after another is disappearing until, except for that of Prince Schwarzenberg, almost none are in existence. Prince Grassalkowitz has reduced his orchestra to a wind band with the great clarinettist Griessbacher as director. Baron von Braun keeps his own wind band for table music.[22]

The Viennese correspondent for the *Allgemeine musikalische Zeitung* of 1800 observed that 'all the noble and wealthy houses that at one time had their own orchestras have disbanded them'.[23] Schönfeld possibly hides a key reason for the general disappearance of orchestras from Vienna

---

[20] Anon., 'Wien', *Kurpfalzbaierisches Wochenblatt* 2/15 (11 April 1801), cols. 243–4.
[21] Dorothea Link, 'Vienna's Private Musical and Theatrical Life, 1783–92, as reported by Count Karl Zinzendorf', *Journal of the Royal Musical Association* 122/2 (1997), pp. 223–31.
[22] Johann Ferdinand von Schönfeld, *Jahrbuch der Tonkunst von Wien und Prag* (Vienna, 1796; repr. Munich: Katzbichler, 1976), pp. 77–8.
[23] *Allgemeine musikalische Zeitung* 2/30 (23 April 1800), col. 520.

among the 'other causes' he cites. The upper-class musicians he cites, whose public and private engagement with the arts was varied and extensive, now often simply lacked the money to maintain an orchestra, owing partly to inflation associated with the Napoleonic Wars. Chamber music was much more feasible and cost-effective. Schönfeld's *Jahrbuch* shows a sizeable growth in musical activity in Vienna more generally in this era, despite the disappearing orchestras.[24]

With the increasing paucity of orchestras, Viennese composers who failed to make it into one of the coveted positions, such as court Kapellmeister or salaried opera composer for the court theatres, might well fall back on writing chamber music to make ends meet. Mozart found himself partly reliant on it when he arrived in Vienna in the 1780s (as the list in Table 1.2 from 1786 reveals). The Viennese thirst for chamber music may also have influenced Beethoven around 1806, when he petitioned unsuccessfully to become an opera composer at the National Theatre: this was when he wrote his five middle-period string quartets (Opp. 59, 74, and 95), and quite a few other chamber works. And both Haydn and Schubert ended up writing a lot more chamber music than opera. They and other Viennese composers met the demand for chamber music with original compositions. Those are the works we usually study, especially the original string quartets and piano sonatas of canonic composers of the era. But a study of publishers' catalogues at this time shows that the demand for chamber music was largely met by arrangements of large-scale works, scaled down for small ensembles. The extent to which the original composers produced these arrangements is explored later in this chapter and later in the book.

Overwhelmingly, opera features in contemporary music catalogues as the preferred genre to be arranged for chamber ensembles. Traeg's 1799 catalogue also shows how opera and theatrical music infiltrates, via arrangements, into all areas of music-making – particularly from stage to salon. His catalogue bears witness to a truly opera-centric culture in what we usually think of as the era of sonatas, string quartets, and symphonies, especially in Vienna. Among opera types, *opera buffa* reigned, so it is hardly surprising to find many arrangements of the works listed in Table 1.1 also appearing in various arrangements in catalogues like Traeg's. Arrangements fit well with the purposes of *opera buffa* – encouraging sociability, interaction, entertainment, and lightly worn learning.

---

[24] See Martin Eybl, *Sammler*innen: Musikalische Öffentlichkeit und ständische Identität, Wien 1740–1810* (Bielefeld: Transcript, 2022), pp. 312–13.

These opera arrangements were 'fruitful' in Beethoven's terms not only because they gave rise to more chamber repertoire. They also brought more money for composers, arrangers, and publishers; and more fame for composers, reaching more places. For listeners and amateur performers they provided greater access to opera (in forms made to measure for amateur performers); more variety in the forms that the work could take (attracting a broader audience and making performance more feasible); and a more intimate knowledge of the work (by way of education through hands-on experience). In general, opera arrangements provided for much sociability through music-making, as well as entertainment and, simply, fun. This last should not be underestimated in a time of political unrest, financial constraint, and social upheaval.

Opera and Musical 'Translation'

Arrangement as musical 'translation' around 1800 often involved converting a large-scale work into a small-scale one. The scaled-down musical product afforded the consumer (the amateur musician) various benefits over the original, including repeated access to the work, which one could now rehear, perform, and even recompose (that is, rearrange) at leisure. So opera was variously translated into 'take-home opera', for varied domestic consumption. This prevalence and variety is evident from Traeg's 1799 publishing catalogue.[25] The catalogue shows a distinction, as well as a correlation, between those composers whose operas were popular in public performances and those whose operas were popular in arrangements. For example in Table 1.3, Paisiello, Salieri, and Martín y Soler figure in the top five opera composers of works appearing in numerous arrangements. But the two most prominent operatic composers in terms of numbers of arrangements in Traeg's 1799 catalogue are Mozart and Weigl, both of whom had been less evident in the Viennese theatres one decade earlier.

There are several reasons for this discrepancy. First of all, some composers' works simply translated more easily and better into arrangements. The distinction between operas that were more or less easily arranged becomes clear where opera arrangements were intended for performance by instrumental ensembles, usually, but not always, without singers (and thus published without text, as many were). In these cases, the realisation of

---

[25] The opera arrangements are in the 'Chamber music' section and the operas in full in 'Theatre music'.

Table 1.3 Numbers of opera arrangements of the top fourteen composers represented in Viennese opera performances, in Johann Traeg's 1799 catalogue

Top fourteen opera composers 1783–92	Composer	Viennese opera performances 1783–92	Numbers of arrangements in Traeg (1799)	Ranked in terms of numbers of arrangements
1	Paisiello	251	40	4
2	Salieri	167	47	3
3	Martín y Soler	140	35	5
4	Cimarosa	127	14	8
5	Guglielmi	112	16	6=7 (tie for 6th place)
6	Sarti	97	16	6=7
7	Mozart	63	99	1
8	Anfossi	51	4	10
9	Storace	41	2	12
10	Weigl	27	44	2
11	Gazzaniga	20	0	13=14
12	Alessandri	15	0	13=14
13	Bianchi	14	3	11
14	Righini	8	8	9

the operatic characters could not depend on words, unless the performers decided to use the instrumental ensemble to accompany singers who used a separate libretto, score, or relied on memorisation (as several performers did). Clear-cut character delineation in ensemble writing was one hallmark of Mozart's operas that his contemporaries recognised. After Mozart's death, Constanze Mozart commented to Mary Novello on 'the extraordinary difference of the melodies he has assigned to the various characters [in a single ensemble] and the wonderful appropriateness of them'.[26] So Mozart's operas 'translate' particularly readily and well into wordless, purely instrumental music for ensemble chamber performance.

Then, the 1799 Traeg catalogue appears roughly a decade after the period surveyed by Platoff. Tastes in opera in Vienna were changing by 1800. Mozart's fame grew after his death in 1791 and publishers capitalised on this in reprints and arrangements. Traeg, in particular, knew Constanze Mozart and her new husband Nissen, who were working to preserve Mozart's legacy and to gain financially through the publication and

---

[26] Vincent Novello and Mary Sabilla Hehl Novello, *A Mozart Pilgrimage: Being the Travel Diaries of Vincent and Mary Novello in the Year 1829* (London: Novello, 1955), p. 94.

Table 1.4 Numbers of opera arrangements of the top eight operas represented in Viennese opera performances in 1783–92, in Traeg's 1799 catalogue

Top eight operas in public performance 1783–92	Opera	Viennese opera performances 1783–92	Number of arrangements in Traeg (1799)	Rank by numbers of arrangements
1	Martín y Soler's L'arbore di Diana	65	11	3=4 (tie for 3rd place)
2	Paisiello's Il barbiere di Siviglia	62	1	8
3	Paisiello's Il re Teodoro	59	6	5
4	Sarti's Fra i due litigant	58	5	6
5	Martín y Soler's Una cosa rara	55	16	1
6	Mozart's Le nozze di Figaro	38	11	3=4
7	Paisiello's La molinara	32	15	2
8	Storace's Gli sposi malcontenti	29	2	7

dissemination of his works. Widening distribution and repeated performance in domestic arrangements brought familiarity and further popularity, helping Constanze's and others' efforts to canonise the composer. As publishers joined the lucrative bandwagon, Mozart's posthumous fame snowballed.

The main subject of operatic arrangements was clearly still Italian opera. Comparison between Platoff's list of operatic greatest hits of the period 1783–92 and the number of arrangements of such works in Traeg's 1799 catalogue reveals the same emphasis on *opera buffa*, but also a discrepancy (compare Tables 1.1 and 1.3). Local composers are favoured in the chamber arrangements of operas listed by Traeg in 1799, and especially Mozart – also Umlauf and Martín y Soler – whereas in the public performances a decade earlier, foreign (Italian) composers and their works were clearly in favour (see Table 1.4). Martín y Soler's *Una cosa rara* and Mozart's *Figaro* were major opera hits, as witnessed by numbers of arrangements in Traeg. Traeg's list also reflects the popularity of Paisiello's *La molinara*, widely 'translated' in various arrangements after its premier in 1788. Besides the reasons already given, these particular operas were preferred for varied arrangements because of their social politics (rags to riches) and sentimental plots, which appealed to a wide audience in terms of gender and class.

In general, the list of opera arrangements in Traeg's 1799 catalogue reinforces the trends seen in Platoff's data on public performances. But certain works and types enjoy prolonged success in private after they have faded from the sphere of public performance. Sentimental opera from the 1770s and 1780s features prominently in Traeg; this affords further insight into tastes and values in the market (upper- and middle-class Viennese amateur performers) around 1800. Quartet arrangements in this list include Niccolò Piccinni's *La Cecchina, ossia La buona figliuola* and Haydn's *La vera Costanza*, for example, while quintet arrangements include Mozart's *Figaro* and *Così fan tutte*.[27] These works would have appealed particularly to opera-going musical amateurs among the bourgeoisie for their memorable and singable tunes, but also for the characters portrayed, who could be realised through the interacting voices of the chamber music. As noted, writers in this genre sought to create believable, appealing characters in real-life situations. Plots were to appeal to 'Everyman', exciting especially pity and sympathy; heroines like Cecchina, and Nina in Paisiello's *Nina, o sia La pazza per amore*, buttonholed many a middle-class operagoer, arousing admiration for the heroines' ingratiating virtues and empathy with their moving expressions of convincing emotion. So these chamber music 'translations' of operas allowed participants (both performers and listeners) to engage with aesthetic and social ideals, such as sympathy and the rewarding of virtue.

Arrangements of German opera (*Singspiele*) are common at this time, which is also evident in Traeg. This reflects a general drive in late eighteenth-century Vienna to boost and support the National Theatre. But German-language theatre had been slow to catch on, possibly owing to some upper-class resistance to Joseph II's politics, which pushed German-language theatre explicitly but restricted theatrical performance more generally. Dorothea Link conjectures that after Leopold II's ascent to the throne in 1790, German-language theatre enjoyed a vogue in the salons, perhaps since they were by then no longer associated with Joseph's social policies.[28] *Singspiele* were for salon entertainment in the 1790s, in various guises with and without text. So the numerous arrangements of *Singspiele* in Traeg, notably of Mozart's *Die Zauberflöte*, might have a sociopolitical

---

[27] On the sentimental aspects of these operas see Stefano Castelvecchi, 'Sentimental and Anti-Sentimental in *Le nozze di Figaro*', *Journal of the American Musicological Society* 53/1 (2000), pp. 1–24; Edmund Goehring, *Three Modes of Perception in Mozart: The Philosophical, Pastoral, and Comic in Così fan tutte* (Cambridge: Cambridge University Press, 2004), especially pp. 138–96; and Waldoff, 'Sentiment and Sensibility in *La vera costanza*', pp. 70–119.

[28] Link, 'Vienna's Private Theatrical and Musical Life', p. 215.

dimension. *Die Zauberflöte* is the most prevalent work of all in Traeg's catalogue, in terms of numbers of arrangements (thirty-five arrangements in total, as noted in the Introduction). More generally, the *Singspiele* arrangements in Traeg evidence the popular acclaim enjoyed by talented Viennese musicians who turned their attention to composing in this genre – composers like Dittersdorf, Winter, and Weigl, whose names are seldom heard today (especially Winter and Weigl).

'Destination' Genres

The genres that were considered the most suitable for the musical translation of opera into chamber music reflected various circumstances. Schönfeld notes that among the nobility a wind ensemble (*Harmoniemusik*) was a popular and much cheaper alternative to a private orchestra. It could be readily made up from the many excellent military wind and brass players in Vienna around 1800. Indeed, chamber music for *Harmoniemusik* was one of the most popular kinds at this time, and not just among the upper classes. Much of the music played by the wind ensembles was arrangement – *Harmonie* was one of the most popular 'destination' genres into which opera was arranged in this era.[29] These wind ensemble arrangements were intended as domestic entertainment as well as outdoor music, but they were also played as dinner music, as we see in the final act of Mozart's *Don Giovanni*. Here a *Harmonie* is playing, as diegetic music, snatches of *Una cosa rara*, *Fra i due litiganti*, and *Figaro* while the Don and Leporello await the stone statue of the Commendatore, invited to dinner. The band plays excerpts from some of the best-known operas of the day, including Mozart's own.

Mozart was drawing on a well-established convention of upper-class households. But among the musical middle-classes, *Harmoniemusik* was likewise popular for an evening's entertainment. Marianne von Martinez (1744–1812), a blind Viennese pianist, held large musical gatherings each Sunday at which guests sang and played fortepiano (see Chapter 3); but sometimes guests could also hear *Harmoniemusik* there for an entire evening. The most popular size for a *Harmonie* was six winds, but an ensemble of eight was a close second. The most popular grouping comprised two clarinets, two horns, and two bassoons; oboe and flute also featured. Both of these

---

[29] See Roger Hellyer, '"Fidelio" für neunstimmige Harmonie', *Music & Letters* 53/3 (1972), pp. 242–53.

groupings allowed arrangers to capture a good deal of the original texture of a large-scale work. The timbral variety they offered was useful for portraying individual characters. As for the repertoire chosen for arrangement for *Harmonie*, Traeg's catalogue, among others, shows composers of Italian opera once again figuring most prominently; and operas, not symphonies or other large-scale works, generally predominate. *Harmoniemusik* was particularly suited to musical translations of opera numbers with a militaristic theme, like 'Non più andrai' from *Figaro*, which is heard thus transformed in the finale of *Don Giovanni*.

Second in popularity for chamber arrangements of operas (that is, arrangements for more than one instrument in general) were those for string quartet. Again, these were not confined to the homes of the downsizing aristocracy, but were also heard in upper-middle-class settings. So, for example, Hofrath Baron von Mayern gave quartet parties during Lent, when the theatres were closed. As with Martinez's gatherings, we have no reported details as to what was played on these occasions. But sources like Traeg's catalogue afford much insight into the kinds of music likely to have dominated their offerings. In addition to Traeg's listing of string quartets, containing 1,100 works in 218 sets, he lists a further 57 sets of arrangements for works. Arrangements for quartets of music from operas and ballet are particularly numerous, with over forty-one entries, including numbers from *Il matrimonio segreto* by Cimarosa; *Der Apotheker* by Dittersdorf; *Una cosa rara* by Martín y Soler; *Die Entführung aus dem Serail*, *Don Giovanni*, *Die Zauberflöte*, and *Le nozze di Figaro* by Mozart; *Il barbiere di Siviglia* by Paisiello; and *La grotta di Trofonio* by Salieri. But just as many arrangements appear for mixed quartets (such as flute quartet) as for string quartet. This kind of quartet was probably popular for the translation of opera because distinctive timbres were useful for portraying distinct operatic characters. But these particular quartet opera arrangements also reflect the general popularity of ensembles comprising a mixture of winds and strings at this time.[30]

The two tables below (Tables 1.5 and 1.6) provide a new angle on the opera composers and works that Platoff cited as the most popular in Vienna in the years 1783–92. These tables show arrangements of operas by these composers, in two very popular genres for opera arrangements: string quartets and wind ensembles of eight players. Again, the entries are drawn from Traeg's 1799 catalogue, which, as it was something of

---

[30] See Sarah Jane Adams, 'Quartets and Quintets for Mixed Groups of Winds and Strings: Mozart and His Contemporaries in Vienna, c. 1780–c. 1800', PhD diss. (Cornell University, 1994).

Table 1.5 Arrangements for string quartet of operas and ballets ('Quartetti aus Opern und Ballets für 2 Violini, Viola e Vllo. arrangirt') in Traeg's 1799 music catalogue; 'g/G' indicates a manuscript; 'M' indicates a publication from Mainz

No.	Name	Work	Arrangement	Publication status	Price (fl.kr)
232	Cimarosa	*Il matrimonio segreto*	2 Vn, Va, Vc	g	5.30
233	Cimarosa	*Angelica e Medoro*	2 Vn, Va, Vc	g	1.30
240	Martín y Soler	*L'arbore di Diana*	2 Vn, Va, Vc	g	5.0
241	Martín y Soler	*Una cosa rara*	2 Vn, Va, Vc	g	6.0
242	Mozart	*Die Zauberflöte*	2 Vn, Va, Vc	g	9.0
242	Mozart	*Die Zauberflöte* (as above, in print)	2 Vn, Va, Vc	M	8.0
243	Mozart	*Die Entführung aus dem Serail*	2 Vn, Va, Vc	g	5.30
257	Mozart	*Don Giovanni*	2 Vn, Va, Vc	G	13.30
246	Paisiello	*Il barbiere di Siviglia*	2 Vn, Va, Vc	g	5.30
247	Paisiello	*La molinara*	2 Vn, Va, Vc	g	5.0
248	Paisiello	*Il re Teodoro in Venezia*	2 Vn, Va, Vc	g	5.0
250	Salieri	*La grotta di Trofonio*	2 Vn, Va, Vc	g	5.0
251	Sarti	*Fra i due litigant il terzo gode*	2 Vn, Va, Vc	g	6.0
253	Storazze [Storace]	*Gli sposi malcontenti*	2 Vn, Va, Vc	g	5.0
254	Weigl	*Das Petermännchen*	2 Vn, Va, Vc	g	5.30
337	Weigl	*Richard Löwenherz*	2 Vn, Va, Vc	g	5.30

a retrospective sales catalogue, shows what was prevalent in the preceding decade. Notable here is that many of these arrangements are available in manuscript copies, rather than prints. In 1784, the opportunistic Traeg had advertised a subscription service in the *Wiener Zeitung*, whereby he would provide sheet music for Viennese house concerts once or twice a week; he even offered to source 'ringers' – skilled players of his acquaintance, to perform where needed – all of which evidences the great appetite for performing chamber music.[31]

We can see that there are recurrent favourite operas for translation into chamber music, but also that quite a range of works by the favoured composers are translated. This suggests that arrangement was not just a way of perpetuating operatic 'hits'. It was also a way of exploring, or

---

[31] Johann Traeg, 'Nachricht an die Musikliebhaber', *Wiener Zeitung* 16 (25 February 1784), pp. 395–6. Discussed in Klorman, *Mozart's Music of Friends*, p. 87.

Table 1.6 Wind ensembles of eight parts ('Harmonie-Stücke zu 8 Stimmen') in Traeg's 1799 music catalogue; 'g/G' indicates a manuscript

No.	Name	Work	Arrangement	Publication status	Price (fl.kr)
85	Cimarosa	*Il matrimonio segreto*	2 Ob, 2 Cl, 2 Hn, 2 Bn	g	9.0
82	Paisiello	*Die eingebildeten Philosophen*	2 Ob, 2 Cl, 2 Hn, 2 Bn	g	9.0
86	Guglielmi	*La bella pescatrice*	2 Ob, 2 Cl, 2 Hn, 2 Bn	g	9.0
99	Guglielmi	*Le pastorella nobile*	2 Ob, 2 Cl, 2 Hn, 2 Bn	g	9.0
103	Martín y Soler	*Una cosa rara*	2 Ob, 2 Cl, 2 Hn, 2 Bn	g	9.0
104	Martín y Soler	*L'arbore di Diana*	2 Ob, 2 Cl, 2 Hn, 2 Bn	g	9.0
105	Mozart	*Die Zauberflöte*	2 Ob, 2 Cl, 2 Hn, 2 Bn	G	9.0
106	Mozart	*Don Giovanni*	2 Ob, 2 Cl, 2 Hn, 2 Bn	G	9.0
107	Mozart	*Così fan tutte*	2 Ob, 2 Cl, 2 Hn, 2 Bn	G	9.0
108	Mozart	*Die Entführung aus dem Serail*	2 Ob, 2 Cl, 2 Hn, 2 Bn	G	9.0
130	Mozart	March from *La Clemenza di Tito*	2 Ob, 2 Cl, 2 Hn, 2 Bn	G	1.30
81	Paisiello	*La molinara*	2 Ob, 2 Cl, 2 Hn, 2 Bn	g	9.0
83	Paisiello	*Il re Teodoro in Venezia*	2 Ob, 2 Cl, 2 Hn, 2 Bn	g	9.0
84	Paisiello	*La frascatana*	2 Ob, 2 Cl, 2 Hn, 2 Bn	g	9.0
98	Paisiello	*La contadina di spirito*	2 Ob, 2 Cl, 2 Hn, 2 Bn	g	9.0
115	Paisiello	*La frascatana*	2 Ob, 2 Cor Anglais, 2 Hn, 2 Bn	g	9.0
168	Paisiello	*La frascatana*	2 Ob, 2 Cl, 2 Hn, 2 Bn	g	9.0
87	Vincenzo Righini	*L'incontro inaspettato*	2 Ob, 2 Cl, 2 Hn, 2 Bn	g	9.0
91	Salieri	*Axur re d'Ormus*	2 Ob, 2 Cl, 2 Hn, 2 Bn	G	9.0
111	Salieri	*La cifra*	2 Ob, 2 Cl, 2 Hn, 2 Bn	g	9.0
112	Salieri	*La grotta di Trofonio*	2 Ob, 2 Cl, 2 Hn, 2 Bn	G	9.0
113	Salieri	*Der Rauchfangkehrer*	2 Ob, 2 Cl, 2 Hn, 2 Bn	G	9.0
114	Salieri	*Il talismano*	2 Ob, 2 Cl, 2 Hn, 2 Bn	G	9.0
88	Sarti	*I contrattempi*	2 Ob, 2 Cl, 2 Hn, 2 Bn	g	9.0
89	Sarti	*Fra i due litiganti il terzo gode*	2 Ob, 2 Cl, 2 Hn, 2 Bn	g	9.0
136	Storace	*Gli sposi malcontenti*	2 Ob, 2 Cl, 2 Hn, 2 Bn	g	1.0
93	Weigl	*Il pazzo per forza*	2 Ob, 2 Cl, 2 Hn, 2 Bn	g	9.0
116	Weigl	*Der Raub Helenens* (Ballet)	2 Ob, 2 Cl, 2 Hn, 2 Bn	G	9.0
125	Weigl	*Richard Löwenherz* (Ballet)	2 Ob, 2 Cl, 2 Hn, 2 Bn	G	9.0
127	Weigl	*Das Sinnbild des menschlichen Lebens* (Ballet)	2 Ob, 2 Cl, 2 Hn, 2 Bn	G	9.0
191	Weigl	*Die Reue des Pygmalion* (Ballet)	2 Ob, 2 Cl, 2 Hn, 2 Bn	G	9.0
192	Weigl	*Die Vermählung im Keller* (Ballet)	2 Ob, 2 Cl, 2 Hn, 2 Bn	G	9.0
188	Weigl	March from *Richard Löwenherz* (Ballet)	2 Ob, 2 Cl, 2 Hn, 2 Bn	G	9.0
195	Weigl	*Alonso e Cora* (Ballet)	2 Ob, 2 Cl, 2 Hn, 2 Bn	G	9.0

becoming acquainted with works by favoured composers, in a variety of guises. Weigl is prominent (much more so than in Platoff's list), in keeping with Traeg's habit of promoting local composers. Mozart, who was a favourite of Traeg, is also prominent (more so than in Platoff's list). But despite this bias in favour of Mozart, Traeg's catalogue gives insight into the relative popularity of different destination genres, and the most popular genres that were arranged ('origin' genres) in Vienna around 1800.

Price is a significant category in Tables 1.5 and 1.6. The opera arrangements for *Harmonie* are more expensive than the opera arrangements for string quartet. This is simply explained by the sheer amount of music – the page count involved. The wind ensembles of eight parts involve approximately twice the amount of music (number of pages) found in the four-part string quartets, and so the wind ensemble arrangements are nearly double the price. There were clearly some economies of scale in the copying process, and in providing more accompanying parts, like cello and viola, which take up less page space than the typically more melodic parts, like clarinet, oboe, and first and second violin. The string-quartet arrangements are on average slightly more expensive than the original string quartets advertised elsewhere in Traeg. A set of six string quartets of comparable length averages around 4 fl. (florin), and the most expensive set of six (Pleyel quartets) costs 6 fl. But an opera arrangement for string quartet averages around 5–6 fl. Opera arrangements were certainly more expensive items to buy relative to publishing or copyist costs, and entailed for the arranger far less labour than original compositions would require from the composer. Like spin-off merchandise today (take-home postcards, T-shirts, and coffee-table books from exhibitions, for example), they can also be seen as money-spinners for their vendors.

After string quartets, solo piano works are the second most popular genre of small-scale chamber music in Vienna at this point, at least according to Traeg's 1799 catalogue. By this time, a general trend had begun towards the piano dominating domestic music. This section in Traeg's catalogue includes a number of arrangements of operas – a large number if we include variations on themes drawn from operas. Variations for piano are borderline in terms of the definition of arrangement at the time. Variations can be a kind of arrangement, but the resulting composition may be so far removed from the original as to be regarded as a completely separate work. They were a prevalent way of 'translating' opera for the home. And their apparent popularity is another index of the prevailing enthusiasm for arrangement. Opera and ballet music were common sources for their themes. The hugely popular category of marches and dances for piano in Traeg includes a few such arrangements.

Traeg's section on sonatas for piano and violin contains several arrangements drawn from opera, the staples *Una cosa rara* and *Die Zauberflöte* coming up yet again. These operas also appear under four-hand piano music, and there are surprisingly few arrangements in this category compared with the wealth that would feature later on.[32] Indeed the keyboard section seems to contain a smaller proportion of arrangements than the section listing the rest of the chamber music. However, this is because there are so many keyboard arrangements that Traeg has categorised them in a separate section, 'Theatre Music'. Here we find ballet and pantomime, *Singspiele*, oratorios, and cantatas arranged for piano; arias, duets, trios, and so forth from German, French, and Italian operas arranged for voice and piano; and even an entire journal in four volumes devoted to the latest opera arias arranged for piano. In 1802, the music lexicographer Heinrich Christoph Koch noted that theatre and chamber music were starting to merge.[33] Traeg's 1799 categorisation of keyboard opera arrangements as 'Theatre Music' (so that some chamber music is listed thus) is an aspect of this merger – as is the culture of opera arrangements *c*.1800 altogether.

Duets for two flutes were a particularly popular medium for opera arrangements. Duets for two violins were also popular. The two types are more or less interchangeable, the flute and violin sharing much the same range and technical capabilities. In this duo repertoire, the arrangements consist of what were originally duets and solos, whereas for representing an entire orchestral texture, quintets and quartets are much more useful. Here, too, we find arrangements comprising collections of arias or hit numbers as well as entire works. Mozart and Martín y Soler are well represented, as usual. A volume of arrangements by Johann Christian Stumpf is typical. Traeg's note for this entry reads: 'Favourite songs from the opera The Marriage of Figaro by Mozart arr. for 2 flutes first booklet ... N.B. All new operas of the most famous composers are being published in a series of volumes, arranged for 2 flutes by Mr Stumpf ('Favorit Gesänge aus der Opera Figaros Hochzeit von Mozart arr. für 2 Flöten erstes Heft ... NB: Auf diese Art werden alle neuen Opern der berühmtesten Komponisten für 2 Flöten arrangiert von Herrn Stumpf Heftweise erschienen'). These arrangements were primarily for entertainment and sociability, but also afforded an educational overview of the music.

---

[32] Christensen, 'Four-Hand Piano Transcription', especially p. 257.
[33] Heinrich Christoph Koch, *Musikalisches Lexikon* (Frankfurt: August Hermann der Jüngere, 1802), s.v. 'Kammermusik', cols. 821–2. Note that Koch's 'Kammermusik' would include symphonies, concertos, and so on. See Klorman, *Mozart's Music of Friends*, p. 4, note 2.

There is a clear preference, demonstrated in Traeg, for larger chamber arrangements of large-scale origin genres such as symphonies, operas, and ballets. Destination genres deploying the piano, such as piano trios and piano quartets, were preferred, not least because the two hands could capture much of the original texture – if not the full weight and power – of an orchestra. The exception here is the duet for two flutes or two violins, but these were intended mainly for popular entertainment, and the interaction of the two melody parts, rather than evoking orchestral texture, is the main point. String quintets and quintets of mixed winds and strings were also popular for arrangements. An entire category of quintets drawn from operas and ballets consists of such mixed quintets. String quartets are similarly given separate treatment. There is an even more sizable section specifically of quartets drawn from operas and ballets; again, these are mostly arrangements of works by local opera composers, and current operatic hits. These discrete categories in Traeg's catalogue suggest by their relative proportions that there were fairly stable types of translations from operas and ballets to mixed quartets and quintets and string quartets. Under the larger chamber groupings are octets, septets, and sextets, including a sizable collection of sextets taken from operas by Florian Leopold Gassmann, Grétry, Salieri, and Umlauf – popular contemporary opera composers, mostly Viennese.

Traeg began as a music copyist, working on an ad hoc basis, and gradually added to his stock with printed editions from other firms. Only in 1794 did he open his own publishing arm. His first advertisement in *Wiener Zeitung* in 1782 emphasises the variety of opera arrangement copies on offer:

From Johann Traeg, in the Pilatisches Haus next to St Peter's on the first floor are to be had all genres of music, such as: symphonies; concertos for keyboard, violin, flute and viola; quintets, trios, duets, sonatas, etc.: oratorios and cantatas; sextets, quintets and quartets from Italian, French, and German operas, all new and select, by the best masters, cleanly and correctly written, at a cheap price.[34]

His 1799 catalogue gives a glimpse into what was in circulation in Vienna seventeen years later, and the forms it took. The prevalence of manuscript opera arrangements, coupled with relatively high prices, suggests high demand and a certain ephemerality – a culture in which people copied out arrangements, or arranged (or rearranged) current hits, chasing their transient popularity.

But the balance was shifting to favour printed over manuscript arrangements, and Traeg was changing his business model to keep up. The flow of

---

[34] *Wiener Zeitung* (10 August 1782), p. 12.

printed arrangements from European publishing houses around 1800, including Traeg's own, suggests the product on offer had a certain stability. Arrangements were becoming less ephemeral, more likely to be kept and reused. The time was right for publishers to cater to the vogue for chamber music with many and varied arrangements. There were no copyright laws to hamper the production of these lucrative editions, and no permission from composers was required, unless of course a publisher wished to assert, validly, the authenticity of a given arrangement. The transition to printed music only was completed by Traeg's son in 1805, when he took over the business. Printed editions of piano music dominate his catalogue (sonatas, variations, dances, and arrangements).

This transition in music print culture in Vienna is reflected in Traeg's 1804 supplementary catalogue. This was his first and last supplement to the 1799 catalogue, and reveals unabated and indeed mounting enthusiasm for opera arrangements. The largest sections in 'Cammer-Music' comprise *Harmoniemusik* (fifty-seven works) and string quartets (fifty-four items). Opera arrangements make up the bulk of the *Harmoniemusik*, and they are more expensive than in 1799, reflecting inflation and continued popularity. The composers have been updated: to Mozart, Salieri, and Weigl are added Cherubini, Ferdinando Paër, and Winter. So too the string-quartet category, where twelve arrangements from contemporary operas and ballets are listed as a separate section (a greater proportion relative to original string quartets than in 1799); there is a notable continued presence of Mozart's later operas in this category (*Così*, *Figaro*, *Tito*, *Don Giovanni*, and *Die Entführung*), also Salieri (*Axur*), but no others from that earlier list, and now with the addition of Paër (*Achilles*), the Overture to Cherubini's *Eliza*, and Winter's *Das unterbrochene Opferfest*, complete – all priced relatively highly compared with original quartets, and typically involving more music.

But the category of solo piano music, which had occupied a fifth of the 1799 catalogue, is most altered and it now takes up one quarter. This growth is due to a higher proportion of opera arrangements. There is now an entire category devoted to opera overtures arranged for solo piano, and what is more, the scores of theatrical works (including *Singspiele* and French and Italian operas) are folded into the piano music category and immediately preceded by lists of piano reductions. Of the 1799 catalogue, Jones writes: 'It is difficult to imagine a more forceful indication of the centrality of the symphony in Viennese musical life'.[35] But on the numbers, both the 1799

---

[35] Jones, *The Symphony in Beethoven's Vienna*, p. 15.

Table 1.7 Mozart's *Figaro* arranged, published by Artaria & Comp., Vienna, 1798–1806

Date	Instruments	Title	Notes
1798	Pf	Overture	
1801	Voice & Pf	Figaro	Entire opera; given to Francesco; Aria Collection
1805	2 Vn, Va, Vc	Figaro	Entire opera in two parts
1805	Pf, 2 Fl.	Overture	Excerpts in collection with other Mozart opera overtures
1806	2 Vn, Va, Vc (2Fl)	Quodlibet [including *Figaro*]	Excerpts; in collection with other Mozart operas http://data.onb.ac.at/rec/AC09155028
1806	Fl, Vn, Va, Vc	Quodlibet [including *Figaro*]	Excerpts; in collection with other Mozart operas http://data.onb.ac.at/rec/AC09198427
1806	2 Fl or 2 Vn	Quodlibet [including *Figaro*]	Excerpts; in collection with other Mozart operas
1806	Pf	Quodlibet [including *Figaro*]	Excerpts; in collection with other Mozart operas
1806	2 Fl or 2 Vn	Figaro	Released at the same time as other versions for the same instrumentation of other Mozart operas
1806	2 Fl or 2 Vn	Figaro	Excerpts and in a collection from all of Mozart's operas, *Duetten von sämtliche Opern*

catalogue and the 1804 supplement provide forceful evidence of the centrality of *opera* arrangements to Viennese musical life.

Table 1.7 takes us beyond Traeg's catalogue and further into the nineteenth century. It shows the variety of arrangements of Mozart's *Figaro* published by Carlo Artaria & Co. in Vienna from 1798 to 1806. Arrangements for piano become prominent at this stage, alongside the ever-popular quartet arrangements and the duets for two flutes or violins. It is particularly clear here that Artaria was cashing in on Mozart opera arrangements in 1806, the fiftieth anniversary of Mozart's birth, using the title 'Quodlibets' (medleys) to designate collections of excerpts from favourite Mozart operas (*Figaro, Don Giovanni, La Clemenza di Tito, Die Zauberflöte*, and so on). The works are realised in this format in four different arrangements: for string quartet (with the possibility of substituting flutes for violins), flute quartet, flute or violin duos, and pianoforte. This packaging emphasises entertainment and sociability – the enjoyment of hit tunes with whichever musical friends happen to be available,

Table 1.8 List of Mozart opera arrangements published by Traeg & Son, in ascending order of plate number

K. 621 March from *La clemenza di Tito*, piano
K. 588 March from *Così fan tutte*, piano
K. 621 March from *La clemenza di Tito*, piano
K. 588 March from *Così fan tutte*, piano
K. 588 Overture to *Così fan tutte*, voice and guitar
K. 588 Aria from *Così fan tutte*, voice and guitar
K. 527 Overture to *Don Giovanni*, piano
K. 621 March from *La clemenza di Tito*, guitar
K. 429 Duet from *Le nozze di Figaro*, guitar
K. 429 Duet from *Figaro*, guitar
K. 429 Aria from *Figaro*, guitar
K. 429 Overture to *Figaro*, four-hand piano
K. 384 Overture to *Die Entführung aus dem Serail*, four-hand piano
K. 298 Quartet, *Die Entführung aus dem Serail*, flute, violin, viola, cello
K. 527 Duet from *Don Giovanni*, voice and piano
K. 527 Aria from *Don Giovanni*, voice and piano
K. 527 Aria from *Don Giovanni*, voice and piano
K. 527 Overture to *Don Giovanni*, piano
K. 620 Overture to *Die Zauberflöte*, piano

for fun rather than serious study. Overtures were beginning to take on a life of their own in the reception history of operas. So it is no surprise that they are produced in chamber music arrangements; they also offered fans of Mozart's chamber music a more self-contained form than the other arrangements of opera excerpts. From 1815, other composers like Rossini and Weber tend to take over in the Artaria catalogue's opera arrangements.

Numerous publishers of this era cashed in on Mozart arrangements and built their publishing reputations around his name. It is typical of the time that less weight was placed on arrangements of his symphonies. Of the forty-one publications released by Traeg and Son (1794–1818), Traeg's own publishing firm, nineteen are opera arrangements and only one is an arrangement of a symphony: K. 551 ('The Jupiter'), arranged for four-hand piano. Table 1.8, showing Mozart opera arrangements published by Traeg himself, reveals other typical trends, notably the favouring of guitar, voice, and pianoforte as destination genres for opera arrangements. They were primarily for women to perform in the home (see Chapter 2). The arrangement of excerpts from operas was also standard around 1800, often of single numbers or selected hits rather than entire works. A preference for whole works, on the other hand, applied to classical symphonies.

Composers and Arrangement *c.*1800

In Vienna around 1800, other operas were in vogue besides the terrifically popular imports identified by Platoff. They include *Una cosa rara* (1786) by Martín y Soler; and also *Singspiele*, like *Das unterbrochene Opferfest* (1796) by Peter Winter, and Joseph Weigl's *Die Schweizer Familie* (1807). This opens a surprising window on reception history. These are works hardly known today; yet around 1800 they were almost as popular as Mozart's operas, sometimes more so, as witnessed by their countless arrangements. Eduard Hanslick recalled, looking back to the early nineteenth century: 'Arrangements of overtures, symphonies and the like [for string quartet] take the place of the four-hand arrangements that are now [in 1869] common'. He even noted that in 1808 the *Allgemeine musikalische Zeitung* was already advertising a string-quartet arrangement of Beethoven's *Eroica* Symphony, and soon thereafter of Weigl's *Singspiel, Die Schweizer Familie*.[36] Of these two works, the Eroica was generally deemed lengthy and difficult, but Weigl's *Singspiel* enjoyed great popularity. The appearance of the string-quartet arrangement of selections from Weigl's *Die Schweizer Familie* (Chemische Druckerei, *c.*1810), first performed with great success on 14 March 1809 in the Theater am Kärntnertor, represents a more typical choice for arrangement than Beethoven's *Eroica* Symphony. By 1810, favourite selections from *Die Schweizer Familie* had been arranged as *Harmoniemusik*, in piano reduction, and for keyboard and voice, and Weigl himself arranged selections from the work as a flute quartet.

Composers derived several benefits from engaging with this culture of musical arrangements around 1800. The most prominent composers of the era, including Haydn, Mozart, and Beethoven, participated actively in the practice of arrangement; they could also sanction known arrangers to do the work for them. In Haydn's correspondence with Artaria regarding the proofs of the *Seven Last Words*, for instance, he was concerned with the idiomatic nicety of an arrangement, but was prepared to hand over

---

[36] Hanslick, *Geschichte*, p. 202. On four-handed piano arrangements in the later nineteenth century see Christensen, 'Four-Hand Piano Transcription and Geographies of Nineteenth-Century Musical Reception'; and Adrian Daub, *Four-Handed Monsters: Four-Hand Piano Playing and Nineteenth-Century Culture* (Oxford: Oxford University Press, 2014).

the actual task of arranging to a musician he could trust.[37] In 1787 Artaria issued three versions of the *Seven Last Words*: the original orchestral version, a quartet arrangement prepared by the composer, and a keyboard arrangement sanctioned by him. Artistic and financial dividends from this practice have already been mentioned: varied versions of a given work meant more sales, better dissemination, and possibly fewer pirate editions – although this last could not be guaranteed. Arranging works for chamber ensemble could also help a composer to learn about composing in a particular genre. It was a typical autodidactic means of learning the art of composition, and rearranging an opera as a string quartet could help a composer learn the art of four-part composition.

But arranging was also fruitful simply as a way of creating more music. Mozart produced his earliest piano concertos by arranging keyboard sonatas by well-known contemporaries (K. 37, 39, 40, 41, all in 1767; and the three piano concertos K. 107, in 1765 or 1771); and his Flute Concerto K. 314 (1777) is an arrangement of his own Oboe Concerto K. 313 (1777–8). Most of Beethoven's own arrangements were of his early chamber music for winds. He also endorsed third-party arrangements of this group of works. He would rearrange chamber music for wind instruments into versions for ensembles of strings and piano. Several of Wranitzky's chamber works are arrangements from his own operas, symphonies, and incidental music. In sum, arrangers' motivations for producing arrangements included learning the art of composition, increasing their fame or recognition (or perhaps inadvertent notoriety), financial gain, and various pedagogical purposes.

Many arrangements were anonymous, but from those that were signed we know that some of the leading musicians of the time produced numerous first-rate arrangements. Among them were, for example, Johann Peter Salomon (1745–1815), Johann Abraham Peter Schulz (1747–1800), Karl Zulehner (1770–1841), Johann Nepomuk Hummel (1778–1837), and Carl Czerny (1791–1857). Not all of them had approval from the composers whose works they arranged. For example, Zulehner in Mainz, who was prolific in opera arrangement, was blacklisted for publishing several masses wrongly attributed to Mozart and for unauthorised editions of Beethoven's music for piano and strings. His extensive career as an arranger, which lasted into the 1830s and produced about 100 works, began in 1788 when he brought out a keyboard transcription of Grétry's *Richard the Lionheart* with Schott. He subsequently completed scores, parts, and arrangements

---

[37] See Hogwood, 'In Praise of Arrangements', p. 84.

for Weber's *Freischütz*, *Euyanthe*, and *Preciosa*, and in 1791 he brought out a piano reduction of *Don Giovanni* for Schott.[38]

It was alongside this wide repertoire of arrangements for varied chamber ensembles that Mozart's operas, and many other works, were performed and received. But it could also be argued that the composition, performance, and reception of Mozart's operas and other prominent works sat *within* this fruitful culture of musical arrangement. As noted, all the composers cited in this chapter engaged in arrangement in order to learn to compose. Composers and performers also arranged when they improvised, if 'arrangement' is understood broadly. This makes sense in relation to works such as potpourris and variations. The kind of self-borrowing by which Mozart produced (and labelled) his early concertos may seem dubious by today's standards. But his contemporaries saw the matter quite differently. There was no clear-cut distinction between an 'original' work and one that was 'derivative'; and even where this distinction was made, there was no automatic assignment of lesser value to derivative work. The devaluing of arrangements was largely the product of a later age.

The valuing and indeed intrinsic position of arrangement in the compositional process around 1800 is most obvious in the case of opera.[39] With opera, arrangement could hardly be seen as a mere step towards 'real composition'. The compositional process involved collaboration in many of its steps, as a function of opera's collaborative nature. Composers of operas worked with librettists, performers, audiences, and even venues or locations to shape their works. So operatic numbers were rearranged to suit particular singers, venues, performers, and tastes (as in the case of insertion arias or 'suitcase arias'), and they were designated as arrangements when composers produced their own piano reductions of their operas, or sanctioned others to do so. In this sense it is more difficult now to determine where any given operatic 'work' ends and the 'arrangement' begins. To put it another way, opera's ontology – its status and conception as a musical 'work' – fit perfectly into the culture of musical arrangement around 1800.[40]

---

[38] See also November, *Beethoven's Symphonies Arranged for the Chamber*, pp. 40–56.

[39] This topic is discussed further in Leopold, 'Von Pasteten und Don Giovannis Requiem: Opernbearbeitungen', especially pp. 86–7.

[40] See also Christine Siegert, 'Autograph – Autorschaft – Bearbeitung. Überlegungen zu einer Dreiecksbeziehung', in Ulrich Krämer, Armin Raab, Ullrich Scheideler, and Michael Struck (eds.), *Das Autograph – Fluch und Segen: Probleme und Chancen für die musikwissenschaftliche Edition; Bericht über die Tagung der Fachgruppe Freie Forschungsinstitute in der Gesellschaft für Musikforschung, 19.–21. April 2013*, Jahrbuch 2014 des Staatlichen Instituts für Musikforschung Preußischer Kulturbesitz (Mainz: Schott, 2015), pp. 99–111.

2 | Kenner und Liebhaber

Meeting the Domestic Market

> You will find few houses in which this or that family is not diverting itself this evening with a string quartet or piano sonata.[1]

In Chapter 1 we saw that in the late eighteenth and early nineteenth centuries Vienna was swept by a vogue for opera, which was 'translated' into chamber music to help to satisfy a voracious appetite for domestic music-making. In this chapter we meet the people at the centre of the vogue: the amateurs who bought, organised, and performed operas in their homes. We consider the profiles of Viennese amateurs, including class and gender, and the meaning of 'amateur' (*Liebhaber*, or *dilettante*) in Viennese music-making around this time. But first we have to find the musical amateurs in question. They are seldom studied, partly because historians tend to concern themselves with high-profile public 'events' rather than the patterns of everyday life, and partly because of an apparent paucity of information. Everyday life is seldom documented closely in the records that survive. There are detailed sources evidencing private-sphere activities, such as letters, memoirs, and diaries, but they do not necessarily include the kind of minutiae of interest here, such as what specifically was performed, by whom, how, and with what outcome.

But there are traces of the everyday details of Viennese music-making around 1800 in surviving documents from this time, including published accounts of amateur musicians and music, which are considered in this chapter. One-off published lists, which group amateurs or 'dilettantes' active in Vienna with their instruments and voices, and reviews of arrangements destined for amateurs, help understand the Viennese amateur in terms of skill level and gender. These accounts have to be read with care, though, as they tend to emphasise the excellence of the Viennese; and they were compiled from sources such as word of mouth, personal knowledge, and newspaper advertisements – certainly not random sampling of the population of musical Vienna. The music itself can be analysed in several ways for what it says about amateur identities and skills. Comparative

---

[1] Ignaz von Mosel, 'Uebersicht des gegenwärtigen Zustandes der Tonkunst in Wien', *Vaterländische Blätter für den österreichischen Kaiserstaat* 1/6 (27 May 1808), p. 39.

analysis of operas arranged into various chamber genres for home use and comparison with the original orchestral scores reveal how the works were 'translated' to suit diverse amateurs. Also revealing is what these opera arrangements left for the performers to do or add (text, for example, or expression) in the process of performing. This analysis affords insights into performance practices and the skill levels required for performing these arrangements, compared with other chamber music from the era.

Public and Private

To understand developments in opera in the Viennese home around 1800, it helps to subdivide the period under consideration.[2] The boundaries of historical (or biographical) periods are necessarily arbitrary: the markers set out below offer just one possible way of parsing this time period, according to turning points in social, political, and musical life in Vienna from Mozart's arrival until the death of Schubert:

1. <u>1781–91</u>: Josephine reforms; building up of National Theatre; establishment of Viennese music presses
2. <u>1792–1803</u>: Decline of old patronage system; educational reforms and a new emphasis on *Bildung* (broad educational and personal development)
3. <u>1803–15</u>: Napoleonic wars; invasion of Vienna (1809); sharp decline in orchestral concerts; founding of the Gesellschaft der Musikfreunde
4. <u>1815–28</u>: Congress of Vienna; secret police and censorship under the Metternich System; pockets of revolutionary unrest; *Biedermeierzeit* – friendship circles, and efforts to cultivate taste and develop sociability while avoiding overt politics; gradual economic recovery from the Napoleonic wars

Developments in the culture of opera in the home do not map neatly onto this scheme. But they were closely related to the opportunities for, and tastes prevailing in, music-making in Vienna, both public and private. And these, in turn, responded to the larger political, social, and cultural trends in the four-part scheme above. In Chapter 1 we saw that arrangements of all kinds flourished when there were limited or no copyright laws, music copying and publishing was burgeoning, and there was a large appetite for chamber music. Opera culture flourished in the home when and where

---

[2] See also Raymond Erickson, 'Music in Biedermeier Vienna', in Pichl, Bernd, and Wagner (eds.), *The Other Vienna*, pp. 229–30.

there was a taste for opera in general, and there was a groundswell of amateur theatre, as there was around 1800. Domestic theatrical performance was a favourite entertainment among the Viennese nobility in the final decades of the eighteenth century. They played social games that were also theatrical. The diaries of Count Zinzendorf from 1783 to 1792, for instance, record many performances of *comédies de société* – recreating recent pieces from the repertory of the national theatre – in the homes of the nobility.[3] The memoirs of Caroline Pichler, daughter of the renowned *salonnier* Hofrath Greiner, give detailed descriptions of his salons, which similarly included private theatrical performances as well as music-making and discussion of literature.[4]

This confluence of chamber music and theatre continues in the early nineteenth century, leading to the popularity of opera arrangements, for example in the salons discussed in Chapter 3, which concentrates on the third period in the schema set out directly above. But opera arrangements can be seen to change, or rather diversify, in type as chamber music is performed in more public settings. Societal and economic changes boosted public performance at intervals. Key factors in the establishment of public chamber music performance were the founding of the Gesellschaft der Musikfreunde at the end of the third period and the economic recovery from the Napoleonic wars in the fourth period.[5] Until the nineteenth century, chamber music had been fundamentally defined by its location in private venues – chambers. It would take time and major ideological shifts before the venues, types, and performers of chamber music would change decisively.

Clemens von Metternich (1773–1859) exerted a decisive influence on the venues and nature of musical life in Vienna, in and beyond the third and fourth periods. He was the Foreign Minister of Hapsburg from 1809 until 1848; an Austrian, he was the main designer of the Congress System. In Vienna, the 'Metternich System' entailed measures introduced by Metternich following the Congress of Vienna in 1815 to attempt to restore political relations in Europe. The system was enforced by efforts to prevent the uprising of opposing or revolutionary groups.[6] Indirectly, this tended to boost private and semi-private musical life in this era.

---

[3] See Link, 'Vienna's Private Theatrical and Musical Life'; on this subject see also Thormählen, 'Playing with Art', especially p. 369.

[4] Caroline Pichler, *Denkwürdigkeiten aus meinem Leben*, 4 vols. (Vienna: Pichler, 1844), see for example vol. 1, p. 51. See also Chapter 3, note 57.

[5] See also my *Cultivating String Quartets*, p. 92.

[6] For background to this era see Paul P. Bernard, *From the Enlightenment to the Police State: The Public Life of Johann Anton Pergen* (Urbana and Chicago, IL: University of Illinois Press, 1991); and Hanson, *Musical Life in Biedermeier Vienna*, pp. 43–60.

Marie Lott would term the venues considered in this book private or semi-private, since there was no public advertising, ticketing, or infrastructure such as would be associated with public music-making.[7] But for Otto Biba, who discusses the case of early nineteenth-century Vienna, the contexts considered here are mostly 'semi-public', because the music made there – particularly in the larger salons – led to the establishment of public musical life, with its standards and ideologies, and genre and performance norms.[8] For the purposes of this book, domestic performances of opera fall into private, semi-private, and semi-public categories. By 'semi-private', I mean concerts in the home, with small, select invited audiences; and neither ticketing nor published music criticism – either of which would have opened up an event to a larger, unknown audience, and, potentially, to public discourse. 'Semi-public' concerts, on the other hand, refers to those that were held in many salons of the time with relatively large audiences, and which were open to guests not necessarily known to the host – friends of friends and Viennese music lovers more generally. Such concerts might have had a commercial aspect (with advertising and/or ticketing), and even press coverage; but they were not truly public in the sense of open access and public venues. There was a continuum from private to public on which any event might sit anywhere; but in early nineteenth-century Vienna, most chamber music, including opera arrangements, was heard at gatherings at or near the 'private' end.

In the musical world, the public sphere embraces public concerts and music publication, and all the activity that allows potentially anyone to partake of and have their say about music, in a potentially open forum.[9] The establishment of music-specific journals and a culture of music reviewing were crucial to developing the musical public sphere. This culture was largely limited to upper-middle-class men, who had the education, time, and money to participate in it. Review culture was slow to get going in Vienna, as was a truly public concert life, mainly because of political repression and war. The various environments of chamber music-making in Vienna around 1800 suggest a public sphere in the process of development. Operatic performances in the Viennese home were a crucial part of this process, fostering the knowledge and popularity of operas at a time when the political situation was conducive to home learning and home-based sociability. In this more private sphere, women could participate and even lead.

---

[7] Lott, *The Social Worlds of Nineteenth-Century Chamber Music*, pp. 18–20.
[8] Biba, 'Public and Semi-Public Concerts'.
[9] On the idea of the public sphere, see Habermas, *The Structural Transformation*, especially chapter 4.

Table 2.1 *Figaro* arrangements available in Traeg's 1799 catalogue, annotated according to the possible gender of performers

Chamber Music/Instrumental Music/Quintets from Operas and Ballets, p. 60
112. First and second acts arranged for string quartet by [Johann Baptist] Kucharz [male performance]

Chamber Music/Instrumental Music/Quartets for Various Instruments, p. 75
490. For clarinet, violin, viola and cello [male performance]

Chamber Music/Instrumental Music/Duets for Two Violins, p. 87
36. [male performance]

Chamber Music/Instrumental Music/Duets for Two Flutes, p. 93
263. [male performance]

Chamber Music/Instrumental Music/ Duets for Two Flutes, p. 94
244. Favourite Songs from the opera *Le nozze di Figaro* by Mozart arranged by [Johann Christian] Stumpf for two flutes, vol. 1. 'N.B. All new operas of the most famous composers are being published in a series of volumes, arranged for 2 flutes by Mr Stumpf' [male performance]

Chamber Music/Instrumental Music/6-Part *Harmonie*, p. 108
160. For two clarinets, two horns, and two bassoons [male performance]

Chamber Music/Clavier Music/Sonatas for Violin and Keyboard, p. 140
148. Sonata for violin and piano composed on themes from *Das Sonnenfest der Braminen* and *Le nozze di Figaro* [male and female performance]

German Arias, Duets, Trios etc., pp. 188–9
11. Nos. 1, 2, 3, 4, 5, and 6 from *Le nozze di Figaro* [male and female performance]
43. Selected arias from *Le nozze di Figaro* [male and female performance]

Italian and French Arias and Duets, pp. 206–7
29. 'Non più andrai', alongside other arias and duets [male and female performance]

Italian, German, and French Arias, Duets, and Trios, with Accompaniment, pp. 213–14
11. Selected arias and duets from operas including *Le nozze di Figaro* and *Don Giovanni* [male and female performance]

Destination Genre and Performers

The genres that were popular as destinations for opera 'translations' are a good starting point for determining what kinds of people performed operas in the Viennese home. This is because certain genres and instruments were associated with performers of a specific social class and gender. So the relative popularity of the various destination genres in publishers' catalogues of the time tells us something about market demographics. Take, for example, Table 2.1, which is a list of *Figaro* arrangements in Traeg's 1799 catalogue. This table shows some of the destination genres most favoured for opera arrangements around 1800. Of the ten items listed here, six would have been performed by all-male ensembles. The very popular string quintet and quartet arrangements of operas and ballets would only have been played by men, and the same goes for those for wind ensembles. Women sang, and played piano, harp, and guitar, but only exceptionally played stringed instruments.

The string quartet was an instrumental group associated with courtly entertainment in the late eighteenth century. Koch was still describing it as a genre for the private pleasure of the ruling prince around 1800, and this courtly setting was still the first and obvious destination for Beethoven's quartets for most of his career.[10] But during the latter part of his career, in the early nineteenth century, the string quartet became a 'public' genre, performed by all-male groups of professional string players (like the Schuppanzigh quartet) that were starting to emerge and play for the public. And it was also the genre par excellence for masculine leisure-time musicmaking in the home. To be sure, there were still associations with the court; this was part of the attraction for the upwardly mobile Viennese businessman, who might use quartet parties with his peers as a means of networking, as well as a source of entertainment.

For opera arrangements, the string quartet was in many respects the ideal vehicle, in that it could realise four-part harmony and allow four players the fun of interacting. A wind ensemble of six or eight players could achieve similar ends, but six or eight wind players – easily assembled from military bands or opera orchestras by the downsizing nobility – were harder to find for a family music-making session. Quartets were a popular choice to accompany an amateur choir and soloists (see Chapter 3 for detail). String quintets were even better for these purposes. A large ensemble could always be formed from a small string-ensemble nucleus when other performers were available. But, as will be seen, quartets and quintet arrangements were gradually being eclipsed by piano arrangements.

Flute duos, which were interchangeable with violin duos, were also played by men. They were terrifically popular for opera arrangements. This was not only because the flute, like the violin, was very popular at the time, but also because it was easy to bring together just two performers. Whereas string quartets and quintets, like keyboard reductions, could be used to accompany voices or a solo singer, and might be performed before an audience, the flute duo and solo arrangements did not lend themselves to accompaniment, so they targeted groups of people who wanted to enjoy music as a private pleasure. This phenomenon of small-scale chamber arrangements designed as 'Musikalische Gesellschafter in einsamen

---

[10] Koch, *Musikalisches Lexikon*, s.v. 'Quatuor', cols. 1209–10.

Stunden' ('musical companions for lonely hours') was already prevalent in the late eighteenth century, and was more prominently marketed as such in the early nineteenth century.[11]

Arrangements for wind bands, a very popular destination genre for opera ensembles, were intended to be performed for the nobility as dinner music, but also in the upper-middle-class home as a cheaper alternative to orchestral music. However, they were also played by military bands as standard repertoire, and in outdoor settings. So of all the destination genres, they were the most diverse in terms of venues and audience. In terms of performers, however, they were not at all diverse. While string-quartet music was lauded for an 'equality' of participation by musicians of different classes, with professional musicians potentially playing alongside amateurs from the nobility, wind ensembles consisted largely of lower-class, professional male musicians.

Harmonie ensembles were often formed of former orchestral musicians in the late eighteenth century, when court orchestras were scaled down as a cost-saving measure. The Viennese Prince Schwarzenberg had a *Harmoniemusik*, which was all that remained of the family's former orchestra by 1780. Prince Alois Liechtenstein created a *Harmoniemusik* in 1789 in Vienna, consisting of horn player Anton Höllmayer, Anton Eisner as the second horn, Johann Harnisch and Franz Steiner as bassoonists, Ferdinand Schleiss and George Klein as clarinettists, and Friedrich Zinke and Joseph Triebensee as oboists. All were professional male musicians who worked for courts and theatres. Triebensee (1772–1846), for example, was oboist in the Viennese Kärntnertortheater for four years before his appointment, and under his direction, Liechtenstein's *Harmoniemusik* developed an excellent reputation. Triebensee was a composer as well as a performer, and composed operas, but particularly music for everyday use. He focused on *Harmoniemusik*, but is also notable for many arrangements of works for *Harmonie*, including major theatrical music:

Mozart's *Don Giovanni*, selections arranged for two oboes, two clarinets, two horns, 2 bassoons, contrabassoon (ad lib)
Mozart's *La clemenza di Tito*, selections for *Harmonie*
Così fan tutte for *Harmonie*
Cherubini, overture and arias from *Medea* for wind octet
Schubert, music from the play *Rosamunde* D. 797 for *Harmonie*

---

[11] Klitzing, *Don Giovanni unter Druck*, pp. 250–5.

When the group disbanded, Triebensee's theatrical career continued. He was second oboist at the Theater auf der Wieden in Vienna in 1791, playing in the premier of Mozart's *Die Zauberflöte*. His example demonstrates how arrangements arose variously in the overlapping spheres (chamber, court, theatre) in which musicians moved, and in response to the need for everyday music.

Chamber music involving piano forms the largest subset of opera arrangements after 1800, even though string quartets were in many respects the ideal vehicle for these arrangements. Arrangements produced in Vienna around 1800 are generally oriented towards the piano, for various reasons. The distinctive powers of the fortepiano (including its registral reach, chordal and textural capabilities, and timbral differentiation) allowed the broadest range of musical genres and styles to be translated for domestic use.[12] For amateur performers, this meant that there was plenty of music that would allow, and invite, female involvement. The boom in piano chamber music in this era was both a function and a product of growing female involvement in chamber music-making in the home. For women, this music-making had multiple functions beyond filling 'lonely hours'. Socialising through music was a way of networking in order to marry 'well', and facilitating others' enjoyment. Piano arrangements also uniquely afford an overview of the entire opera, with one or two (four-hand) performers only. So they served an educational as well as an entertainment function, and of course were a simple way of accompanying arias – one of the most popular forms of chamber music at the time.

Women also played a growing role in the musical education of children, for which they might use arrangements of well-known music. Ignaz von Mosel observed of domestic music-making in 1808:

[T]he practice of musical art has [in Vienna] become a permanent and indispensable article in the series of items of knowledge that all parents that are at all well-to-do have their children taught. One would consider the opposite an unforgiveable neglect in the education of their family on the part of the former, and it has indeed become a kind of rarity to see a boy or a girl from a house of the educated middle class to whom this art has remained foreign ... no ceremonial opportunity passes that is not glorified by this art.[13]

Publishers cashed in on this function of arrangements as it became more apparent, just as they marketed musical arrangements as 'companions for

---

[12] Parakilas, 'The Power of Domestication', p. 17.
[13] Mosel, 'Uebersicht des gegenwärtigen Zustandes der Tonkunst in Wien', p. 39.

lonely hours'. The use of arrangements to educate children predates the publishers' use of title pages and slogans to advertise this application. In the early nineteenth century, the Viennese firm Diabelli, Schott (Mainz), and Simrock (Bonn) all rearranged *Don Giovanni* and other operas into pedagogical editions, specifically reduced in scale and difficulty to cater to beginners. Publications like Diabelli's *Little Pieces* (*Kleinigkeiten*) and the series *Selection of Beloved Melodies for the Pianoforte with Attention to Little Hands* (*Auswahl beliebter Melodien für das Piano-Forte mit Berücksichtigung Kleiner Hände*), together with the later *Recreation Musicales* (1840) and *Le premier début* (1846), all take this pedagogical approach.

The mapping of specific genres onto characteristics of the musical market in Vienna (such as age, gender, class, location of performance) is by no means straightforward. The difficulty may be illuminated by Michel de Certeau's idea of consumers' creative resistance to norms of public life, which can be extended to performance, reception, and meaning in Vienna's musical scene.[14] Men might buy and perform arrangements marketed for 'little hands'; women might perform string quartets (Schönfeld lists three talented female violinists in Vienna in 1796[15]), or add percussion to arrangements of military music;[16] and middle-class families might enjoy a concert with *Harmoniemusik*.[17] There was not yet a 'normal' public musical life. Any norms were developing gradually, so such actions on the part of consumers may not have been perceived as unusual, transgressive, or aspirational, as the case might be.

Class, Gender, and Performance Standards

In 1791, Joseph Haydn sent a keyboard arrangement drawn from his Symphony No. 95 to his friend Maria Anna von Genzinger in Vienna (Haydn was in London). When the score appeared to be lost in the post, Haydn told her that she could make the arrangement of that symphony, and one of No. 96, herself. This might seem a difficult task for an amateur. Genzinger would have been described as a 'dilettante' in her time, but she was what we would today consider an advanced or skilled

---

[14] Michel de Certeau, *The Practice of Everyday Life*, trans. S. Rendall, 3rd ed. (Berkeley, CA: University of California Press, 2011), especially pp. xiv, 73, 167.

[15] Schönfeld, *Jahrbuch der Tonkunst*, pp. 6, 10, and 14; one of them, Miss Brunner, is explicitly listed as a skilled quartet performer.

[16] Discussed further in November, *Chamber Arrangements of Beethoven's Symphonies, Part 2*, xv.

[17] Link points to many undocumented concerts in middle-class homes in late eighteenth-century Vienna: 'Vienna's Private Theatrical and Musical Life', p. 210.

amateur. She played the piano and continued her studies into adulthood. Haydn, who knew her well, must have known that she was up to the task. In fact, their friendship developed in correspondence about arrangements. Here is the text of her letter, dated 10 June 1789:

Most respected Herr v[on] Hayden,

With your kind permission, I take the liberty of sending you a pianoforte arrangement of the beautiful Andante from your so admirable composition. I made this arrangement from the score quite by myself, without the least help from my teacher; please be good enough to correct any mistakes you may find in it. I hope that you are enjoying perfect health, and I wish for nothing more than to see you soon again in Vienna, so that I may demonstrate still further the esteem in which I hold you. I remain, in true friendship,

    Your obedient servant,
    Maria Anna [noble] v. Genzinger
    Born [noble] von Kayser

My husband and children also ask me to send you their kindest regards.

Haydn responded with high praise:

Nobly born and gracious Lady!

In all my previous correspondence, nothing delighted me more than the surprise of seeing such lovely handwriting, and reading so many kind expressions; but even more I admired the enclosure, the excellent arrangement of the Adagio, which is correct enough to be engraved by any publisher. I would like to know only whether Your Grace arranged the Adagio from the score, or whether you took the amazing trouble of first putting it into score from the parts and only then arranging it for the pianoforte; if the latter, such an attention would be too flattering to me, for I really don't deserve it.

Best and kindest Frau v. Gennsinger [sic]! I only await a hint from you as to how and in what fashion I can possibly be of service to Your Grace. Meanwhile I return the Adagio, and very much hope to receive from Your Grace some demands on my modest talents; I am, with sincere esteem and respect,

    Your Grace's
    most obedient servant,
    Josephus Haydn [m.p]ria.
    Eszterháza, 14th June 1789.

P.S. Please present my respectful compliments to your husband.[18]

---

[18] Marianne von Genzinger to Haydn, Vienna, 10 June 1789; and Haydn to Genzinger, Eszterháza, 14 June 1789, in H. C. Robbins Landon and Dénes Bartha (eds.), *Joseph Haydn: Gesammelte Briefe und Aufzeichnungen* (Kassel: Bärenreiter, 1965), pp. 207–8.

Accounts of the late eighteenth and early nineteenth century list numerous female 'dilettantes' and amateur performers who would have been able to create, and may even have published, arrangements of complex music.[19] This would often have been done starting with individual performance parts, rather than scores, which were not so often published in this era – a time-consuming but educational process. The term musical 'dilettante' referred to a musican who did not earn money through musical performance, and covered a broad range of skill levels from beginner to almost professional.[20] Most of the female Viennese dilettantes were singers and pianists. Ignaz von Mosel's 1808 listings of Viennese performers on stringed instruments include both lower-born and upper-class men. Women are scarce among performers of stringed instruments in Vienna in the early nineteenth century: Mosel lists only one female violinist, under 'Dilettanten'; and Anton Ziegler, whose 1823 listing of Viennese musicians is considered in Chapter 6, has none. The (masculine) amateur string-playing tradition was still going strong in early nineteenth-century Vienna, but amateur keyboard playing was also flourishing, in this case especially among women. Mosel notes: 'an excellent [female] keyboard player is to be found in almost every distinguished family'.[21] Schönfeld and Mosel both list numerous Viennese pianists, both male and female, 'Dilettanten' and 'Künstler/innen'.

There is a clear gender imbalance reflected in Schönfeld's long list of talented pianists in Vienna in 1796, among whom women outnumber men by thirty-six to twenty-five.[22] In Ignaz von Mosel's list (1808), women outnumber men by twenty to thirteen (the same ratio, 3:2). Most of these people are from the upper-middle class or the nobility: pianos were still expensive; the mass production of uprights would not happen until later in the century. In Mosel's account there are fifty pianists in total, among them seventeen professionals and thirty-three dilettantes; among the professionals are four females, and among the dilettantes twenty-one. He notes 'The dilettantes of the piano enjoy with pride that Abbé Gelinek had the good fortune to be Most High Music Master of Her Majesty the Empress'.[23] In other words, these sources reveal that piano-playing was on the increase, especially among the upper middle classes, and one of the reasons for this was the leadership of the former Empress (Maria Theresa).

---

[19] See especially Schönfeld, *Jahrbuch der Tonkunst*; and Mosel, 'Uebersicht des gegenwärtigen Zustandes der Tonkunst in Wien'.
[20] Biba, 'Public and Semi-Public Concerts', p. 259.
[21] Mosel, 'Uebersicht des gegenwärtigen Zustandes der Tonkunst in Wien', *Vaterländische Blätter für den österreichischen Kaiserstaat* 1/7 (31 May 1808), p. 52.
[22] Schönfeld, *Jahrbuch der Tonkunst*, pp. 3–68; see also Eybl, *Sammler*innen*, pp. 313–14.
[23] Mosel, 'Uebersicht des gegenwärtigen Zustandes der Tonkunst in Wien', pp. 51–2.

As to other instruments popular in Vienna at this time, published arrangements for instruments such as harp, guitar, and harmonica can be understood as efforts to generate repertoire for enthusiastic amateurs who otherwise had little music to play. Mosel notes the high price of the pedal harp, which explains why there are fewer amateurs to mention than for piano; they are all women, whereas the only performers of guitar he considers worthy of mention are men.[24] Typically, there are no women listed as performers of wind instruments or any of the lower string-family instruments (viola, cello). Regarding professional harpists, his nationalist bias is still readily apparent:

The talents of the court harp player and chamber virtuoso, Josephine Müllner . . . are too well known at home and abroad to be allowed further mention here. All foreign artists on this instrument, who have been through here, have had, by comparison to her, to give way.[25]

Viennese Dilettantes: Facts and Fictions

In general, Viennese accounts of local dilettantes around 1800 tend to be full of praise. These accounts need to be read carefully. The *Newest Portrayal of the Customs of Vienna* (*Neuestes Sittengemählde von Wien*), a series of fictional letters based on factual observations published by Anton Pichler in 1801, came in for some contemporary criticism for caricature and ignoring the lower classes. It is also problematic for other reasons. The author was one of several Viennese at the time to boast that Vienna, of all cities, offered the greatest variety and quality of musicians: 'In general', the writer opined, 'I believe that there is possibly no other city in which so many great artists in all subjects of music live, as here'.[26] Allowing for exaggeration and bias, it is clear that music-making was the most prominent form of social entertainment in early nineteenth-century upper- and middle-class Viennese homes. Indeed, domestic chamber music (confined at first to family members) was an important factor in the development of new semi-private and semi-public social circles in Vienna. The same writer alludes to reasons for the prevalence of private music-making in Vienna. In

---

[24] On Mosel, see Eybl, *Sammler*innen*, especially, pp. 114–16.
[25] Mosel, 'Uebersicht des gegenwärtigen Zustandes der Tonkunst in Wien', p. 52.
[26] Anton Pichler (ed.), *Neuestes Sittengemählde von Wien* (Vienna: Pichler, 1801), p. 160.
A scathing review appeared in *Annalen der österreichischen Literatur* 1/13 (February 1802), cols. 103–4.

particular, as Mosel noted, musical instruction was considered essential to good upbringing and was obtained by every well-off family.[27] Pichler also notes that it was easy to get together a group of talented amateurs for a private house concert.[28]

Mosel's account, seven years later, is in much the same vein, but adds a new concern with 'equality', which was starting to surface in discourse about chamber music-making in this era:[29]

If one could assume that the culture of music keeps pace with the formation of the mind, then one would have much reason to congratulate the inhabitants of this capital: for nowhere else is this divine art so widely practised, so much loved, and so eagerly practised, as here; nowhere else will one find among the dilettantes on almost all instruments so many accomplished practitioners, some of whom may rank themselves alongside the professors of this art, indeed some may even surpass them. The art of composition works the miracle every day that was otherwise attributed only to love: it makes all classes equal.[30]

Schönfeld's earlier account foreshadowed these observations. It details the private and semi-private house concerts that evolved in his day, and by and for whom they were given. Under 'Konzert', in a short section on the current state of music in Vienna, he mentions numerous private house concerts.[31] In a more extensive section he covers 'Dilettantakademien' (amateur concerts). He lists twelve Viennese patrons, mostly nobility, who 'occasionally or at fixed times give large concerts or even only quartets'.[32] Schönfeld goes on to say that in many other private houses both large and small concerts are held during the year. He, like other writers of the time, wishes to emphasise the 'openness' of the music-making in these settings.[33] But under 'Dilettantakademien' he also notes several that are exclusive or 'closed': Baroness von Puffendorf runs a 'closed society' (*geschlossene Gesellschaft*) for singing and piano performance, largely of more 'learned' works like fugues and church music; and Baroness Zois likewise runs 'a small musical coterie or friendship circle' (*eine kleine musikalische Kotterie*) for singing and piano. Schönfeld can only list four musical salons that welcomed foreigners: those of Herr Henikstein, Count Grenier, Marianne Martinez, and himself.

---

[27] See n. 14. [28] Pichler, *Neuestes Sittengemählde von Wien*, p. 161.
[29] On 'equality' and string-quartet ideals at this time see also my *Beethoven's Theatrical Quartets*, pp. 10–13.
[30] Mosel, 'Uebersicht des gegenwärtigen Zustandes der Tonkunst in Wien', p. 39.
[31] Schönfeld, *Jahrbuch der Tonkunst*, p. 98. [32] Ibid., p. 69.
[33] See Eybl, *Sammler*innen*, pp. 312–13.

Many of these gatherings offered more pretence of openness than actual freedom of entry. Despite their ubiquity, Viennese private concerts around 1800 fostered exclusivity in terms of both class and gender. The many salons frequented by Zinzendorf were given by and for the 'upper crust' of Viennese society. Zinzendorf, a government official of high rank from an old but no longer wealthy noble family, expected to be invited to all major social events in the city; but even he was sometimes overlooked.[34] And the amateur concerts mentioned by Schönfeld were mostly put on by male members of the nobility, which was typical in Vienna at the time. Often the emphasis was on music-making for a select group of listeners, sometimes just for the participants themselves, and string-quartet performance figured prominently among small-scale works. He lists twelve men who put on such concerts, all of them members of the nobility, including Lobkowitz, Lichnowsky, various court councillors, and two wholesale merchants.

Both before and after 1800 there is appreciably more emphasis on male leadership in Viennese salons than in the traditional French salons. Important male salon hosts from late-eighteenth-century Vienna who supported musical activities include Hofrat Franz von Grenier, Baron Gottfried van Swieten, Prince Galitzin, Prince Liechtenstein, and Count Etienne Zichy. Women figure frequently in accounts of the salons, but often as performers (singers, pianists), rather than hostesses. Fanny von Arnstein was an exception, and Grenier's daughter, Caroline, would become an important salon hostess in the early nineteenth century, as would Arnstein's daughter. These women set examples that would help other women to take the lead. Van Swieten ran string-quartet parties in the 1780s, which featured serious works in learned style. He was instrumental in bringing important aspects of the Berlin salons to Vienna, especially an emphasis on *Bildung* (well-rounded personal development) through music-making (specifically chamber music and 'ancient' music). Van Swieten encouraged the arrangement and performance of chamber music with his Sunday-morning musical sessions in the Imperial Library, commissioning Mozart among others to arrange keyboard fugues by Bach for string trio and quartet. This was not the place for amateur performances of opera arrangements.

Male dominance was especially typical of string chamber music around 1800 (as evidenced above), which certainly included some amateur performance of opera arrangement. Looking back on the era, Hanslick confirmed that the string quartet was the favoured genre for private

---

[34] Link, 'Vienna's Private Theatrical and Musical Life', p. 206.

music-making in Vienna at this time, but he was focusing on male music-making: 'practically every music-loving family gathered together their [string] quartet of amateurs [Liebhaberquartett], mostly on a given day of the week'.[35] Accounting for the Viennese quartet boom in the 1800s, he noted: 'musically talented sons were to learn violin and cello, whereas nowadays [the 1860s] music instruction in the home is completely absorbed by the piano'.[36] Earlier in the century, sons who received music instruction usually learned stringed instruments and were thus well placed to participate in a family string quartet, while daughters typically received instruction in piano and singing.

Hanslick tended to ignore female music-making and the prevalence of the piano in the early part of the century. However, singing and piano performance were as popular as or even more popular than string quartets in music-making in the Viennese home around 1800. Dorothea Link observes, from documentary evidence, that keyboard-accompanied song and especially operatic excerpts took centre stage in Viennese domestic music-making at this time.[37] For instance, before a dinner party attended by Count Zinzendorf on 29 November 1786, given by the Envoy of Saxony, a group of three noble women sang the trio from *Il barbiere di Siviglia*; and that same year the professional singer Josepha Duschek is reported to have given various performances of opera arias at salons of the nobility. Duschek was one of the few professional musicians to have been admitted into such social circles. But among the nobility, singers of near-professional talent (both male and female) were in plentiful supply in Vienna around 1800, as we see in the accounts of music-making in Vienna by Schönfeld and Mosel, and the retrospective *Memoirs* on Vienna in the 1820s by Leopold von Sonnleithner.[38] They would have been accompanied mainly by piano reductions, which were produced in great numbers for the most popular operas.

---

[35] Hanslick, *Geschichte*, p. 202.   [36] Ibid.
[37] Link, 'Vienna's Private Musical and Theatrical Life', p. 207.
[38] Otto Erich Deutsch (ed.), 'Leopold von Sonnleithners Erinnerungen an die Musiksalons des vormärzlichen Wiens', *Österreichische Musikzeitschrift* 16/2–4 (1961), pp. 49–62, 97–110, 145–57; Mosel, 'Uebersicht des gegenwärtigen Zustandes der Tonkunst in Wien', pp. 50–1; and Schönfeld, *Jahrbuch der Tonkunst*, pp. 3–68. Sonnleithner's *Memoirs* were first published in Leopold von Sonnleithner, 'Musikalische Skizzen aus "Alt-Wien"', *Recensionen und Mittheilungen über Theater, Musik und bildende Kunst* 7/47 (1861), pp. 737–41 and 753–7; 8/1 (1862), pp. 4–7, 8/12, 177–80, and 8/24, 369–75; and 9/20 (1863), pp. 305–25; they are translated in Alexandra A. Vago, 'Musical Life of Amateur Musicians in Vienna, ca. 1814–1825: A Translated Edition of Leopold von Sonnleithner's "Musikalische Skizzen aus 'Alt-Wien'" (1861–1863)', MA thesis (Kent State University, 2001).

Table 2.2 Ignaz von Mosel's list of the best male and female singers in Vienna (in order of importance) c.1800, categorised as artists and professors (*Künstler und Professoren*)

Artists and professors (female)	Artists and professors (male)
Antonia Campi (1773–1822)	Carl Weinmüller (c.1765–1828)
Anna Pauline Milder-Hauptmann (1785–1838)	Julius Radichi (1763–1846)
Antonie Laucher (c.1786–1871)	Giuseppe [Joseph] Tomaselli (1758–1836)
Josepha Fischer-Vernier (1782–1854)	Giovanni Liverati (1772–1846)
Marianne Marconi [Schönberger-Marconi] (1785–1882)	(Franz) Joseph Fröhlich (1780–1862)
Katharina [Kathinka] Buchwieser (1789–1828)	Anton Haitzinger [Haizinger, Halzinger] (1796–1869)
Luise Müller (1778/79–1838 or later)	Ignaz Saal (1761–1836)
	Johann Michael Vogel (1768–1840)
	Leopold Pfeiffer (1759–1831)
	Friedrich Sebastian Mayer (1773–1835)

Amateur Singers and Changing Tastes

In Mosel's listing of singers in Vienna around 1800 the number of excellent female 'Dilettanten' is the highest. He first lists the names of seven professional female singers, giving extensive descriptions of the voices of three of them (see Table 2.2). Antonia Campi (1773–1822) was a Polish operatic soprano for whom Paër created *Sargino, ossia l'allevo d'amore* (Vienna, 1803), who was appointed first Imperial Singer in 1818. Pauline Anna Milder-Hauptmann (1785–1838) from Constantinople made her debut in Schikaneder's troupe at the Theater an der Wien in 1803 in Franz Xaver Süßmayr's *Der Spiegel von Arkadien*, and sang the title role in the first performance of Beethoven's *Leonore*. And the German soprano Antonia Juliana Laucher (1786–1871), with her sister Cäcilia, was employed as a singer by the Viennese Court Opera. Then, following a list of nine male professionals, he names twelve female 'Dilettanten', but could clearly go further:

By the way, we are quite surprised to find the names of at least a hundred really excellent dilettantes of singing, who are not known and for the reason that their talents amuse only the limited circle of their acquaintances, and could never be admired in public.[39]

A time was approaching in which these semi-professional singers (as we might consider them) would receive early operatic experience in private

---

[39] Mosel, 'Uebersicht des gegenwärtigen Zustandes der Tonkunst in Wien', p. 51.

settings and then go on to make professional careers. Chapter 3 discusses private and semi-private salons where these dilettantes featured in performances of opera excerpts and even entire operas. Several of the most important of these salons were run by Mosel's favoured *Dilettant* singers, mostly men: Professor Johann Zizius, Prince Lobkowitz, Kiesewetter, Henikstein, and Sonnleithner. It is also notable that Mosel's listing of *Dilettanten* includes fewer members of the nobility than does Schönfeld's list from twelve years prior. Now the increasingly monied upper classes had time and energy to devote to music-making. Or some of them did. Mosel notes gloomily of Herr Doctor Rathmayer that he is a 'Tenor of rare perfection' but that 'it is very regrettable that more serious business has forced him to neglect this talent'.[40]

Mosel reinforces the perceived primacy of vocal music in Vienna around 1800, giving preference to the listing of dilettante and professional singers in his report on Viennese musicians. Revealing a certain xenophobia, he does not include foreign musicians in his lists: 'Foreign artists do not appear here for the reason that their existence here, as only temporary, can have no influence on the popular state of music in Vienna, of which we are speaking here.'[41] Of course there are a number of Italians who then resided in Vienna among the singers he lists, and the first two professional female singers he lists were essentially 'foreigners'. But a key reason for his bias in favour of German nationals becomes clear in his views on Italian opera, which had reached a new height of popularity. His diatribe begins by lamenting the absence of a music conservatorium, or any similar institution, in Vienna:

It is most palpable with regard to opera, for which suitable singers would emerge from such an institute, while the theatre management, with all its effort and all its trouble, is unable to find an excellent tenor for German opera, and for this reason is unable to put many a great classical work on the stage, with which it would otherwise have promoted good taste and amused the public. In view of the preference which the inhabitants of Vienna, to the great praise of their taste, now give to the German *Singspiele*, whose music strives for truth of feeling, for correctness of expression, for power of representation, over the Italian, whose usual platitudinous monotony and mindless gurgling have for many years made the enlightened connoisseur bored ... It is all the more regrettable that, due to the aforementioned obstacle, the means are lacking to keep the public on this good path and to provide burgeoning good taste, skill and persistence.[42]

---

[40] Ibid., p. 51.   [41] Ibid., p. 44.   [42] Ibid., pp. 41–2.

Table 2.3(a) Opera arrangements advertised by the forerunner to Diabelli and Cappi's Viennese firm, 1817

Plate no.	Composer/arranger	Opera, instrumentation (publisher)	Advertisement date
19	Rossini (arr. Diabelli)	*Tancredi*, flute, violin, and guitar	-
29	Rossini	Overture to *L'italiana in Algeri*, piano	22 March 1817
?	Rossini	Cavatina 'Soffri o Cor' from *L'italiana in Algeri*, Cavatina, voice and piano	22 March 1817
33	Rossini	'Papatacci' trio from *L'italiana in Algeri*, Terzetto, voice and piano, Mechetti	-
40	Mauro Giuliani (on an opera by Friedrich Heinrich Himmel)	Guitar variations 'on the favourite romance from the opera *Fanchon*', Op. 88,	20 September 1817

But the real reason for Mosel's disgruntlement was the increasing preference of the inhabitants of Vienna for Italian opera. A glance at the opera arrangements in Viennese publishing catalogues from this time reveals the unstoppable direction of the Viennese taste for opera. Tables 2.3a and 2.3b shows opera arrangements that were advertised by the forerunner to Diabelli and Cappi's Viennese firm, 1816–18. Overwhelmingly, Rossini features. There is a smattering of *Singspiele*: Carl Maria von Weber's *Das Waldmädchen* (1800) and Adalbert Gyrowetz's *Der Augenarzt* (1811).

The extensive catalogues of Artaria and Company show that this rage for Rossini opera arrangements takes off in earnest in the late 1810s. Before then, Mozart is very well represented, as are the Italian composers of Italian opera mentioned in Chapter 1. But there are a few newcomers and a focus on *Singspiele*, noted by Mosel, and on multilingual arrangements. An example of the latter is Austrian composer Paër's opera *Sargino*, a *dramma eroicomico* in two acts that was premiered in Dresden in 1803. In Artaria's catalogue, various piano arrangements of *Sargino* are published with both German and Italian text, with separate plate numbers. Other Austrian newcomers include Josef Eybler, Jakob Haibel, Franz Anton Hofmeister, Wenzel Müller, Franz Alexander Pössinger, and Josef Wölfl. Haibel (1762–1826) offers a good example of an Austrian composer caught up with the folk-music movement – which around 1800 offered escape from the trials of war into the 'simple

Table 2.3(b) Opera arrangements advertised by the forerunner to Diabelli and Cappi's Viennese firm, 1816–18

Catalogue no.	Composer/Arranger	Opera, instrumentation (publisher)	Advertisement date
351	Wenzel Johann Tomaschek	Overture to *Seraphine*, piano	16 December 1816
351	Giuliani (on an opera by Nicolo Isouard)	Variations 'on the duet from the opera *Jeannot et Colin*', guitar, Mechetti	16 December 1816
20	Jean Baptiste Fier (on an opera by Rossini)	Variations on 'Di tanti palpiti' from *Tancredi*, Op. 50, guitar	25 January 1817
68	Rossini	Cavatina, 'Soffri o cor' from *L'italiana in Algeri*, voice and guitar	23 March 1817
68 (+ Pl. No. 28)	Rossini	Cavatina 'Per lui che adoro' from *L'italiana in Algeri*, voice and guitar	23 March 1817
68	Rossini	Aria, 'Oh! che muso' from *L'italiana in Algeri*, voice and guitar	23 March 1817
68	Rossini	Cavatine 'Di tanti palpiti', from *Tancredi*, voice and guitar	23 March 1817
90	Rossini (arr. Diabelli)	*L'italiana in Algeri*, flute or violin and guitar	19 April 1817
90	Rossini	Quartet, 'Ah se giusto', from *Tancredi*, voice and guitar	19 April 1817
90	Rossini	*Tancredi*, flute or violin and guitar	19 April 1817
90	Rossini	Overture, piano	19 April 1817
90 (+ Pl. No. 29)	Rossini	Overture to *L'italiana in Algeri*, piano	19 April 1817
90	Rossini	Rondo 'Pense alla patria' from *L'italiana in Algeri*, piano	19 April 1817
69	Rossini	Variations on Rossini's 'Polacca' from *Tancredi*, Op. 51, guitar	27 March 1818
283	Adalbert Gyrowetz (arr. Friedrich Starke)	Variations on 'Mir leuchtet die Hoffnung' from *Der Augenarzt*, Traeg	10 December 1818

life' of the country – and of the fashion for plots with lightly moralising social commentary. He joined Emanuel Schikaneder's company at the Theater auf der Wieden in 1789. In 1796, his opera *Der Tiroler Wastel*, a light 'Volkstück mit Musik' composed in collaboration with Schikaneder, received rave reviews, and was performed 118 times at that theatre – this is far more often than the most popular Italian operas of the 1780s and early 1790s.

The plot of *Der Tiroler Wastel*, like many of the time, appeals with engaging comedy on the everyday, with familiar (and familial) characters and plot. The simple farmer Wastel and his wife Liesel have come to the big city, Vienna, to stay with his well-to-do brother. There he encounters

Example 2.1 *Der Tiroler Wastel*, by Jakob Haibel, arranged for *Harmonie* by Franz Joseph Rosinack Schörtzel (fl. 1800), bars 1–9

confused family relations, born of the easy and unscrupulous view of life prevailing in the city. He is disgusted, but then brings order to his circumstances with good sense. Schikaneder created the role of Wastel himself, drawing on his own observations of character and dialect in Innsbruck. It led to various spinoffs, including Tirolean costumes for Viennese women, plays based on Tirolean folk characters, and also musical arrangements. The work was immediately arranged for home use, including a *Harmonie* arrangement by Franz Joseph Rosinack Schörtzel (Example 2.1), which made the everyday drama readily performable in everyday settings.

Overwhelmingly, though, the 'take-home' opera in these early nineteenth-century publishing catalogues is music for piano, and piano and voice. This means that it is music in which women could readily participate. A spin-off effect of opera's heightened popularity at this time was numerous variations on themes from well-known operas.[43] So, for example, there are Joseph Gelinek's Variations on 'Ein Mädchen oder Weibchen' from *Die Zauberflöte* and two sets of variations drawn from *La clemenza di Tito*. One thinks also of Beethoven's Clarinet Trio, Op. 94; 12 Variations on 'Se vuol ballare' from *Figaro*, WoO 40; and variations for piano and cello, such as WoO 46 and Op. 66. And from Hummel there are variations on 'Vivat Bacchus, Bacchus liebe!' from *Die Entführung aus dem Serail* as well as his Viola Fantasie/Potpourri, Op. 94. These numerous piano arrangements allowed hands-on experience and reliving of operatic hits by gifted amateur pianists in the home, and also served the purposes of canon formation, by promoting the repetition and familiarisation of works. They drew attention to pianism generally, and specifically the talents of the well-known pianists who created them. Some of these pianists, such as Hummel, Clementi, and Friedrich Kalkbrenner made arrangements with their own performance in mind. This trend of arranging in order to draw attention to the skill of the (pianist) arranger, discussed in Chapter 6, would become more pronounced over the first half of the nineteenth century, culminating in the arrangements of Liszt.

But in these catalogues there are also many variations on lesser-known works, carried out by lesser-known composers, which served primarily to provide more fun with familiar repertoire for more amateurs in the home. An example is the work of Pössinger, who wrote arrangements for flute Op. 27, on 'Wenn sie mich nur von weitem sieht', and the flute variations Op. 31, on 'Wer hörte mich nur von weitem sieht', both from Weigl's *Die Schweizerfamilie*. Pössinger is a significant figure in the history of opera for the Viennese home in this period. He lived in Vienna and played violin in the Vienna Hofmusikkapelle. In 1786, he joined the Viennese court theatre orchestra and in 1798 was appointed violinist-violist in the imperial court orchestra, a position he held until his death on 19 August 1827. Pössinger mainly wrote music for string quartet. He also made arrangements. He was particularly successful as an arranger of contemporary works, mostly of popular contemporary operas for string quartet, including Weber's *Oberon*; Rossini's *Tancredi*, *Zelmira*, and *La gazza ladra*; and Beethoven's *Fidelio*. Arrangements of works with nationalist overtones, such as Weber's *Der Freischütz* and *Oberon*, helped these works retain their resonance throughout the nineteenth century.

---

[43] This topic is discussed in detail by Axel Beer, 'Die Oper daheim: Variationen als Rezeptionsform', in Hinrichsen and Pietschmann, *Jenseits der Bühne*, pp. 37–47.

The Role of the Performers

We have seen that many Viennese dilettantes were competent enough to perform arrangements, and that there was a particular proliferation of talented string-quartet performers in Vienna around 1800, just about all of them male, and numerous talented female pianists. Complex characters set by sophisticated composers meant that there were arrangements to be found to showcase the talents of the most able amateurs; but even Mozart's notoriously complex operas contained numbers that could be 'translated' for such amateurs. A comparison of Examples 2.2 and 2.3 illustrates this point. Example 2.2 shows Papageno's aria 'Der Vogelfänger bin ich ja', of Mozart's *Die Zauberflöte* (Paris: Sieber, n.d.), bars 1–14, from an early nineteenth-century anonymous quartet arrangement. The texture is a simple melody and accompaniment, and the melodic material is given wholly to the first violin. The arrangement is within the reach of performers

Example 2.2 Papageno's aria 'Der Vogelfänger bin ich ja', bars 1–14 (bar 14 is missing in the original), from an early nineteenth-century quartet arrangement (anonymous) of Mozart's *Die Zauberflöte* (Paris: Sieber, n.d.)

Example 2.3 'Porgi amor' from Mozart's *Le nozze di Figaro* (Cavatina, No. 11), arranged for string quartet in Artaria's complete arrangement of *Figaro* (Vienna: Artaria, 1806), bars 1–25 (editorial slurs are shown with dotted lines)

of modest skill (by any standard), even the first violin part. This should not be surprising; after all this is a song sung by a 'simple' character, and Mozart's music invariably reflects the character he is setting.

But when we turn to 'Porgi amor', from *Figaro* (Cavatina, No. 11), arranged for string quartet in Artaria's complete arrangement of *Figaro*, bars 1–25 of which are shown in Example 2.3, the story is different. In the operatic original, this is the Countess's first aria and Mozart uses it to portray a complex and troubled psyche. This is a prayer to the God of Love, to grant freedom from the sorrows inflicted on her by her deceiving husband; the Countess offers to accept either the restoration of his love or her own death. The melodic line is rich with ornamentation, and fluctuating in affect, which contributes to a difficult first violin part in the arrangement (the vocal line commences in bar 18). Again, the lower parts are essentially accompanimental; but, as often in Mozart's orchestration, the accompaniment also contributes to the characterisation. The extensive introduction, in which all parts play important roles, sets the background for understanding the Countess's state of mind, and this function is here transferred onto the four parts of the string quartet. When the vocal line commences in bar 18, there are still subtle interactions between voice and accompaniment, which adds interest to the lower parts in the string-quartet version.

These early nineteenth-century arrangements can vary in difficulty independently of the sophistication of the sources. There is another layer of 'translation' to be considered, which contributes to relative difficulty. This is the fact that performers reading from musical parts around 1800 often had quite a lot to do in order to 'realise' the music. Back then, amateur performers did not read from scores that had been carefully edited to reflect composers' performance expectations in detail. We know from the correspondence of composers such as Haydn, Mozart, and Beethoven that the parts (rather than scores, then much less common) of their original chamber music that were produced and sold often came riddled with errors into the hands of buyers, despite composers' remonstrations.[44]

In practice this meant that amateur performers were still 'arrangers' in a certain sense – they wore the responsibility of tidying up the arrangement to the degree they wanted or needed to in order to enjoy and follow the music in a satisfying way. So, for instance, in Example 2.2, bar 14 is missing in all parts. Performers who were familiar with the work would spot an error, and could probably supply the omission to resolve the problem

---

[44] For an example involving Beethoven and Steiner, see my *Beethoven's Theatrical Quartets*, p. 47.

collaboratively. In Example 2.3, several slurs and other articulation (later in the movement) would need to be added to bring parts into vertical alignment – which the performers might or might not want. Non-uniform bowing and articulation, for example, were accepted ways of individualising the parts in chamber music performance.

Example 2.4 contains a more challenging passage, in which performers would need to take steps to 'realise' the notation if they cared about vertical uniformity and sought to observe Mozart's instructions in the operatic original. This is an excerpt from the Finale in Mollo's string-quartet arrangement of *Don Giovanni*, Act 2 Scene 15. In bars 15 and 16, the fluctuating dynamics that are so crucial to the invocation of the sublime in this music are wholly missing from the lower strings. Even in this small-scale format, this music exhibits aspects of the musical sublime such as stark contrasts of dynamics and register, thought to invoke a sense of incommensurability, which was associated with the sublime.[45] The lower strings needed to fill in unspecified dynamics, drawing on other parts and their knowledge of the opera, to evoke this.

This example presents further challenges for the performers from another angle: the *way* it is arranged. The Commendatore is represented by first violin, but in bar 10 that part takes on an eerie circular chromatic motif, last heard in the overture. In bar 12, viola chips in with Leporello's nervous chatter; then all parts join in with the fluctuating dynamics. This blending and sharing of vocal parts and accompaniment between the performing parts in the arrangement creates difficulties for performers more used to a tidy division of melody and accompaniment in the easier chamber music of the day. But this kind of part writing was wholly in keeping with the *thematische Arbeit* (thematic working) of the more challenging string quartets of the time. All this was well within reach of the talented middle- and upper-class Viennese male performers who could afford to buy this sheet music, and who were after all often talented minor composers. A little bit of recomposition and adaptation would have been no object to such performers, and indeed contributed to the collegiality and camaraderie offered by quartet music around 1800.

Each original edition, because of its deficiencies (by modern editorial standards), provides some scope for performers to exercise compositional skills. For example, in the 1806 Artaria string-quartet arrangement of

---

[45] On the mathematical sublime, relevant here, see James Webster, 'The Creation, Haydn's Late Vocal Music, and the Musical Sublime', in Elaine Sisman (ed.), *Haydn and His World* (Princeton, NJ: Princeton University Press, 1997), pp. 59–60.

Example 2.4 Excerpt from the Finale in Mollo's string-quartet arrangement of *Mozart's Don Giovanni*, Act 2 Scene 15, bars 1–21 (editorial dynamics are shown in parentheses)

Figaro, the viola player will need to delete an entire bar near the end of No. 4 so that the parts add up. There are also several bowing and articulation discrepancies between the parts, including missing triplet signs in the cello in No. 5, all of which can be resolved through careful listening on the part of the performers. It should be noted, however, that quartet players at this time, even the professional performers who were starting to be heard in public, were not necessarily given to much rehearsal. An article from 1810, 'Performance of Instrumental Quartets' (1804) for the *Allgemeine musikalische Zeitung*, signed 'Cambini in Paris' but probably written by Friedrich Rochlitz, the journal's editor at the time, suggests as much. The theatrical metaphor he deploys here suggests a tricky mediating role for performers in the instrumental quartet in the more public performance contexts that were emerging. He argued that music will be meaningless to an audience unless the performers have rehearsed sufficiently:

The best actor would not dare to give a scene from a significant play without having gone through it: it causes me grief and I must shrug my shoulders involuntarily, when I hear musicians say: Come on, let's play quartets! – just as lightly as one says in society: Come on, let's play a game of Reversis! Then must music indeed remain vague and without meaning.[46]

In a properly realised string-quartet performance, the performers need rehearsal to produce 'perfect performance' (*vollkommene Ausführung*), as he terms it. But in this article the author protests that quartet players are not achieving this standard; his complaint, together with evidence discussed by Klorman, suggests that extensive rehearsal was not considered normal or necessary, even for professionals.[47] This seems to have remained true into the 1820s: in a conversation book of 1825, professional violinist Karl Holz observed to Beethoven, 'We rehearse only your quartets, not those of Haydn and Mozart, [which] work better without rehearsal'.[48] As to amateur performers of opera arrangements, they were left to work out a good deal in performance – and were probably striving more for a fun sight-read than 'perfect performance'.

---

[46] Giuseppe Cambini [Friedrich Rochlitz], 'Ausführung der Instrumentalquartetten', *Allgemeine musikalische Zeitung* 6/47 (22 August 1804), col. 783.

[47] See Edward Klorman, 'The First Professional String Quartet? Reexamining an Account Attributed to Giuseppe Maria Cambini', *Notes, the Quarterly Journal of the Music Library Association* 71/4 (2015), pp. 629–43.

[48] Dagmar Beck, Grita Herre, and Karl-Heinz Köhler (eds.), *Ludwig van Beethovens Konversationshefte*, 11 vols. (Leipzig: Deutscher Verlag für Musik, 1968–2001), vol. 8 (1981), p. 259.

Many opera arrangements for domestic use were far from complete in the sense of representing the original in chamber form: recitatives are missing, and arrangers often cherry-picked the lyrical numbers most suitable for setting. So, for example, in Artaria's 1806 arrangement of *Figaro* for string quartet, the piece labelled No. 5 is actually No. 10 in the original – Figaro's 'Non più andrai', and No. 6 in the arrangement is No. 11 in the original, 'Porgi amor' (see Table 2.4). These were hit solo numbers, well known to everyone who saw the opera in the opera theatre – and to many who did not, thanks to numerous arrangements. More to the point, these arrangements themselves are hardly 'complete' in the sense now assumed: modern editions of chamber music of this era specify just about everything that the performer needs to know about his or her part in standard, detailed notation.

Take, for example, the Artaria string-quartet arrangement of 'Non più andrai' (an excerpt from which is Example 2.5). Articulation is often only

Table 2.4 *Le nozze di Figaro* numbers included in Artaria's 1806 arrangement, listing both the scene number in the respective act and the song number. Bracketed tempo indications in the first column are indicative only

Number in arrangement (tempo)	Number in *Neue Mozart-Ausgabe*	Scene
Overtura	Sinfonia	
Atto primo/Act One		
No. I (Allegro)	No. 1 Duettino (Susanna, Figaro)	I–II
No. II (Allegro)	No. 2 Duettino (Susanna, Figaro)	I–II
No. III (Allegretto)	No. 3 Cavatina (Figaro)	I–II
No. IV (Allegro assai)	No. 7 Terzetto (Susanna, Basilio, Il Conte)	VI–VII
No. V (Allegro)	No. 10 Aria (Figaro)	VIII
Atto secondo/Act Two		
No. VI (Larghetto)	No. 11 Cavatina (La Contessa)	I
No. VII (Andante)	No. 12 Arietta (Cherubino)	II
No. VIII Finale (Allegro molto)	No. 16 Finale (multiple characters)	VI–XI
Atto terzo/Act Three		
No. IX (Allegretto)	No. 21 Duettino (Susanna, La Contessa)	X
No. X (Grazioso)	No. 22 Coro (Soprano I, II)	XI–XIV
No. XI (Marcia)	No. 23 Finale (Susanna, La Contessa, Il Conte, Figaro; Coro)	XI–XIV
Atto quarto/Act Four		
No. XII (Andante)	No. 28 Aria (Susanna)	IX–X
No. XIII (Larghetto)	No. 28a Rondo KV 577 (Susanna) [Mozart's 'Al desio di chi t'adora', K577, composed 1789; replacement aria for original No. 28]	X

Example 2.5 String-quartet arrangement of 'Non più andrai' from Mozart's *Le nozze di Figaro* (Vienna: Artaria, 1806), bars 57–9

partially specified in these early editions, and its application is left to performers. This early edition uses staccato dots throughout, but they are applied sparingly and not uniformly. So here, as in many editions of chamber music from around 1800, modern performers or editors need to decide on the degree to which unmarked notes should be shortened. This would have been easily resolved by contemporary performers. For early nineteenth-century music, a non-legato technique was the norm for unslurred, unmarked notes. The theorist Heinrich Christoph Koch noted that unmarked notes were typically played in a detached style, and he also noted, in the entry on 'staccato' (Abstoßen) in his *Musikalisches Lexikon* of 1802, that non-legato performance was especially common in music with fast tempi:

[I]n passages of faster tempi … there are many types of passages to which performers are accustomed in which notes without special markings are to be detached from one another; to this end composers take care never to mark these passages with the staccato sign.[49]

On the basis of Koch's testimony, and of similar directives in early-nineteenth-century string-performance treatises, 'Non più andrai', marked Allegro (and 'vivace' in the manuscript, but not in Mozart's hand) requires a basic non-legato style throughout (that is, for all unmarked notes, as in the cello in Example 2.5). For 'Porgi amor', however, the reverse applies. The opening tempo designation ('Larghetto'), flat key (E-flat major), presence of numerous slurs, and melancholy affect (including written-out sighs

---

[49] Koch, *Musikalisches Lexikon*, s.v. 'Abstoßen oder absetzen', col. 44.

and syncopation) all combine to suggest a fundamentally legato style. Performers of the time would have 'read' all these signs and performed in this way automatically, without needing the detailed articulation markings that we assume to be necessary today. Missing dynamics and accents are more tricky – they can be inferred from the affect, and from careful listening to the other performers.

Performers of arrangements could probably often remember at least parts of popular items from live public performances, or from hearing others playing popular arrangements. Mozart reported as follows to Baron Gottfried von Jacquin, writing from Prague in January 1787:

> I looked on, however, with the greatest pleasure while all these people flew about in sheer delight to the music of my 'Figaro', arranged for contredanses and German dances. For here they talk about nothing but 'Figaro'. Nothing is played, sung or whistled but 'Figaro'. No opera is drawing like 'Figaro'. Nothing, nothing but 'Figaro'. Certainly a great honour for me![50]

Arrangements were a useful spin-off from the success of the Prague premier of Mozart's *Le nozze di Figaro* (following comparatively less success in Vienna in 1786[51]): they helped broker this difficult music to a public eager for the popular sentimental plot and revolutionary touches like the militaristic 'Non più andrai', which was a great success. Still, the second violinist performing from Artaria's arrangement of this work for string quartet would need to be reminded not to play p on note 2 in bar 7, where everyone else had *mf* in a unison passage, and to start the crescendo at the beginning of bar 59, like everyone else, rather than at the end of the bar (as marked in the Artaria part; see Example 2.5); and the first violin might need reminding to perform triplets at the end of this number, where the triplet sign is lacking in the Artaria part.

Passages could be freely adapted to suit the performers' capabilities. So, for example, where a passage is too high or too fast for them to perform with ease, the performer can rearrange the part one octave lower or in larger rhythmic units, adapting it to his or her abilities. Thus the first violin triple-stops at the end of 'Non più andrai' could be simplified by performing the upper note or top two notes of each chord.

String-quartet arrangements from around 1800, destined for use mainly by gentlemen at leisure, tended to provide a satisfying, fun performance

---

[50] Bauer et al., *Mozart: Briefe und Aufzeichnungen*, vol. 4, *1787–1857* (1963), p. 10; trans. Anderson, *The Letters of Mozart and His Family*, p. 903.

[51] On the Viennese premier, see Simon P. Keefe, *Mozart in Vienna: The Final Decade* (Cambridge: Cambridge University Press, 2017), pp. 367–8.

experience for the four performers. Contemporary arrangements that would have involved women operated in the same way, but also provided some additional benefits for the female performers. The culture of musical arrangements in early nineteenth-century Vienna granted female performers (pianists and singers) roles denied to them in other areas of musical life, and with them opportunities to advance their musical education through the arrangement and performance of orchestral music. The precise roles and opportunities on offer are implied by the music itself. Four-hand piano transcriptions at least offered women a chance for hands-on experience of music they might otherwise never perform, and a chance for some social, exciting, and possibly subversive interaction, entailing hand-crossing and shoulder-rubbing.[52] These transcriptions became increasingly prominent.

As we have seen, around 1800, women were most commonly deployed as singers or piano accompanists in the performance of opera in the home – in Vienna as elsewhere. The publication records of the firm of Tranquillo Mollo, who took over from Artaria, show the kinds of scores available around this time. Like many other firms of the day, Mollo cashed in on the thirst for things theatrical, arranged for the chamber. Artaria had published substantial numbers of piano reductions from current operas and of individual arias, and Mollo took these over (the pieces appeared between 1787 and 1804 with a special 'Raccolta' – collection – number). Mozart opera figures prominently among the arrangements offered by Mollo from these early years. After 1804 music by new, popular composers, including Paër and Rossini was increasingly represented.

An example drawn from Mollo/Artaria's complete piano reduction of Mozart's *Die Entführung aus dem Serail* (initially released in 1798 and reprinted twice) shows the complexity these piano parts could incorporate. This is the opera Joseph II is claimed to have said had 'too many notes', and it does indeed contain virtuoso vocal parts (especially for Osmin and Constanze, but also for Belmont; see Example 2.6), with complex and sometimes soloistic orchestral writing (especially in 'Marten aller Arten'; see Example 2.7). But the general point here holds true of all piano reductions and many piano chamber arrangements: the pianist recreates the orchestral texture. So where string-quartet and *Harmonie* arrangements, for example, afforded men an entertaining play through repertoire they might also perform in more public contexts, piano reductions and piano chamber arrangements afforded women a chance to take on a challenging leadership role with repertoire they would not play in any other context.

[52] On this subject see also Christensen, 'Four-Hand Piano Transcription', pp. 255–98.

Example 2.6 Belmont's first aria in Mollo's piano reduction of *Die Entführung aus dem Serail* (Vienna, n.d.), bars 20–36

Women figure frequently in accounts of the salons (detailed in Chapter 3) as performers rather than hostesses, and certainly not always with difficult parts or leadership roles. Where all-string chamber music featured, we have observed that the spotlight was on men and on male

Example 2.7 Orchestral introduction to 'Marten aller Arten' in Mollo's piano reduction of *Die Entführung aus dem Serail*, bars 1–28

connoisseurship and sociability.[53] But arrangements were a good way to include women, foregrounded or otherwise. So, for example, Louis Spohr rearranged some of his salon music to include harp, in order to involve his wife Dorette, who played both harp and piano. This simple fact of inclusion

---

[53] On this subject see also Lott, *The Social Worlds of Nineteenth-Century Chamber Music*, pp. 13–18.

becomes important when we consider the otherwise isolated lives of women in the early nineteenth-century Viennese home. Opera in the home was being made into the everyday music of everyday people. What it offered for both women and men was the potential for new roles in music-making, and a trying-on of various roles afforded by opera plots. Opera in the home was not only a way to understand current affairs, ideas, and aesthetics, but also a retreat and respite from the constraints of everyday life under the Metternich System.

3 | Female Agency in the Early Nineteenth-Century Viennese Musical Salon

> Katharina *Hochenadl*, who lost her mother at an early age, soon made use of her talents to lighten the burdens of the household by teaching music. At the same time, she most devotedly supported her father's wish to cultivate genuine art in his house through regularly recurring events. This was done in two ways: first, attention was paid to chamber music (piano sonatas with and without accompaniment, string quartets, solo songs for one and more voices); and then larger works, such as oratorios, cantatas, or older operas, accompanied by piano amplified by a violoncello, were performed. These efforts began and took effect especially in a period in which these particular branches of music were neglected in public musical life, and so it is quite understandable that precisely the most eager musical friends gladly joined this circle, and participated as willingly as they listened.[1]

Just off the ring road that surrounds central Vienna today as it did in 1800, and directly opposite the Kärntnertortheater, was the Bürgerspital. Originally the medieval citizens' hospital, this capacious building was transformed into an apartment complex between 1783 and 1790, comprising some 10 courtyards, 20 staircases, and 220 apartments. Here there lived many artists from the Kärntnertortheater, and also musical amateurs like Josef Hochenadl (1752–1842), an official at the Court War Accounting Office. His daughter Katharina (1785–1861) eventually became a concert pianist in Vienna, but early in her career she was instrumental in building up Vienna's semi-private musical life. The Hochenadl salons were hosted by her father, who held them at his handily situated home from the middle of November through the winter until Easter, on Sundays at noon. This calendar of private soirées was typical of Vienna at the time. They continued until the winter of 1824–5. Sonnleithner, whose account of Katharina is quoted at the beginning of this chapter, started attending the salons in 1815, some time after their inception. He recognised Katharina's central role in these events. However, history has all but demolished the

---

[1] Deutsch (ed.), 'Leopold von Sonnleithners Erinnerungen', p. 53 (italics original).

record of women's roles in the Viennese salons of this time, which came to life after the theatres' doors had closed for the week and for the season.

This chapter explores environments, such as the Hochenadl salon, where arrangements were performed in early nineteenth-century Vienna, and the purposes they fulfilled, such as fostering sociability and advancing social and aesthetic understanding. I examine prevalent plots and themes in arranged works and various types of opera arrangements to consider how they might have extended the meaning and experience of public concert-going. For instance, as noted at the end of Chapter 2, they could allow domestic performers and listeners to engage with ideas about political freedom, class, and nationalism that were being raised in the Viennese salons more generally. Audiences for opera in Viennese salons could listen to works with revolutionary themes and potentially politically inflammatory plots that would not be tolerated in other art forms or more public venues. For example Cherubini's *Les deux journées* (1800), a 'rescue' opera about an incident in the French Revolution, was very popular in arrangement. The continued popularity of Mozart's *Die Zauberflöte* and Gluck's *Iphigénie en Tauride*, in arrangements, into the era of the Congress of Vienna (1814–15) was perhaps related to their prominent theme of hope, which would have spoken also to the city's populace.[2]

This book is about arranging public music, and specifically operas, for private performance. But it is also about the crucial contribution of private-sphere music-making to creating Vienna's public reputation as the 'City of Music' in the early nineteenth century. In particular, the book is about the middle-class people (women as well as men) who worked behind the scenes to develop a new music culture – arguably by rearranging an old one – to reflect middle-class ideals, values, and a new idea of nationhood. The salon was an important space for this rearrangement, where women could take on roles and leadership not offered to them in public. It can be seen as a zone of transaction between public and private spaces, and musical arrangements as a currency in this transaction.[3]

It was no small matter to arrange – in the sense of bringing about and organising – musical opportunities, and ultimately the cultural shifts they facilitated. The second part of this chapter considers three prominent

---

[2] On this subject, see Hilary McSherry, '"Komm Hoffnung!": Hope, Opera and Diplomacy at the Congress of Vienna', MA thesis (Dalhousie University, 2019).

[3] On the salon's mediating role see Habermas, *The Structural Transformation*, p. 45; discussed in Ruth A. Solie, 'Biedermeier Domesticity and the Schubert Circle: A Rereading', in *Music in Other Words: Victorian Conversations*, California Studies in 19th-Century Music (Berkeley, CA: University of California Press, 2004), pp. 123–6.

female 'arrangers' who were significant agents in rearranging the social order in early nineteenth-century Vienna, and paving the way for female musicians like Katharina Hochenadl: Fanny von Arnstein (1758–1818); Caroline Pichler (1769–1843); and Maria Theresia von Paradis (1759–1824). I discuss the musical and literary activities they organised, and the degree to which class and gender mixing persisted in their more-or-less private music-making, especially through the vehicle of musical arrangements. Their activity spans a long period, and a shift from small-scale, semi-private music-making towards large-scale, semi-public performances. These women were helping to establish a new public sphere of musical life in Vienna – as Hanslick puts it, the 'stately image' (*stattliches Bild*) of musical Vienna.[4]

Viennese Salons

What exactly is a salon, as the term applies to Vienna around 1800? Recent researchers tend to use a broad definition of salons – as regular heterosocial gatherings of intellectuals, artists, patrons, and professionals, meeting primarily to pursue sociability and knowledge – which encompasses most of the private and semi-private gatherings in Vienna around this time.[5] If the definition of salons were extended to include amateur musicians, who might cross over into the categories of 'professionals' or 'artists', and also 'patrons' and 'intellectuals', little of Vienna's private and semi-private middle- and upper-class domestic social life would be excluded. Cypess has argued that 'salon' can misleadingly evoke an exclusive, high-society environment, whereas applied (anachronistically) to the early nineteenth century, it takes in events ranging from large informal gatherings to intimate gatherings of family and friends.[6] Sonnleithner's evidence suggests that this inclusive understanding of musical salon participation is warranted after 1800, and indeed that it

---

[4] Hanslick, *Geschichte*, xi.
[5] For selected sources defining salon, see especially Anja Bunzel and Natasha Loges (eds.), *Musical Salon Culture in the Long Nineteenth Century* (Woodbridge: Boydell & Brewer, 2019); also Marjanne E. Goozé, 'What Was the Berlin Jewish Salon Around 1800?', in Cypess and Sinkoff, *Sara Levy's World*, pp. 21–38. On salon culture more generally in the nineteenth century, see Verena von der Heyden-Rynsch, *Europäische Salons: Höhepunkte einer versunkenen weiblichen Kultur* (Zurich: Artemis & Winkler, 1992).
[6] Rebecca Cypess, 'Ancient Poetry, Modern Music, and the *Wechselgesang der Mirjam und Debora*: The Meanings of Song in the Itzig Circle', *Bach* 47/1 (2016), pp. 21–65.

was so before this. Looking back to the early nineteenth-century Viennese salon, he wrote:

The enjoyment of pursuing music on a small-scale, non-professional level [was] one of the long-standing characteristic hallmarks of German and Viennese music lovers. France and Italy used the word dilettanti to describe only the active attendees of musical programs: the enthusiastic concert- and theatre-going public. However, on the other hand, when we Germans speak of musical dilettantes, we are thinking of people who themselves sing, play a string or wind instrument, direct or compose. Even if the results of our dilettantes cannot easily compete with the more careful performance of outstanding professional artists, when they are effectively prepared such results contribute to the spread of knowledge of solid musical works of art and thereby to an enhancement of taste as a whole.[7]

Some of these gatherings took place weekly 'in the season' (that is, not in summer, when the wealthy left town for their country residences). The Hochenadl salons, for instance, took place on this kind of schedule. Others were less regular, being held around birthdays and other special occasions.

There is evidence of a broad spectrum of salons in terms of content, and participation from the aristocracy as well as the middle classes – after 1800 as well as before. Music, although not always the centre of attention, was a regular feature, although *Salonmusik* was recognised as a category only in the 1830s. As Hanslick defines it, *Salonmusik* is basically a vapid display, which flourished in an era dominated by the virtuoso (beginning around the 1820s and 1830s, especially with Liszt). If we follow Hanslick, it would be surprising if *Salonmusik* contributed much to Viennese musical culture, in the sense of 'high art' as he sought to define it. The musical 'public sphere' of serious discourse would only develop with the later flourishing of concert life.[8]

But Hanslick's telling of Viennese music history suggests a misunderstanding of the breadth of salon culture and the purposes of the salons. They were also considered a microcosm of polite society, and potentially a place for personal and social improvement on the part of the participants.[9] Hanslick's account also supposes that *Salonmusik* had nothing to do with these laudable purposes. But the nineteenth-century salon can be understood as an integrated practice or process rather than as events or an environment, and its 'objects' or 'products' (including *Salonmusik* itself)

---

[7] Deutsch (ed.), 'Leopold von Sonnleithners Erinnerungen', p. 101; trans. Vago, 'Musical Life of Amateur Musicians in Vienna', p. 3 (italics original).
[8] Hanslick, *Geschichte*, xii.
[9] See Peter Gradenwitz, *Literatur und Musik in geselligem Kreise: Geschmacksbildung, Gesprächsstoff und musikalische Unterhaltung in der bürgerlichen Salongesellschaft* (Stuttgart: Steiner, 1991).

as part of this practice. In the salons, composers and performers, professionals and amateurs, intellectuals and artists, listeners and critics met at least superficially on more informal terms than they did in the concert hall. As Sonnleithner says of the Hochenadl salons, 'the most eager friends of the true art of music gladly joined this circle, and participated as willingly as they listened'.[10] Scores and works were adapted by the performers to meet the social and cultural needs of the moment. Instrumentation was freely changed, and 'arrangements' of various sorts were produced – in new performing scores or in improvised, unnotated versions – to serve the purposes of musical sociability, entertainment, and *Bildung*. Within the salon, musical scores enabled sociable interaction, which allowed the rise of musical practices that might not otherwise have developed, by people who otherwise lacked such opportunities – especially female performers.

The practice-oriented character of salons in Vienna is indicated by the kinds of activity they involved. Link has explored the private entertainments that took place in Count Zinzendorf's circle in the period 1783–92, dividing the 166 entertainments into 5 broad categories: domestic music-making; music to enhance social events such as dinners; concerts; *comédies de société* (the greatest number); and Italian plays and poetry readings. Of the events that Zinzendorf attended, the concerts are borderline in terms of narrower definitions of the salon, because of their scale (almost public). Conversely, domestic music-making was sometimes too small in scale to serve the socialising function, even where it took place regularly. But all of these events were potentially geared to educational and, especially, social ends. This is clear from the activities chosen, which frequently mixed the arts – music, poetry, theatre – and were interactive. Interest in theatre extended to the imitation of public performances and performers. The theatrical character of these entertainments, which persists into the nineteenth century, is quintessentially Viennese.

The emphasis in Viennese salons before and after 1800 was firmly on theatre, including theatrical musical works, especially opera. The much-favoured *comédies de société* were theatrical performances in the homes of the nobility, who re-enacted works that had been staged at the National Theatre, often with some mimicry of particular actors.[11] Other participatory theatrical entertainments in salons included *Geschichten spielen* (pantomiming of scenes from famous plays); *tableaux vivants* or *lebende Bilder* (posing like characters from famous historical paintings); and

---

[10] Deutsch (ed.), 'Leopold von Sonnleithners Erinnerungen', p. 53.
[11] Link, 'Vienna's Private Theatrical and Musical Life', pp. 205–57.

Attitüden (acting out emotions depicted in paintings).[12] They meant that the Viennese did not have to resist their appetite for theatre once Vienna's five theatre doors closed for the day, or for the season.

The purposes of these theatrical pursuits extended beyond entertainment. All of them involve 'arrangement', in a sense parallel with musical arrangement, and a making one's own of public, large-scale art forms; they served to develop self-actualisation, empowerment, and agency – all components of *Bildung* – in the middle classes. Participation in salon practices helped people understand the social and political commentary that underpinned a great deal of theatre around 1800. Pierre Beaumarchais' *Le Mariage de Figaro*, for example, which was initially banned by the censors, observes that class does not necessarily correlate with virtue – the early admiration and success of Mozart and Lorenzo Da Ponte's *Figaro* underscores the popularity of the trope, and the rapid permeability of music by theatrical and political influence. Taking on theatrical personae also allowed the participants to try on roles that might otherwise be forbidden to them, for example by uttering manservant Leporello's subversive lyrics. Trying on these roles was a way of defining oneself in contradistinction to the aristocracy/ruling class, and thus exerting a kind of power. Rescue plots were in vogue around 1800, in the wake of the French Revolution – in operatic hits like Spontini's *La Vestale* or Weigl's *Die Schweizer Familie* involving heroism, political freedom, and personal choice (as in marriage for love). Even where they appeared to offer sheer entertainment, or pure escapism, opera arrangements also helped to define their arrangers' and performers' sense of freedom – a freedom of choice regarding what they heard, where they heard it, and how.

To be sure, the extent to which a salon was taken up with *Bildung* varied with the host and his or her connections. But Brian Vick points out the error, typified by Hanslick, of viewing salons as 'feminine' or 'limited' environments where contentious topics should be avoided. In fact the salons, and the music-making they hosted, often served serious political and religious functions and involved a great deal of debate among a fascinating cross-section of society, and women played various important roles, including that of hostess.[13]

Viennese salons built on the character and functions of those of Paris. But they differed from the Parisian salons in three major ways: the division

---

[12] Thormählen, 'Playing with Art', especially p. 370.
[13] Brian E. Vick, *The Congress of Vienna: Power and Politics after Napoleon* (Cambridge, MA: Harvard University Press, 2014), pp. 112–52.

of classes; male domination; and the prevalence of music – especially opera, arranged in many and various forms. As regards class, the traditional French salons were designed as microcosms of polite society, bringing together men and women of various social strata (though in practice mostly the upper levels) to pursue intellectual topics of contemporary interest. In Vienna there was less mixing of the classes from the outset, and especially after the Congress of Vienna in 1815. But even before 1800 this was probably more an ideal than a reality, depending on the particular salon. The salons of Arnstein included distinguished middle-class intellectuals such as Wilhelm von Humboldt, August Wilhelm Schlegel, and Friedrich Schlegel. During the Congress of Vienna, she was also visited by famous aristocrats like the Duke of Wellington, the Prince of Talleyrand, and Prince Karl August of Hardenburg. But her salons were an exception in this respect. Arnstein herself, arriving from Berlin with a noble heritage, frequently encountered class obstacles related to Jewish prominence among the upwardly mobile middle classes.

Male domination was much more pronounced in Viennese salons, both before and after 1800, than in French salons. Important male salon hosts figure from the late eighteenth century. In the early nineteenth century, male singers as cited by Mosel started to dominate as salon hosts, especially Kiesewetter and Sonnleithner; Schubert, too, exerted considerable influence on the Viennese musical scene through his Schubertiads.

The greater emphasis on music most distinguishes Vienna from Paris in the salons. Publishing catalogues in Paris around 1800 certainly speak to a great enthusiasm for opera arrangements. But before 1800, all of the types of salon frequented by Zinzendorf might offer music, whereas in Paris the primary emphasis was on literature. Even at Viennese salons centred on Italian plays or poetry readings, the poetry might be replaced or complemented by music-making. As for what was played at these salons, and how, we have memoirs, iconography, and accounts in newspapers by way of indication. A few detailed programmes are discussed later in this chapter, but programmes were rarely preserved. The repertoire depended, again, on the host and the nature of the salon, and followed changing tastes. But we can assume that the publishers' catalogues of this time provide a reliable index. They show a voracious and wide appetite for chamber music; a particular penchant for arrangements of large-scale works for chamber ensembles or piano solo; and, specifically, vast enthusiasm for opera arrangements.

These distinctive aspects of the Viennese salon persisted, and intensified in the early nineteenth century, as musical salons became a vehicle for middle-class aspiration. The rich salon culture, supported by the middle class and the aristocracy, contributed greatly to the vitality of Viennese musical life, especially around the time of the Congress of Vienna. Chamber music flourished among the middle classes, partly because the Viennese nobility and rulers were themselves often interested or involved in music and were emulated by aspiring middle-class families, in their new salons that now opened up and remained distinct from those of the nobility. Francis I, Emperor of Austria (r.1804–35) for example, was an amateur violinist; and his second wife Maria Theresa was a competent pianist. These were influential people in Viennese social and musical life. The desire for 'things domestic' (domestic activities) observed by Schönfeld in 1796 continued, encouraged by the government in the following decades, since it kept people (especially men) engaged at home, rather than meeting with others, and possibly conspiring to bring about another revolution.[14]

While the new salons of the bourgeoisie in early nineteenth-century Vienna involved some emulation, they also developed a distinctive character, especially post-Congress. They shared a new emphasis on simplicity rather than ostentation, and good manners rather than studied elegance. They also ostensibly sought to cultivate civil harmony and avoid political agitation. But the reality was sometimes otherwise. Arnstein's salon, for example, became known as a centre of conspiracy against Napoleon, attracting great attention after Napoleon's defeat and especially during the Congress of Vienna. The salon ended in 1818, when Arnstein died. New amusements, such as walking parties, were adopted alongside music-making, in pursuit of the 'harmonious' ideal; Schubert's circle among others took up and modelled such new, light-hearted pursuits.[15] Not all Schubert's music was deemed appropriate for the salons; his more 'serious' chamber music, such as string quartets, was typically excluded.[16] Perhaps this music reflected too clearly the melancholy and disillusionment that lay not far beneath the surface of salon life. The Sonnleithner family's history and Pichler's writings, for example, are filled with references to early death, suicide, and depression.[17]

---

[14] See also Donald G. Daviau, 'Biedermeier: The Happy Face of the Vormärz Era', in Pichl, Bernd, and Wagner (eds.), *The Other Vienna*, p. 23.
[15] Heindl, 'People, Class Structure, and Society', p. 50.
[16] See also Alice M. Hanson, 'Vienna, City of Music', in Erickson, *Schubert's Vienna*, p. 110.
[17] Burkhard Bittrich, 'Österreichische Züge am Beispiel der Caroline Pichler', in Karl Konrad Polheim (ed.), *Literatur aus Österreich, österreichische Literatur: Ein Bonner Symposion* (Bonn: Bouvier, 1981), pp. 167–89; for details of the Sonnleithner family history see Vago, 'Musical Life of Amateur Musicians in Vienna', pp. 13–24.

Salonmusik Doing Cultural Work

Modern scholars' conviction that the politically powerless early nineteenth-century bourgeoisie sought out innocuous pastimes and engaged in trivial pursuits to avoid attracting suspicion of conspiring – especially in early- to mid-nineteenth-century German lands – does not hold up in general.[18] The word *Biedermeier*, coined 1855–7, was originally used to label the middle class from that period as arrogant and self-righteous.[19] Today it refers to the style and art of the period in Germany from 1815 to 1848. The derogatory connotations have faded; but there remain problematic implications of triviality. A more balanced view has emerged as scholars examine the *Biedermeier*-era practice of salon music-making and the music it fostered. The private music-making and small-scale art of this era are then revealed as performing important social and cultural functions, helping to mitigate any small-mindedness, even when they seemed light-hearted and innocuous. This music-making and art gave the middle classes chances for cultural emulation and communication (sometimes covert), and also entertainment, and it gave women a chance to participate, as pianists in particular.

Salonmusik offered opportunities for personal expression that were not to be found in other arts. Consider the varied arrangements of themes from topical operas of the day, as in the potpourri. This very popular form was a medley of tunes that were not developed; the genre amounted to a form of musical arrangement. Around the end of the eighteenth century it came to be applied to strings of melodies from an opera or operas, as for example in the *Potpourri tiré des airs de 'Zauberflöte', 'Don Juan' et 'Figaro'* for piano (1820) by Gelinek.[20] Gelinek (1758–1825), a Czech-born composer and pianist, lived in Vienna for most of his career; he was known particularly for composing variations and had connections with Mozart, whom he met in Prague for a performance of *Don Giovanni*.

The potpourri was also developed by the German composer and violinist Spohr, who seems to have been particularly inspired by Viennese opera.

---

[18] On this subject see especially Daviau, 'Biedermeier: The Happy Face of the Vormärz Era', pp. 11–27.

[19] See Hanson, *Musical Life in Biedermeier Vienna*, p. 1.

[20] Andrea Klitzing lists eighteen potpourris in her catalogue of arrangements of Mozart's *Don Giovanni* printed in German-speaking countries up to 1850: 'W. A. Mozart: Don Giovanni. Arrangements – Gedruckt im deutschsprachigen Raum bis 1850' (2020) www.vandenhoeck-ruprecht-verlage.com/media/pdf/c3/2f/03/TABELLE-V-R-W-A-MOZART-DON-GIOVANNI-ARRANGEMENTSJJ7FAJWC1dwHu.pdf.

Most of Spohr's potpourris were originally intended for his own performance in concerts, but he regularly rearranged them for salon performance. Operas chosen for Spohr's potpourris included those with socially and politically interesting plots, such as the Potpourri in F-sharp minor on themes from Mozart's *Die Zauberflöte*, Op. 50 (composed in 1820; published in Leipzig, 1821), which is itself a rearrangement of the second movement of the Sonata for Violin and Harp, Op. 114. The huge popularity of *Die Zauberflöte* in arrangements in the early nineteenth-century German home is witnessed by contemporary publishing catalogues. Spohr would have encountered this vogue during his stay in Vienna (1812–15).

Spohr's Potpourri Op. 56 (composed 1821; published in Leipzig, 1822) is also based on a topical *Singspiel*, this one by another Viennese composer – Winter's *Das unterbrochene Opferfest* (premiered 1796), which took as its subject conflicts between Europeans and Incas in the sixteenth century. Again, this is a rearrangement of a work by Spohr, the Potpourri for Clarinet and Orchestra, Op. 80. The heroic-comic plot, in which the English hero shows bravery and benevolence in the face of oracular powers and foreign forces, seems to have fitted well with European tastes in contemporary salons: it was very popular in and beyond Vienna, and was variously arranged for domestic enjoyment and edification. Keith Warsop notes the compositional sophistication of Spohr's potpourris, which generally go beyond the typically more-or-less random mixture of favourite operatic hits strung together; they deploy variations on themes, carefully designed transitions, and recapitulations to make musically satisfying and coherent pieces.[21]

Repertoire performed at concerts, public or private, in Vienna at this time is often difficult to ascertain, since programmes are often non-existent or non-specific (where they do exist). But we do know that the Viennese salons offered varied musical fare, and reflected offerings in the more public arena. At the Hochenadl salons around 1820, for instance, Sonnleithner reports that the following excerpts from operas, songs, and sacred vocal works were heard between the instrumental items (accompanied by Katharina at the piano and a cellist 'for reinforcement'):

Wolfgang Amadeus Mozart, first finale from *Don Giovanni* (1787); arias for soprano from *Die Zauberflöte* (1791)

---

[21] Keith Warsop, 'Spohrs Potpourris', *Spohr Journal* 33 (2006), p. 15, www.spohr-society.org.uk/spohr_journal_33_2006_p15_warsop_spohrs_potpourris.pdf.

Ludwig van Beethoven, 'Adelaide'

Joseph Haydn, duet from *The Seasons*

Louis Spohr, tenor aria from *Faust* (*Singspiel*, 1813 – when Spohr had taken up a post at the Theater an der Wien)

Joseph Weigl, pieces from *L'Uniforme* (heroic-comic opera, 1800)

Ferdinando Paër, duets from *Camilla* (1798–9) and *Agnese* (*opera semi-seria*, 1809); trio and Finale from *Sargino* (heroic-comic opera, 1803)

Gaspare Spontini, duet from *Die Vestalin* (*La Vestale*, 1807)

Franz Schubert, 'Erlkönig' (1815), 'Gretchen am Spinnrade' (1814)

Friedrich Ernst Fesca, 'Die Geburt' (c.1819)

Étienne Mehul, trio from *Beiden Füchsen* (*Une folie*) (*comédie en vers mêlée*; 1802)

Friedrich Götz, composer of German opera and theatre director in Berlin, duets and trios

Gioachino Rossini, duet, trio, and finale from *L'italiana in Algeri* (1813); aria from *Sigismondo* (1814); aria and duet from *Semiramide* (1823); trio from *Zelmira* (1822)

Simon Mayr, duet from *Ginevra di Scozia* (1801)

Ernesto Nicolini, aria, duet, and finale from *Carlo magno* (1813); aria from *Quinto Fabio* (1811)

Valentino Fioravanti, quintet from *I virtuosi ambulanti* (1807); scale trio from *Le cantatrici villane* (1801)

Giovanni Paisiello, aria from *La molinara* (1788)

Saverio Mercadante, duet from *Elisa e Claudio* (1821)

Puccita [or Vincenzo Pucitta?], duet for two sopranos

Pierre Rode, variations [possibly the Variations on 'Nel cor più non mi sento' from Paisiello's *La molinara* (1821)]

Johann Nepomuk Hummel, 'La Sentinelle' (original for 3 voices, guitar, piano, violin, cello 1, cello 2 (ad lib))

Ignaz Moscheles, 'Der Abschied des Troubadours' (original for violin, guitar, and piano, by Moscheles, Mayseder, and Giuliani)

Most popular choruses: Nikolaus von Krufft, 'Die Wanderer im Walde'; Luigi Cherubini, Introduction from *Elisa* (1794); Carl Maria von Weber 'Lützow's Jagd'; Johann Peter Pixis, 'Räubenchor' from *Almazinde* (1820); and Andreas Romberg's 'Die Mache des Gesanges'[22]

---

[22] Deutsch (ed.), 'Leopold von Sonnleithners Erinnerungen', pp. 53–4.

In other words, opera, in excerpted and arranged form, for soloists and chorus, was central to the repertoire performed at the Hochenadl gatherings. Some of the operas chosen were fairly recent, despite Sonnleithner's report that 'old opera' was performed, including works premiered at the Kärntnertortheater across the road some years before. From 1797 to 1802 Paër was musical director of the Kärntnertortheater, where his most successful opera, Camilla, was produced in 1799. The contemporary works of Rossini were evidently the most popular in these salons, together with recent works by Fioravanti and Nicolini – two names rarely heard today. But some operas from Platoff's list of hits of the 1780s, cited in Chapter 1 – notably works by Mozart and Paisiello – made it into these salons. This music was 'old' in early nineteenth-century terms, where a culture of contemporaneity still prevailed in musical life, especially regarding opera.[23] So salon performances of excerpts were an important way to keep these earlier operas in the active repertoire; this, in turn, started to create an operatic performing canon uncoupled from theatrical production, discussed further in Chapter 4.[24]

There is an emphasis in the list above on theatricality: the Lieder cited are substantial and lend themselves to theatrical presentation – Schubert's 'Erlkönig' and 'Gretchen' (both based on texts by Goethe). The variations listed sit at the virtuoso end of the spectrum, and like the opera excerpts (which they often included), they are popular public music of the time, arranged for private performance by skilled amateurs. Hanslick notes the public performance by Ignaz Moscheles with Giuliani and Joseph Mayseder around 1817 of arrangements like 'La Sentinelle' and 'Der Abschied des Troubadours'.[25] The repertoire also reflected the occasion. During Carnival, the Hochenadl salons featured comic arrangements, lending themselves to theatrical presentation:

Haydn's Berchtesgadener Symphony for children's instruments
A sung symphony
The first finale from Wenzel Müller's [Das] lustige Beilager (with the master
   of the house performing the carriage driver with raw comedy)
Franz Joseph Aumann's duet 'Das Gevatterbitten'

---

[23] On this phenomenon in the eighteenth century, see William Weber, 'The Contemporaneity of Eighteenth-Century Musical Taste', *The Musical Quarterly* 70/2 (1984), pp. 175–94.

[24] On the concept of the 'performing canon' see William Weber, 'The History of Musical Canon', in Nicholas Cook and Mark Everist (eds.), *Rethinking Music* (Oxford: Oxford University Press, 1999), p. 340.

[25] Hanslick, *Geschichte*, p. 217.

Pietro Generali's 'Aria in one tone'
The Pappataci-trio and the first Finale from the *L'italiana* [Rossini] etc.[26]

The community-forming power of performing comedy at this point in Viennese social history should not be underestimated. In Müller's *Das lustige Beilager*, for example, the master of the house performs the carriage driver with base comedy, a play on roles with particular resonance in Vienna in these times when class distinctions were being more keenly felt, perhaps especially in the salons. Salon music-making with such works afforded some kind of relief from social pressures, by way of entertaining critique. The carnival topic and tradition of social inversion can be seen to confirm either traditional order or social mobility depending on context, and, on occasion, provided an acceptable vehicle for smuggling in the latter.

Among the prominent Viennese salons of the era, those of Arnstein, Pichler, and Paradis were particularly important musically, but they also served important purposes socially, culturally, and politically.

Arnstein's Salon and *Toleranz*

Social pressures were never far from the surface for Jewish people living in early nineteenth-century Vienna. Most Jews had lived apart from Christians and had not been allowed by the government to own immovable property. There were exceptions for the more affluent Jews; those who were wealthy or who established factories received preferential treatment by Maria Theresa. But there were restrictions on the rest of the Jewish community. Joseph II was the first to attempt to shift these attitudes and eliminate sanctions on the majority of the Jewish population. The 1781 Patent of Toleration allowed certain rights and recognised the existence of non-Catholic religions in the Habsburg Empire. Then the Edict of 1782 allowed Jewish students to attend schools and universities, and Jews were permitted a wider range of occupations, including that of banker and factory owner. But restrictions remained on the Hebrew language and literature and on religious ceremonies, and immigration was tightly restricted. It was only through the 1867 Constitution that Jews were accorded the unrestricted right to reside and to practise their religion throughout Austria.

---

[26] Deutsch (ed.), 'Leopold von Sonnleithners Erinnerungen', p. 54.

It is against this backdrop that we need to understand the salons of Arnstein, daughter of the banker of Friedrich II of Prussia, who grew up in Berlin in a wealthy and sociable family.[27] After marrying Viennese banker Nathan Adam Arnstein in 1776, she moved to Vienna, where she founded her first salon four years later – the first Jewish salon in Vienna. She virtually dominated Vienna's salon life between 1780 and 1818. Subsequently Arnstein's daughter, Henriette von Pereira-Arnstein, would become an important salon hostess herself. The Jewish bankers of Vienna, to whom these women were related, were generally excluded from the social circles of Austrian aristocrats.[28] So these families fostered their own salons, which became centres of learning and art.

Nathan was upwardly mobile. He was ennobled by Emperor Francis and became the first unconverted Jewish baron in Austria in 1798; he went on to co-found the Austrian National Bank. But Jewish families could not take civic rights for granted; naturalisation could be rescinded and could not be applied to children. The husband of Fanny's daughter, Henriette, baptised their sons, taking steps towards naturalisation to establish an enduring belonging that would include their daughters. Jewish families like the Arnsteins also played a consciously prominent role in the patriotic fervour that took over in the early 1800s. Friedrich Schlegel's wife was Jewish and his son fought in the Napoleonic Wars, and both sons converted to Christianity. Jewish community music-making contributed publicly to the war effort, and 'soft diplomacy' was carried out in the salons.

Around 1800 Arnstein's salon became the centre of a cooperating salon network of intellectual and musical women in Vienna, with close ties to Berlin, where Arnstein's sisters, Sara Levy and Rebecca Ephraim, lived.[29] Her sisters took part in the patriotic surge and were groomed to marry well and so thrive despite restrictions. They directed lively musical and literary salons, and Levy visited Arnstein's salon in Vienna. In 1800 Arnstein's other sister Caecilie Wulff (1760–1836) married Bernhard von Eskeles, an associate of Arnstein's husband Nathan von Arnstein, and came to Vienna; and in 1805 Rebecca also came to Vienna. Other women in Arnstein's circle (who kept literary salons themselves) were Bernhard von Eskeles' sister Eleonore Fliess and Arnstein's two nieces

---

[27] See also Peter Seibert, *Der literarische Salon: Literatur und Geselligkeit zwischen Aufklärung und Vormärz* (Stuttgart: Metzler, 1993), pp. 103–4.

[28] See also Hanson, *Musical Life in Biedermeier Vienna*, p. 114.

[29] See also Cypess and Sinkoff, *Sara Levy's World*; see also Cypess, *Women and Musical Salons in the Enlightenment*, pp. 200–32; and Petra Wilhelmy-Dollinger, *Der Berliner Salon im 19. Jahrhundert: 1780–1914* (Berlin: De Gruyter, 1989), pp. 140–50.

Regina Frohberg and Marianne Saaling; Mariane von Eybenberg; and Dorothea Schlegel, wife of Friedrich Schlegel. Sarah, Fanny, and Caecilie were all musical.

The soft diplomacy of Fanny's early salons is described by Johann Pezzl, a playwright and Enlightenment writer who lived in Vienna from 1784. He carefully avoided mentioning anyone by name (ostensibly protecting female modesty). But he writes about certain influential women in the context of discussing 'a core of businessmen who work hand in hand with the stars of first magnitude in the State'; the businessmen would include Nathan:

> As these persons' gatherings are not quite so rigorously barricaded against honest, but earthly beings as those of the nobility, the enlightened way of thinking is spread through them to many others, and through these again to many classes of the public. Here it is particularly helpful that some ladies from these houses combine the masculine way of thinking with feminine charm, and are thereby doubly agreeable.... These are Musarion's pupils: their company is as instructive and tasteful as it is charming; in their houses one does not while away the evenings with miserable card-shuffling. Little concerts, confidential chats among friends, literary novelties, discussions about books, travel, works of art, the theatre; the events of the day, and interesting news related, judged and illuminated with a little spice, make up the entertainment, and shorten the long winter evenings for the intimate circle. There one makes the acquaintance of most of the resident scholars as well as the foreign ones who occasionally travel through Vienna.[30]

Operating as charming hostesses, certain women in Viennese society became, according to Michael Wise, 'a sort of muse for intellectual exchange and progressive activity – that helped pave the way for a more liberal era in which no longer the aristocracy alone, but an enlightened bourgeoisie, determined the cultural agenda'.[31]

Arnstein's style of leadership was geared to supporting and developing people, and above all inspiring them to bring about change for the better. She sought to create strong emotional bonds and collaborative conditions, encouraging participation by bringing together a new and diverse variety of

---

[30] Johann Pezzl, *Skizze von Wien*, vol. 1 (Vienna: Krauss, 1786), pp. 89–91; *Musarion oder die Philosophie der Grazien (Musarion or the Philosophy of the Graces)* is a poem in three books, a philosophical verse narrative by Christoph Martin Wieland. He worked on it between 1764 and 1767, but did not publish it until 1768 (Leipzig: Reich).

[31] Michael Wise, 'Introduction', in Hilde Spiel, *Fanny von Arnstein: Daughter of the Enlightenment* (New York, NY: New Vessel Press, 2013), xi.

thinkers in her salons. This was a new level of societal mixing. Hilde Spiel notes the new freedom of exchange it afforded:

> Here one could listen to free speech and good music, converse about writers – including those with rebellious or progressive leanings – without being prevented by an abbé, meet interesting foreigners, artists and scholars, such as were never admitted among the high nobility.[32]

Arnstein's social 'arrangements' in the salons created a kind of chemical experiment in the sense implied in the Fragments of Friedrich Schlegel (1772–1829). These provocative aphorisms appeared in his literary magazine *Athenaeum*, published 1798–1800, and might well have been discussed in the salons of Arnstein, especially those attended by Schlegel himself. For Schlegel, 'chemistry' is a metaphor for thinking, philosophising, and especially wit ('reason is mechanical, wit chemical, and genius organic spirit'), leading to some kind of change of state, or transformative process.[33] Arnstein operated not by the force of her own personality or opinions, but by bringing the right mix of people together, and by modelling the process of interacting – with conversation (in various languages), wit (her lively intellect was well known), and music-making.

This conception of the salon can be related to Schlegel's philosophical system, in which coexisting multiplicity, totality, and unity are distinguished. Moving away from the notion of organic unity, which had dominated his earlier thinking, the late Schlegel speaks metaphorically of a 'chemical system', which entails a merging (*Verschmelzung*) of disparate elements. He referred to his own literary fragments in the *Athenaeum*: they were brief, pithy (almost prickly) statements, each exhibiting an internal unity ('A fragment, like a small work of art, has to be entirely isolated from the surrounding world and be complete in itself like a hedgehog', *Athenaeumsfragment* 206). The 'unity' of the individual fragments reflects Schlegel's view that things do not come together as a totality but constitute a 'chaotic universality' of infinitely opposing forces and positions.[34] Something akin to a critical mass – a plenitude of fragments – would act as a kind of forcefield of reciprocal pressures and attractions, ultimately combining the fragments to form a dynamic whole. The assembling of

---

[32] Spiel, *Fanny von Arnstein*, p. 126.

[33] See Matthew Tanner, 'Chemistry in Schlegel's Athenaeum Fragments', *Forum for Modern Language Studies* 31/2 (1995), pp. 140–53; and Michel Chaouli, *The Laboratory of Poetry: Chemistry and Poetics in the Work of Friedrich Schlegel* (Baltimore, MD: Johns Hopkins University Press, 2002).

[34] Allen Speight, 'Friedrich Schlegel', in Edward N. Zalta (ed.), *The Stanford Encyclopedia of Philosophy* (2016), https://plato.stanford.edu/archives/win2016/entries/schlegel.

diverse people at a salon, or indeed musical pieces (*Stücke*) into collections (as in *Salonstücke*), sought to create something greater than, or at least productively different from, the sum of its parts.[35] This did not mean that each piece (or person) was somehow incomplete. Each was self-contained, although there might be commonalities, and it was the diversity of the individuals that ultimately bound them.

Arnstein clearly valued music in the blending of classes, cultures, and disciplines that was a hallmark of her salons. It is not easy to determine how this conception played out in her musical salons, simply because we lack evidence of exactly what was played and how. Regarding her own musical tastes, we know that she was an admirer of Mozart, who in 1781 moved into a room (servants' quarters) in the Arnstein's centrally located house at 1175 Graben. He lodged there for over eight months leading up to his marriage to Constanze Weber and it was there that he wrote *Die Entführung aus dem Serail*.[36] Fanny attended the 1781 premier of *Die Entführung aus dem Serail* and all of Mozart's subscription concerts, and she was also associated with the Bach revival.[37] Cypess investigates music subscriptions and musical collections owned by women of the Itzig family (Fanny's family), noting that 'although their collections consist overwhelmingly of instrumental music, they also sang'.[38] We know that she frequented the Italian opera. In one unfortunate incident, an argument arose between two of her admirers who wanted to escort her there in December 1795, and in the resulting duel Prince Carl Liechtenstein was killed.

Around 1800, Fanny's salons were open to a regular stream of important guests and literati virtually throughout the afternoon and evening, outside theatre hours. In November 1808, for example, the German composer, writer, and music critic Johann Friedrich Reichardt arrived in Vienna and went immediately to the Hofburgtheater to hear Joseph Weigl's new opera *The Orphanage*. There he met the diplomat and friend of Fanny, Jacob Salomo Bartholdy, who

> assured me [Reichardt] that one could attend the evening assembly at the Arnsteins', which he had left not long since in full swing, even in boots and traveling clothes; and I gladly hastened thither with him at once. There, too, I found quite a new Vienna; for perhaps half of the very imposing and numerous

---

[35] See also my 'Louis Spohrs Salonmusik im Kontext', *Spohr Jahrbuch* 5 (2021), pp. 9–30.
[36] Spiel, *Fanny von Arnstein*, p. 67.
[37] Nicholas Temperley and Peter Wollny, 'Bach Revival', *Grove Music Online* (2001), https://doi.org/10.1093/gmo/9781561592630.article.01708.
[38] Cypess, 'Ancient Poetry, Modern Music', p. 58.

assemblée were indeed wearing boots. The noble, splendid lady of the house, the most interesting friend of my youth from Berlin, and her excellent sister, Frau von Eskeles, received me.[39]

No musical performance is mentioned on this occasion, which was apparently mostly given over to gaming and was, we learn from this account, relatively informal (witness the wearing of boots). But Reichardt met Vienna's most popular amateur pianist, Magdalene von Kurzböck, whose playing, according to Mosel's account of the same year 'is most similar to the late Mozart, and who also possessed a very fundamental knowledge of music theory'.[40] Such performers were well able to create arrangements at sight from orchestral scores, as was the Italian writer and composer Carpani, whom Reichardt met shortly thereafter at 'a pleasant dinner of Herr von Pereira's' (the husband of Fanny's daughter), with whom he spent 'a pleasant half hour at the fortepiano'.[41]

By the time of the Congress of Vienna, Arnstein's salon had reached its peak, and the role of music in it was more formalised, if still thoroughly integrated with other elements. Every Tuesday Arnstein presented musical salons, in addition to her other salons – with Arnstein herself taking a leading role in the music-making, as amateur pianist and singer. Formerly, she had regularly invited young women amateurs as well as professional virtuosi to perform in her home. At the time of the Congress of Vienna, there were lavish dinners, *tableaux vivants*, and piano performances by the likes of the young Jewish opera composer Giacomo Meyerbeer, and the young Jewish pianist Ignaz Moscheles, both of whom could also be counted on to deliver effective piano arrangements. During the Congress of Vienna, the music publisher Carl Bertuch heard Moscheles play the overture to *Fidelio*, vocal duets, and other chamber music at a soirée. He also heard Meyerbeer play piano variations and choruses from the oratorio *Timotheus* or *die Gewalt der Musik*.[42]

This particular Handel oratorio seems to have been a favourite. The work describes a banquet held by Alexander the Great and his mistress Thaïs in the captured Persian city of Persepolis, during which the musician Timotheus sings and plays his lyre, arousing various moods in Alexander until he is finally incited to burn the city down in revenge for his dead

---

[39] Johann Friedrich Reichardt, *Vertraute Briefe geschrieben auf einer Reise nach Wien und den Oesterreichischen Staaten zu Ende des Jahres 1808 und zu Anfang 1809*, vol. 1 (Amsterdam: Kunst und Industrie-Comtoir, 1810), pp. 144–5; trans. Spiel, *Fanny von Arnstein*, p. 196.
[40] Mosel, 'Uebersicht des gegenwärtigen Zustandes der Tonkunst in Wien', p. 52.
[41] Cited in Spiel, *Fanny von Arnstein*, p. 197.   [42] Ibid., p. 259.

Arnstein's Salon and Toleranz 91

Greek soldiers. It might have had particular resonance for Jewish musicians who had lost close family members in the Napoleonic Wars. In 1812, as part of the war effort, Arnstein combined forces with Joseph Ferdinand Sonnleithner, secretary at the Hofburg theatre (uncle of Leopold von Sonnleithner, and librettist of Beethoven's *Fidelio*), Prince Lobkowitz, Count Moritz Fries, and Countess Marianne Dietrichstein, to help organise a money-raising public performance of *Timotheus* or *die Gewalt der Musik*, in an arrangement by Mozart. The event, which was suggested by Arnstein and strongly supported by Sonnleithner, was a success and a direct precursor to the formation of the Gesellschaft der Musikfreunde in 1812.[43] Immediately before this event, and so also precursors to the Gesellschaft der Musikfreunde, were a sequence of private events organised by a group of twelve noble women, Arnstein among them. In 1811, she was elected to their new charitable society, the Society of Ladies of the Nobility for the Promotion of the Good and the Useful.[44]

In salon performance, as well as in public settings, Arnstein herself tended to retreat into the background to let others shine in musicmaking. Schönfeld reported in 1796:

Frau von Arnstein: the most instructive and difficult compositions are her favourite pieces. She reads very well, has a light touch and masterly attack. She excels in pieces requiring rapidity. It is to be regretted that for some years she seems to have lost her taste for playing, for she hardly touches the fortepiano any longer. Persons of her powers should not desert their necessitous art, which always, more and more, is in need of encouragement. She also has a very pleasant voice and fluent throat. Her little daughter likewise shows promise of many musical talents.[45]

Reichardt's account of Arnstein's daughter Henriette's performance in 1808 allows us a glimpse into the performance of musical arrangements at this time – so ubiquitous that it seldom attracted detailed attention. Here we see how musical arrangements, like the social arrangements of Fanny's salon, could inspire and promote the people involved, leading perhaps to something greater than the sum of the parts, and possibly to transformation. Reichardt was invited to a Sunday concert at the home of Henriette's tutor, the piano maker Andreas Streicher (1761–1833). Streicher had arranged for two pianos (four hands) the Piano Quartet in F minor, Op. 6, by Prince Ferdinand of Prussia (1806) for Madame Comtesse de Majan (née Franziska von Spielmann). Mosel listed Franziska von Spielmann as

---

[43] See Richard von Perger, *Geschichte der K. K. Gesellschaft der Musikfreunde in Wien*, vol. 1: *1812–1870* (Vienna: K. K. Gesellschaft der Musikfreunde in Wien, 1912), p. 6.
[44] Spiel, *Fanny von Arnstein*, pp. 226–7.   [45] Schönfeld, *Jahrbuch der Tonkunst*, p. 5.

one of his chosen dilettantes in 1808 and described her as 'a pupil of Streicher admired as a very excellent performer'.[46] The arrangement was published in 1814 by the firm Riedl in Vienna. Of a performance involving Henriette and Kurzböck, Reichardt reports:

Thus, on a beautiful bright morning in [Andreas] Streicher's apartment, on two of the most beautiful fortepianos of this master, we heard beautiful artistic hands perform this highly ingenious composition with such perfection as one rarely hears. The tender artistic souls entered with so much spirit and feeling into the sublime and beautiful thoughts and fantasies of the composer, and exercised the greatest difficulties with so much precision and roundness, that they truly conjured up a whole world of music around us.[47]

Reichardt opens a window on the perception of female performers in the Viennese private sphere at this time. The performance of this arrangement shows off the prowess of Streicher as arranger, and, moreover, as instrument maker. It also displays the two performers to best advantage as women: they are shown as both beautiful and accomplished, highly desirable virtues for women wishing to climb the social ladder in early nineteenth-century Vienna. However, we are told, the performance goes further, towards a transformative experience for the listeners, thanks to the performers' exceptional skills. The listener comes to believe that he or she is listening to an original composition, as it is being composed ('tender artistic souls entered ... into the sublime ... fantasies of the composer'). Several other reviews of arrangements from this time also suggest a transformation or 'change of state': a good arrangement was capable of allowing the listener to 'complete the work' or enter into the composer's imagination, discussed further in Chapter 6.[48]

German performers of exceptional skill were on show in Arnstein's home at the time of the Congress of Vienna. A published account of a salon in the Arnstein home helps clarify how music-making in private, and especially opera, could evade censorious political scrutiny but still talk politics in the wider sense. The report needs to be treated with some caution, since it is retrospective and possibly idealised; it is a supplement to the *Blättern für Musik, Theatre und Kunst* edited by Leopold A. Zellner, a New German enthusiast, published in Vienna in 1855 by playwright Moritz Bermann as 'A concert at Baroness Fanny Arnstein's at the time of

---

[46] Mosel, 'Uebersicht des gegenwärtigen Zustandes der Tonkunst in Wien', p. 52.
[47] Reichardt, *Vertraute Briefe*, pp. 346–7.
[48] See also my *Beethoven's Symphonies Arranged*, p. 163.

the Vienna Congress' ('Ein Conzert bei Baronin Fanny Arnstein zur Zeit des Wiener Congresses').[49] This gathering, allegedly held on 20 November 1814, was at the upper end of the social spectrum, with international guests including Lord Castlereagh, leading the British delegation; Karl August von Hardenberg, chief representative of Prussia; and Prince de Talleyrand, representing French foreign affairs. The programming choices apparently spoke subtly against the repression felt by many Viennese at this time.[50]

The operas in the Arnstein salon were reportedly performed by excellent singers on this occasion, with accompaniments from piano arrangements. They were probably strategically chosen, foregrounding the German language, but more significantly the triumph of good, rational people over evil dictators: Mozart's *Die Zauberflöte*, Weigl's *Die Schweizer Familie*, and also Gluck's *Iphigénie en Tauride*.[51] The last is pointedly relevant in terms of plot – a family drama speaking of the tragic aftermath of war. These excerpts from earlier operas framed a programme that otherwise foregrounded local talent, both performers and composers:

1. Aria of the Queen of the Night from *Die Zauberflöte*, performed by court opera singer Sophie Schröder accompanied by Ignaz Moscheles
2. Recitation: scene from *MacBeth*
3. Piano Concerto by Johann Nepomuk Hummel played on a Conrad Graf piano
4. Recitation: Idylls (Count Bindemonte)
5. Franz Clement playing his own violin concerto
6. Peter Hänsel ("Haydn's student"; violin) playing his own trio together with Hummel (piano) and Ferdinand Kauer (flute)
   – Intermission for conversation –
7. Weinmüller sings Sarastro's aria and recitative from *Die Zauberflöte*
8. Recitation: from *Phädra* (Frau von Weißenthurn)
9. Aria from *Die Schweizer Familie* ('an opera, which, although already five years old still disperses its magic')
10. Paradis playing a piano sonata dedicated to her by Leopold Kozeluch
11. Franz Wild 'incites enthusiastic admiration' with his performance of Oreste's aria from *Iphigénie en Tauride*

---

[49] Fully reported in Gradenwitz, *Literatur und Musik in geselligem Kreise*, pp. 258–67.
[50] Daviau, 'Biedermeier: The Happy Face of the Vormärz Era', pp. 17–18.
[51] Gluck's French opera might seem to be the outlier. But the revised version was the only opera Gluck wrote in German – Gluck's 'tragic *Singspiel*', according to modern scholars. See, for example, Amanda Holden, *The New Penguin Opera Guide* (London: Penguin, 2001), p. 325.

In the Arnstein salon, the conversation was witty and intellectual but light-hearted, the musical repertoire and dramatic readings apparently primarily showing off local virtuosity and skill. But by playing off Sarastro against the Queen of the Night, Arnstein asked listeners to think about the triumph of reason and good over irrationality and evil. The 'magic' subject of an opera like *Die Zauberflöte* was politically safe and potentially useful. *Die Zauberflöte* could attest to the powers of German composers and musicians, and also speak in veiled language about Enlightenment ideals, especially the attainment of freedom through wisdom. Of course, salon hosts' political intentions cannot be precisely divined – overt political agendas would have been problematic in the climate of surveillance and censorship. But the repertoire of the Viennese musical salons at this time includes morally uplifting or instructive music of the recent past, such as Haydn's *Die Schöpfung*, along with more abstract symphonies, concertos, and sonatas, which were 'safe' but still could be evocative, being rousing and emphatically German.

Andrea Klitzing notes particular conventions governing the language used on the title pages of arrangements that were tied up with German nationalism. For piano reductions of Mozart's operas, German or Italian were used almost invariably, and after 1818 the proportion of German title pages for such arrangements increases significantly.[52] German publishers tried to advertise arrangements of German music as national cultural products by using German on title pages, where once French and Italian were often seen ('senza Parole' and so on), especially after the Congress. Musical arrangements of certain operas were becoming an appealing, safe means of social and political discourse among middle-class musicians in *Vormärz* Vienna (before the March revolution of 1848) – and were perhaps the only way for women to take part in such discourse.

During the first months of 1815, Arnstein's Prussian friends tried to get their ideas about civil rights for Jews incorporated into the constitution of the German Confederation. But they did not persist when the matter became difficult. Slight changes in the wording, introduced by reactionaries, left the German states free to reject any progress made under the influence of French law during the occupation. Similarly, a petition to Emperor Franz to improve the situation of the Austrian Jews (Nathan von Arnstein was among the petitioners) failed in April 1815.

---

[52] Klitzing, *Don Giovanni unter Druck*, p. 257.

Pichler: A Voice for Middle-Class Women

Otto Biba finds that economic, political, and social developments after the Congress of Vienna promoted rapprochement of traditionally quite separate classes.[53] While this was true of Arnstein's salon, it became generally less true in a time of diminishing social mobility. After Arnstein's death in 1818, Henriette continued her mother's social duties, but moved to Baden. Arnstein-Pereira's guests, like those of her mother, included Pichler (née von Grenier), who held an exemplary post-1815, middle-class Viennese salon. Senior civil servants, scholars, musicians, painters, and especially writers frequented her salon in the prosperous district of Alsergrund. A centre of patriotic renewal, it was also a gathering place for German Romantics, and a prominent literary forum for cultural and intellectual exchange in Vienna in the first third of the nineteenth century. Guests of Pichler, like those of Arnstein, included leading thinkers and writers of the day, such as the Schlegel brothers; the playwright Grillparzer; the author Ludwig Tieck; the poet, dramatist and preacher Zacharias Werner; the poet and novelist Clemens Brentano; and the polymath Wilhelm von Humboldt. They read new literature and discussed theatre, books, and music. Her salon was also frequented by Beethoven and by Schubert, who set some of Pichler's poems.

Pichler's salons were less open than those of Arnstein, and this was typical of the new era. Her family had very close links to the house of Habsburg and, on the face of it, were conservative. But Pichler's writings show a healthy scepticism and free thinking, especially about class. Gunilla Budde points to Pichler's description of the Viennese aristocracy as musically disengaged, double-faced, and slightly poisonous:

> Just as the enjoyment of music united, it also marked boundaries. The Viennese salonnière Caroline Pichler, a cosmopolitan between upper middle-class and aristocratic milieux, was amazed to see how the courtly commentary, which had little interest in music, took the shine off a performance of her music society. Whereas at the dress rehearsal one had been able to garner the applause one deserved in front of families and friends, at the actual premiere the aristocratic audience, with its 'apathy', exuded a 'chilling' atmosphere.[54]

---

[53] Biba, 'Public and Semi-Public Concerts', p. 257.
[54] Gunilla-Friederike Budde, 'Stellvertreterkriege: Politik mit Musik des deutschen und englischen Bürgertums im frühen 19. Jahrhundert', *Zeitschrift für moderne europäische Geschichte* 5/1 (2007), p. 106.

Baroness de Montet, who lived in Vienna from 1810 until 1824, likewise observed Viennese salon culture among the upper classes. She participated in numerous aristocratic salons and evening parties and made pointed comments on the vanity and arrogance of the nobility and the split between classes: 'There is a great germ of hatred and perhaps revolution in the arrogant and contemptuous morgue of the high Austrian aristocracy and the wounded vanity of the second society ... The poet, the man of genius cannot cross the stupid barrier that separates him from the elegant and aristocratic salons'.[55] These comments concern exclusion from some salons on grounds of class; this split was to widen.

Perhaps most importantly for the development of the salon, Pichler was accepted by men as a leader, even though she was reticent about her work and gentle in her influence, like Arnstein. This gentleness has made her something of a controversial figure among modern-day feminists. Susan Kord describes her as 'not feminine enough' for the nineteenth century and 'not feminist enough for the twentieth', and re-examines the canonical casting of Pichler as a conservative author, observing discrepancies between Pichler's actions and her writings.[56] But this is to apply anachronistic terminology. Like Arnstein and Paradis, Pichler exploited a leadership style that was more affiliative than authoritarian, and did not of itself preclude women from leadership.[57] She married a wealthy businessman and then paved the way for other women by becoming knowledgeable about the male world of business and economics. She seldom foregrounded her own talents but, by hosting salons, provided a platform for others to mix and catalyse new ideas in the Viennese private sphere.

Pichler is generally important because through her own writings and the attitudes she modelled, she helped to define and pinpoint a distinctively Austrian outlook or voice – one that may also be discerned, albeit less clearly, in the plots and themes of the arranged works that I discuss in this book. The themes include idealising ancient times; escaping into history and nature for healing; valuing of family; freedom for Austria; and

---

[55] Alexandrine Prévost de la Boutetière de Saint-Mars du Montet, '1825, Vienne – Paris, 1826', in *Souvenirs de la Baronne du Montet, 1785–1866*, 2nd ed. (Paris: Plon-Nourrit et Cie, 1904), p. 264.

[56] Susanne Kord, '"Und drinnen waltet die züchtige Hausfrau"? Caroline Pichler's Fictional Auto/Biographies', *Women in German Yearbook* 8 (1992), pp. 141–58.

[57] See also Judith E. Martin, 'Caroline Pichler's and Johanna Schopenhauer's Restoration Conformity: Corinne as Underground Artist', in *Germaine de Staël in Germany: Gender and Literary Authority (1800–1850)* (Lanham, MD: Fairleigh Dickinson University Press, 2011), pp. 151–208.

safeguarding (while also defining) 'national treasure'.[58] These values were also projected in Pichler's documented actions, for example, in her choosing to wear 'old German' national dress at the Congress of Vienna.[59] And they are evident in her artistic and literary choices. Spohr, for example, collaborated musically with Pichler, who wrote celebratory and political poetry, working with her on the cantata *Das befreite Deutschland* (*Germany liberated*), WoO 64 (1814). This is one of many ceremonial works composed to celebrate the return of Austrian Emperor Franz I to Vienna after Napoleon's defeat at the Battle of Leipzig in October 1813. An arrangement of this work for piano, four hands, suitable for salon performance, was released in Vienna in 1830.

As for the music performed at her salons, few specifics are recorded. Pichler was herself musical and her memoirs are full of evenings of music-making, including the performance of opera arrangements. She makes a distinction between treating an arranged piece 'as theatre' and not so doing, and also between the performance of excerpted numbers and entire works. Thus, for example, in 1809, in the company of amateurs, she noted that a bravura aria was to be sung 'or to be produced in theatre at the fortepiano'.[60] It is possible that the distinction refers primarily to whether the item was sung or not. Most piano reductions of operatic works included text, but at this time they might be published with no text at all and intended purely as instrumental music: many of the ensemble chamber music arrangements of operas from this time were without text. Pichler played piano reductions of Johann Gottlieb Naumann's operas – mostly Italian, composed in the period 1762–1801 (and surviving 'old opera' as in the Hochenadl salons) – and oratorios, with the blind Viennese piano virtuosa Paradis, 'mostly without theatre and play'.[61]

Pichler owned a fine 'organisirtes Fortepiano' – a hybrid instrument that could be used either as a piano or as a positive organ. This was an ideal instrument for the performance of arrangements, since the timbre and texture could be readily adapted. A number of developments in pianos around this time helped to make them well suited to the numerous piano arrangements that were being published, and also the many more created at the hands of amateur and professional pianists. One such was the Streichers' piano. Nannette Streicher (1769–1833) was a respected fortepiano maker in Vienna. Mozart owned a fortepiano made by her father,

---

[58] Bittrich, 'Österreichische Züge am Beispiel der Caroline Pichler', especially p. 187.
[59] Vick, *The Congress of Vienna*, p. 55.
[60] Pichler, *Denkwürdigkeiten aus meinem Leben*, vol. 2, p. 82.   [61] Ibid., vol. 1, p. 217.

Johann Andreas Stein (1728–92), one of the most respected piano builders of the time, and she carried on his legacy by making fortepianos for Beethoven and others. She and her son, Johann Baptist, became important manufacturers, producing fifty to sixty-five grand pianos each year by the early 1820s. These instruments were more robust than previous models, and, like the French and English instruments of the time, expanded the compass of the instrument, making the performance of arranged orchestral repertoire more feasible (see also Chapter 6). Nanette Streicher was not just a piano maker. She also contributed to Viennese musical life by organising private concerts in her apartment. From 1812 onwards she organised a piano salon, offering young artists an opportunity for semi-public performance in front of an audience that included friends and customers of the firm.

Paradis: Piano Salons and *Bildung*

If sociability and *Bildung* were central purposes of the early nineteenth-century Viennese salons, the educational function was particularly prominent in Paradis's salon. She organised important piano salons in the same era as Streicher. She became blind at the age of three, but was nonetheless a touring virtuoso in her early years, travelling to Germany, France, England, and Holland. She returned to Vienna in 1786, and largely withdrew from public appearances, devoting herself to teaching and composing. Her compositions include piano pieces, operettas, cantatas, and ballads. She was active as a salon host up to her death in 1824, and was mentioned as such by Schönfeld in his 1796 account of private musical entertainments in Vienna (see Chapter 2). After 1815, Schönfeld became a member of the musical circle that gathered at her home, No. 482 at the Bergel; she lived on the fourth storey with retired official Johann Riedinger, who managed her domestic affairs.

Paradis gathered her students together for rehearsals and performances; according to Sonnleithner at least, she operated on the principle that the desire to learn is awakened and nurtured by rivalry.[62] Students, among them schoolgirls, performed piano music with and without accompaniment at regular evening entertainments on Sundays of Advent and Lent. The programme was varied, with several vocal and solo instrumental pieces

---

[62] Deutsch (ed.), 'Leopold von Sonnleithners Erinnerungen', pp. 98–100; trans. based on Vago, 'Musical Life of Amateur Musicians in Vienna', pp. 152–6.

following the pattern of formal concerts in the usual mixed programming style of the day. Parents and friends of the students and singers attended, and a few others such as travelling professionals and amateurs.

Sonnleithner's description makes it clear that arrangements were played at these events, with opera arrangements prominent among them. Of the vocal works performed, he says they 'first consisted of songs, arias, duets, and trios from the most popular operas of the time'.[63] It seems that some of these arrangements were accompanied by a one-per-part orchestra made up of amateurs, others by piano reductions. Sonnleithner described an 'instrumental accompaniment' made up of 'loyal friends ... with kind devotion':

Dr Anton Peck, lawyer ... later Herr Eugen Frölich von Fröhlichsthal, then Herr Georg Hellmesberger, played the first violin. Herr Josef Kläckl ... the viola. Herr Franz X. Rabel ... the violoncello. Together with others, I helped with all string instruments, and sometimes I even played the contrabass in the concert tuttis. Later the contrabass changed to the much more competent hands of Herr Johann Hindle. The merchant Herr Franz Schober worked tirelessly as flautist; Fräulein Julie Engelhardt and Herr Franz Barthioli represented the guitar section.[64]

Piano reductions were used for rehearsals, provided by Herr Peter Decret, Herr Johann Schmiedel, and Sonnleithner himself. He provides a list of thirty female singers, soprano and alto, who took part. Most of them were amateurs, with the exception of Aloisia Lange (née Weber), Mozart's sister-in-law and an important interpreter of his work. Lange had been a coloratura soprano of considerable range and great success at the Kärntnerthortheater and Burgtheater. She sang the role of Donna Anna at the first Viennese performance of *Don Giovanni*, and premiered the Queen of the Night. She undertook concert travels, and was engaged at various concert houses in Europe, then went into exile in Zurich during the Napoleonic invasions; during this time she had also begun teaching. Only around 1818–19 did she return to Vienna, when she took part in the Paradis salons. In 1820, this circle performed the vocal quartets, choruses, and first finale from *Don Giovanni*, with Lange singing Donna Anna, together with 'other larger works'.[65] Sonnleithner notes that this performance, and an 1818 performance of Haydn's *Creation*,

---

[63] Deutsch (ed.), 'Leopold von Sonnleithners Erinnerungen', p. 100; trans. Vago, 'Musical Life of Amateur Musicians in Vienna', p. 155.
[64] Ibid., pp. 98–9; trans. Vago, 'Musical Life of Amateur Musicians in Vienna', p. 153.
[65] Ibid., p. 99; trans. Vago, 'Musical Life of Amateur Musicians in Vienna', p. 153.

were exceptions, being vocal repertoire from an earlier time, while the rest was contemporary.

Regarding the arrangements, it is not clear who carried them out, only that musicians capable of doing so were in abundant supply. Sonnleithner records:

> The orchestra part [of the *Creation* and *Don Giovanni*] was arranged for two pianos for four hands and was performed by the outstanding schoolgirls of the house. Other schoolgirls participated diligently in the choir. You can imagine what happy and joyous impressions such performances and rehearsals made on the young students.[66]

So although Sonnleithner believed Paradis' pedagogy turned on competition, this was evidently just part of her recipe. The performance of these arrangements gave the students a foothold in the musical world through aspirational and collaborative experiences, where they worked alongside professional (or professional-level) musicians on 'real' repertoire from the public sphere. It is possible that these students also had a hand in the arrangements, but if not they would still have gained considerable insight into the works through the practical performing experience that arrangements afforded.

* * *

Sonnleithner's *Memoirs* show how women were included as key agents in the Viennese musical salons, even if they were not usually the main hosts, especially because of their musical contributions in singing and on piano. The soirées he attended and ran were an ideal environment for nurturing female singers. Outstanding performers at the Hochenadl salons were Georg Hellmesberger, Leopold von Sonnleithner, Caroline Unger-Sabatier, Anna Fröhlich, and Barbara Fröhlich, and other singers from Schubert's circle such as Josef Barth, Josef Götz, and Adalbert Rotter. But female pianists, in particular, could move into powerful leadership roles.

Such a pianist was Katharina Hochenadl: her father was an enthusiastic music lover who gave Katharina her earliest lessons. For several years from 1803, her piano teacher was the Mozart pupil Anton Eberl, beside whom she gave her first public concert at a professional level in the Jahnische Saal in January 1804. There were at least six further public concerts: 1804 at the summer concerts in the Augarten, January 1805 with Eberl in the Jahnische Saal, December 1806 with Eberl at a benefit concert in the Burgtheater, December 1807 at a benefit concert in the Kärntnertortheater, and

---

[66] Ibid; trans. Vago, 'Musical Life of Amateur Musicians in Vienna', pp. 155–6.

March 1817 at the concert of the Gesellschaft der Musikfreunde in the Universitätssaal. But Hochenadl's reputation as one of the best pianists in Vienna, distinguished by powerful playing, precision, virtuosity, and technical ease, was still based primarily on concerts in private or semi-public settings, especially the family's modest flat in the Bürgerspital. They began as early as the end of the eighteenth century, extending to regular Sunday winter concerts up to around 1825. These series were interrupted only for performances by the Gesellschaft der Musikfreunde, of which Hochenadl was one of the first members.

The purpose of these house concerts moves on from the social and educational functions of the earlier salons towards musical and political ones. Their aim was the intensive study of older, 'classical' music, considered to be substantial, by composers such as Mozart, Haydn, Beethoven, Schubert, Cimarosa, Cherubini, Paër, Spontini, Rossini, Eberl, Weigl, and so on. Particularly noteworthy were performances of eight oratorios and two operas (by Gluck and Naumann), accompanied by Hochenadl on piano and her half-brother, Thomas Hochenadl, on cello. Kiesewetter, who regularly attended these concerts and also participated as a singer, arranged at least two oratorios (Handel's *Judas Maccabaeus* and Graun's *Der Tod Jesu*) in piano reduction especially for these performances. The manuscripts of these reductions, held in the Österreichische Nationalbibliothek, show that Kiesewetter's arrangements are similar in level of difficulty to contemporary opera piano reductions.[67]

These private salons performed the vital function of promoting agency for middle-class and amateur musicians. Choosing where and how to perform chamber music gave them a sense of purpose in an era of stifling oppression. Participants – women among them – planned and sometimes arranged the repertoire, dictated the standards, and assessed the results. Because the piano parts of published arrangements from this time frequently contained much of the original texture (they were often designed to be performed with or without other instruments, as detailed in Chapter 2), they offered a chance for female leadership, and even virtuosity. Times were changing, though. Viennese salons had once fostered some intermixture between the aristocracy and middle classes, at least in critical discourse on art; this parity was perhaps already waning in the late eighteenth-century salon, and the split between classes widened further in the early nineteenth century. Parity also declined between the sexes in the salons. In the 1820s the younger generation of writers now tended to meet in inns and

---

[67] See Österreichische Nationalbibliothek shelf marks Mus.Hs.31260 and Mus.Hs.31261.

coffeehouses, without women.[68] But in the musical salon, leaders like Arnstein, Hochenadl, and Paradis had set a powerful precedent for women in the Viennese public sphere, and for musical women generally.

---

[68] On this shift see Johann Sonnleitner, 'Vom Salon zum Kaffeehaus. Zur literarischen Öffentlichkeit im österreichischen Biedermeier', in Pichl, Bernd and Wagner (eds.), *The Other Vienna*, pp. 71–83.

4 | Canon Formation, Domestication, and Opera

Histories of music have typically treated the home as a music-making venue on the periphery, if they consider it at all. The history of musical culture in Vienna, for example, has focused on the public sphere: the rise of concert life, celebrated public figures, and public music-making in general.[1] Recent musicology, including the preceding chapters, has turned to the home, with new consideration, especially, of women's roles in music-making as we have seen in Chapter 3.[2] But there has been little discussion of the consequences of domestic music-making, or of its centrality to musical life, including its contribution to the development of public musical life – especially in Vienna. An exception is James Parakilas' 1995 article 'The Power of Domestication in the Lives of Musical Canons'. Whereas Weber had theorised various types of canon formed in the public sphere – the performing, pedagogical, and scholarly canons – Parakilas examines the role of domestic music-making in the process of canon formation.[3] He criticises scholars' tendency to emphasise the 'supply' side of musical culture when consumers also have a large role in shaping canons: 'instead of representing musical publics as inert recipients', he proposes that discourse about canons can 'describe the process of negotiation between authorities and publics over the canonic'.[4] Citing Pierre Bourdieu's work on consumers' roles in the cultural market, Parakilas identifies 'domestication' as a key process linking the 'relatively independent logics' of production and consumption, and examines its role in canonisation.[5]

This chapter takes Parakilas' work further. I investigate various strands of influence, seeking to understand the role of musical 'domestication' in canon formation in the early nineteenth-century Viennese home. Answers

---

[1] On Vienna see Hanslick, *Geschichte*; also Botstein, 'The Patrons and Publics of the Quartets'; Hanson, *Musical Life in Biedermeier Vienna*; Jones, *Music in Vienna*, especially pp. 95–6 and 102–17; Weber, *Music and the Middle Class*; and Morrow, *Concert Life in Haydn's Vienna*.

[2] See for example Heindl, 'People, Class Structure, and Society', pp. 36–54, Liu, 'Die Rolle der Musik im Wiener Salon bis ca. 1830'; Peham, *Die Salonièren und die Salons in Wien*; and Jones, *Music in Vienna*, especially pp. 95–6 and 102–117.

[3] Weber, 'The History of Musical Canon'; Parakilas, 'The Power of Domestication'.

[4] Parakilas, 'The Power of Domestication', pp. 5–6.   [5] Ibid., pp. 6–7.

are sought to fundamental questions: how the performance of music in the home influenced the creation of an authoritative list of musical 'works' to be championed in public; which genres were thus canonised, and how opera, which dominated 'domesticated' music, fared in the developing canon; and who were the 'authorities' and 'publics' in Vienna around the time of the Congress (1814–15 and just afterwards).

As Mark Everist has shown, to analyse and properly critique canons, we need to examine the real agents behind them, the *people* who create them.[6] Here I focus on middle-class circles, especially the salons Sonnleithner held and attended. Thanks to middle-class agency, repertoires were perpetuated and recreated, rethought and re-evaluated through musical arrangement and domestic performance. So in early-to-mid-nineteenth-century Vienna, concert life would develop in significant areas – repertoire, performance practices, and listeners' behaviour, tastes, and values – largely in the middle-class home. Weber suggests we keep in mind reciprocal relationships between the classes in this era.[7] This approach is particularly valuable when considering the upper echelons of the Viennese middle class, who were in part seeking to emulate the aristocracy in their musical values and activities at this time. To understand how opera arrangements figured in the canonising process and how they relate to the canonised repertoire in Vienna, we can also revisit publishing catalogues to see consumer choice at work. This perspective is mainly left to Chapter 5.

The Salon as a Centre for Canon Formation in Early Nineteenth-Century Vienna

The *Memoirs* of Sonnleithner (1797–1873) provide a counterweight to Hanslick's emphasis on the public sphere and his denigration of the early nineteenth-century salon (discussed in Chapter 3). The *Memoirs*, written in 1861–3, are of salons Sonnleithner attended in Vienna around 1814–25.[8] This detailed account of private and semi-private music-making balances the public historical record with an ideographic perspective, by studying the individuals concerned as unique instances of agency related to their unique life histories, rather than focusing on 'laws' and grand historical

---

[6] Mark Everist, 'Reception Theories, Canonic Discourses, and Musical Value', in Everist and Cook, *Rethinking Music*, pp. 378–402.

[7] William Weber, 'The Muddle of the Middle Classes,' *19th-Century Music* 3/2 (1979), especially pp. 181–2.

[8] Deutsch (ed.), 'Leopold von Sonnleithners Erinnerungen'.

narratives as Hanslick did.[9] The *Memoirs* are retrospective, and were subject to gaps, personal bias, and inaccuracies, but they remain an important line of evidence as to how the music-making in these salons influenced, intersected with, and departed from the trends of the emerging public concerts.

Looking back from the late nineteenth century, Sonnleithner reports the centrality of music-making in the Viennese home, a result of the Napoleonic Wars and their aftermath:

> Until about the year 1813 the system of associations which today unites the participating friends of the musical arts in splendid rehearsals and performances had not yet taken first root – because of the public situation in Germany at that time. Activities allotted to dilettantes were limited to house music (string quartets were common) and participation in church music, which, particularly in Catholic countries, offered singers and instrumentalists ample opportunity to practice their talents to the glory of the church without being subject to criticism.[10]

The era of 'splendid rehearsals and performances' was beginning in private around 1813, precisely in connection with the house music Sonnleithner is talking about. What was missing, aside from any formalised institutions ('system of associations'), was public review or criticism – an absence that arguably kept these events private or semi-private, and which Sonnleithner sees as benefiting the development of musicians. But the means of public review were being established. Middle-class amateurs themselves would determine the general standard and judge the results against it. Standards pertaining to listening were a case in point. At this stage, modes of listening in the home and the salon were influenced by participation in church music, as Sonnleithner suggests. The performance of sacred music alongside other repertoire in the home fostered the development of silent, reverent, thoughtful listening by audiences. Such listening practices still remained largely foreign to public concert and theatre life, although they were an important component of the thinking behind and process of canon formation.

Sonnleithner describes a variety of musical salons in Vienna in this era, differing in their locations, repertoire, tastes, agendas, and behaviour, and thus in respect of canon formation. In Chapter 3 I considered some of these salons, in which women played a large part. Here I will revisit the various house-concert series that Sonnleithner attended, especially the larger-scale

---

[9] Hanslick himself was to take a much more idiographic approach in later works after *Geschichte*.
[10] Deutsch (ed.), 'Leopold von Sonnleithners Erinnerungen', p. 101.

series hosted by middle-class men, looking in more detail at repertoire choices, 'domestication' (especially via arrangements), and emerging standards and tastes – the ideology underpinning canon formation. I discuss a process by which the larger salons where arrangements were performed emerged from string-quartet parties; I then consider the importance of smaller-scale music-making in the home, based around the piano.

One of the earliest of the larger salons was held in the home of Sonnleithner himself. His father, Ignaz, was an influential personality in the Viennese musical scene; he helped found the Gesellschaft der Musikfreunde in 1812, leading to the emergence of public concerts. Ignaz was a composer of church music, symphonies, and quartets, and probably encouraged the young Leopold to take part in the social performance of string-quartet arrangements. A long-time family friend, Wilhelm Böcking, recalled Leopold's youthful engagement with quartet arrangements, giving an indication of the repertoire choices:

But the young man already had such a mature judgement that he did not overestimate his own talent and preferred to become a capable jurist rather than a mediocre artist. At the same time, music remained his favourite pastime during his leisure hours. In the autumn of 1813, together with several school friends, he organised Sunday quartet practice in his father's house, which were diligently continued in the following years. The quartet arrangements of the overtures and symphonies, as well as entire operas and oratorios, which were very popular at that time, were soon also used and gave rise to multiple instrumentation of the voices, and to the addition of the double bass, a flute, and French horns (*ad libitum*).[11]

These musical gatherings involved anything from four to forty people, who performed a mixture of vocal and purely instrumental works, with a clear preference for the former. The desire to include other family members and acquaintances led to choral rehearsals in parallel with string-quartet practice, which allowed these ensembles to perform finales from operas by Mozart, Spontini, and others. It is likely that both Leopold and his father conducted and organised these rehearsals.[12] Choral music arrangement, above all, contributed to the creation of communities of musicians outside public spaces, fostering empathy, and building agency and leadership – all important drivers of canon formation.

Around 1813, Franz Schubert, too, was taking part in family quartet rehearsals in his home, which were to expand into mini orchestral performances. Sonnleithner, who was a friend of Schubert's, describes this

---

[11] Ibid., p. 107. [12] Vago, 'Musical Life of Amateur Musicians in Vienna', p. 32.

process of expansion. When Schubert's home became too small, the meetings moved into the more spacious home of businessman Franz Frischling, at Dorotheergasse No. 1105. Here the group could perform the smaller symphonies of Haydn, Pleyel, Rosetti, Mozart, and others. Towards the end of 1815 the meetings moved to the yet larger home of violinist Otto Hatwig, a former member of the Theater auf der Wieden and Burgtheater orchestras, in the Schottenhof. Here larger symphonies could be staged, and talented schoolgirls performed solo pieces with orchestral accompaniment. These performances were no longer primarily arrangements, but full orchestral versions. The orchestra comprised businessmen, tradesmen, and city officials – and a very few properly professional musicians. But despite their scale, these performances were still home entertainments. The group also met in 1818 in the home of Anton von Pettenkoffer, where the expanded repertoire included oratorios by Haydn and Handel. This domestic music-making, born largely of arrangements, was familiarising audiences with the orchestral and theatrical works of composers as well as their chamber music, opening up the possibility of such large-scale music becoming canonic in a time of limited concert performances.

The salons of Hochenadl focused more on vocal music than those of the Schubert circle. Sonnleithner observes (above) that string quartets were common repertoire in this era for house music in Vienna. But as we have seen in the preceding chapters, and as Sonnleithner remarks elsewhere in his *Memoirs*, there was a great thirst for vocal music.[13] We have also seen that the two repertoires were not entirely distinct: string-quartet arrangements could be used for exploring vocal music, including opera. Like those that developed from the Schubert circle, these salons became quite large in scale. But they remained more clearly an alternative or substitute for public concert life: the group met regularly on Sundays at noon from November until Easter, and during Lent, when the Gesellschaft der Musikfreunde did not operate.

Hochenadl's salons provided an alternative to concert life not only in terms of timing, but also of repertoire. The aim was to present music that was otherwise rarely heard in Vienna. Key works in the Hochenadl repertoire dated back to the eighteenth century, including Handel's *Judas Maccabeus* and *Messiah*; vocal music by C. P. E. Bach, Johann Adolph Hasse, and Carl Heinrich Graun; as well as works by Mozart, Beethoven, and Andreas Romberg. By contrast with these salons, the early nineteenth-century Viennese theatre maintained a culture of contemporaneity in

---

[13] Deutsch (ed.), 'Leopold von Sonnleithners Erinnerungen', p. 107.

music; benefit concerts, too, tended to display recent works.[14] By reminding enthusiastic amateur musicians of earlier repertoires that were within their reach for study and performance, Hochenadl's salons fostered the formation of canons of earlier music. They helped create both a 'scholarly canon' (of music studied in theoretical terms) and a 'performing canon' (the active repertoire of publicly performed music) via private or semi-private performances; and also, indirectly, a pedagogical canon of older works emulated by newer composers.[15]

Weber observes that the performing canon entails more than the presentation of earlier works: works that become canonised are 'organized as repertoires and defined as sources of authority regarding musical taste', so that 'a performing canon is more than just a repertory: it is also a critical and ideological force'.[16] In other words, the repetition of earlier works in the salon is not enough to make them canonic. There has to be an exercise of choice and judgement; and these choices and judgements need to be shared. A musical canon is an ideological force because it represents an agreement about which musical works are exemplary. Various discourses project these views, so that they are endorsed, and a consensus emerges in time.[17] A straightforward example of discourse is a review, which endorses or condemns particular works and composers, and thus shares and influences opinions, standards, and choices.

In salon culture, canon-forming discourses usually take place 'in-house' and are verbal, rather than public and published; they consist in conversations, gestures of approval, and plans for performance and reperformance. We know from Sonnleithner that in the Hochenadl salons musical works 'were excellently rehearsed, well known to the performers as well as to the regulars among the listeners, and therefore provided a rare artistic pleasure in a period that was not very favourable for serious music'.[18] The organisers of these musical salons encouraged the valuing of certain earlier music as 'serious' and drew a distinction between this approved repertoire and the bulk of contemporary musical culture. The repertoire thus distinguished received careful attention to its performance and rehearsal at a time when this was uncommon, implying respect for the composer as a source of authority. Knowledge as well as pleasure was to be gained from repeated performance of such repertoire.

---

[14] On this subject, with regard to eighteenth-century Europe, see Weber, 'The Contemporaneity of Eighteenth-Century Musical Taste'.
[15] Weber, 'The History of Musical Canon', pp. 339–40.   [16] Ibid., p. 340.
[17] Terry Eagleton, *Ideology: An Introduction*, rev. ed. (London: Verso, 2007), p. 19.
[18] Deutsch (ed.), 'Leopold von Sonnleithners Erinnerungen', p. 54.

So the salon organisers were helping to develop an audience who would value this music in their terms, according to their ideas of what was 'serious' and worthy of close study. This shared understanding – of music deserving repeated close attention and analysis – would then lead to further repetition, new insights, and wider sharing. In other words, the salon organisers and participants were constructing the mechanism of canon formation. The reason they were doing so with such enthusiasm in Vienna at this particular time is linked to who they were: mostly middle-class musicians with good education (if they were men), and time, money, and talent for music, but little power beyond the reach of their low- or middle-ranking government and civic positions. They eagerly sought *Bildung*, or personal and educational development, often with a view to improving their agency and power in society.

Key among the Viennese agents of canon formation was Raphael Georg Kiesewetter, who attended the Hochenadl salons and had a hand in arrangements, writing out piano excerpts from oratorios. He would later contribute significantly to canon formation in his own house concerts, stressing *Bildung* as a foundational value.

Bildung, Professional Performance, and Attentive Listening

Early nineteenth-century Viennese salons promoted *Bildung* by providing a kind of internship or training ground, especially for opera singers. This was important for the development of musical life in Vienna before the 'system of associations' mentioned by Sonnleithner had developed, because it boosted professionalism. Professionalism in performance facilitates the formation of canons – it is part of the process of revering musical works and composers, and sharing this admiration. Mosel had lamented the lack of professional training for German singers in Vienna in 1808.[19] In the 1810s and 1820s this was changing. Sonnleithner himself remained an amateur, without extensive training. But Katharina Hochenadl, who sang alto in a choir, studied piano with Anton Eberl and became very proficient. Of the other outstanding musicians who participated in the Hochenadl salons, the Fröhlich sisters (depicted in Figure 4.1) built up their own professionalism. Anna Fröhlich taught voice from 1819 to 1854 at the Universität für Musik und darstellende Kunst, Vienna (established in 1817), and was the first woman to assume the role of a professor there. Schubert

---

[19] See Mosel, *Uebersicht*, pp. 41–2.

Figure 4.1 *A Schubert Evening in a Vienna Salon* by Julius Schmid (1897). Centralised women (next to Franz Schubert, at the piano) from left to right: Katharina Fröhlich; the actor and singer Sophie Müller (standing); Anna Fröhlich (partly hidden); Barbara Fröhlich; [Schubert]; Josephine Fröhlich (with music in her hands). Courtesy of Alamy Images

wrote the solo part in two of his major compositions for Josephine Fröhlich, who studied from 1819 to 1821 and, like Anna, sang with the Gesellschaft. Josephine made her operatic debut in *Die Entführung aus dem Serail* in 1821, before undertaking European tours as an opera singer.

There are many other examples of this internship function of salons, and of the transfer of skills learned in private or semi-private settings to public musical life. For example, the Hochenadl salons exerted this kind of influence on the career of Georg Hellmesberger, who joined the circle in 1819. He came to Vienna in that year and 'was recommended to Dr Sonnleithner and ... appeared at Sonnleithner's evening concerts and achieved through his efforts the means for a broader education, which opened to him an honourable artist's way'.[20] Hellmesberger became conductor of the Imperial Opera in 1829.

After 1815, Sonnleithner became a member of the musical circle that gathered at the Paradies home. Operas and other large-scale works in arrangements were core repertoire at these salons; for example Mozart's *Don Giovanni* was performed in 1820 and Haydn's *Creation* in 1818. So to

---

[20] Deutsch (ed.), 'Leopold von Sonnleithners Erinnerungen', p. 151.

some extent these salons, like those of Hochenadl, revived earlier repertoire and had a canon-forming function. However, much of the repertoire performed in this salon was contemporary. The Paradies salons also provided crucial early training and performance experience for developing musical professionals, allowing them to perform challenging repertoire in a supportive environment.

With the Viennese salons of Ignaz Rohrer, whose sons Anton and Franz played piano and violin respectively, we see a move away from the private end of the spectrum: admission was now charged for concerts. Another gesture towards public musical life was a growing insistence on professionalism in performance, and on the formation of taste. So, for example, Vinzenz Neuling and Adam Hutschenreiter hosted musical evenings from 1817 to 1822, seeking to 'perform only good works and present them with only the best musicians'.[21] The standards and tastes being endorsed by the house concerts, which foreshadow the conditions that would become expected in the public arena, were again linked to the performance of earlier music – helping form what Weber would term the 'performing canon'. Repertoire was often music by Haydn and Mozart. There was a performance of Haydn's *Creation* with Johann Nestroy (director, bass singer, and popular playwright) and Johann Schmiedel (bass), who 'dared to tackle Haydn's *Creation* with quintet accompaniment'.[22] This comment implies the reverence this repertoire was attracting, but also the zeal with which performers took on the challenge of performing it. At this time (1817–22), Nestroy was a law student. Again, the salons helped an initially amateur musician forge a career in music. In 1822 he abandoned his studies and joined the Kärntnertortheater, first singing Sarastro in *Die Zauberflöte*. From 1825 he began to tour Europe, before returning to Vienna in 1831 to continue his career as a singer and playwright.

The Viennese salons perhaps most important for canon formation were those of government official and musicologist Kiesewetter, who hosted musical evenings in his home after 1816.[23] His apartment was larger than Sonnleithner's and suitable for small orchestral rehearsals. Bach's music was played – so we can talk about a Bach revival before the more famous one in Berlin in 1829, where Mendelssohn conducted the *Saint Matthew*

---

[21] Ibid., p. 154.   [22] Ibid.
[23] See also Herfrid Kier, 'Kiesewetters historische Hauskonzerte. Zur Geschichte der kirchenmusikalischen Restauration in Wien', *Kirchenmusikalisches Jahrbuch* 52 (1968), pp. 95–119.

Passion.[24] Indeed, revivalist sentiment was already taking effect in Vienna before Kiesewetter. His concerts involved musical arrangements and adaptations to cater to the performers who were available. According to Sonnleithner, Kiesewetter 'frequently rewrote individual voices into chorus parts, transcribed the music into contemporary notes and keys, and thus made the music accessible to everyone'.[25] Favourite repertoire included vocal works by Giovanni Perluigi da Palestrina, Francesco Durante, Niccolò Jomelli, Domenico Scarlatti, and Handel. Kiesewetter not only hosted concerts of music from the sixteenth to eighteenth centuries; he also arranged many concerts featuring contemporary music, at which Schubert's compositions became ever more prominent. Musicians ranged from amateurs to professionals. Conducting from the piano were musicians such as Johann Hugo Worzischek, Franz Gebauer, Franz Pechaczeck, and Johann Jenger – all professional musicians. The vocal works were accompanied by piano, and also by strings where they were available. Alois Fuchs, who regularly sang bass, also played cello and possibly supplied basso continuo. The performance standards were high, as was the amount of repetition, study, and reverence accorded to the music.

High standards and repeated performance do not foster study and reverence without attentive listening; and the salons were helping to develop this practice, too. The retrospective painting reproduced in Figure 4.1, from the late nineteenth century, shows the Fröhlich sisters and Schubert at a soirée, and may depict the performance of operatic arias and songs in the salon. Most pertinent here, though, is the artist's depiction of listeners and listening. One man tries to distract Barbara Fröhlich, who is shown in the centre – he is probably the flautist Ferdinand Bogner, whom she later married. But otherwise the listeners are focused and attentive. Nobody speaks. Eyes are closed for silent contemplation or turned to the centre of the room, where the music-making is taking place. There, Schubert sits at the piano, Josephine Fröhlich stands to sing, and musical scores – objects of study and devotion, conveyors of the revered works – are clearly in evidence. Of course this depiction is probably idealised – more about what the artist hopes to see in the salon than what happened there most of the time; and this imagined moment might be inflected by late-nineteenth-century thinking. However, ideals are precisely of interest here. The picture belongs to a series of illustrations by various artists from across the nineteenth century which,

---

[24] On this topic see Celia Applegate, *Bach in Berlin: Nation and Culture in Mendelssohn's Revival of the St. Matthew Passion* (Ithaca, NY: Cornell University Press, 2005).
[25] Deutsch (ed.), 'Leopold von Sonnleithners Erinnerungen', p. 56.

I have argued, emphasise listeners and attentive listening in private-sphere contexts.[26] This visual culture offers an alternative view to the typically satirical association of salon culture with incessant conversation.[27] The main theme in Figure 4.1 is silent and thoughtful listening, a key mechanism for *Bildung* and a requisite for canon formation. It illustrates the understanding of attentive listening to which the culture of these salons ultimately led, rather than its habitual character.

Salon Types, 'Classics', and Canonic Systems

> Classic [Classique]: A term that is applied to composers who are generally admired and who are regarded as authoritative: Palestrina, Durante, Leo, Piccini, Cimarosa, Handel, Hasse, Gluck, Mozart, Haydn, Méhul, Chérubini, Catel, these are classic composers. The word is used moreover in connection with works that are regarded as masterpieces, or at least as excellent, and which have been adopted as models for teaching purposes. Oratorios by Handel, Jommelli, and Haydn, cantatas by Pergolesi, psalms by Marcello, masses by Palestrina, Mozart, and Cherubini, Leo's Miserere, Pergolesi's Stabat Mater, symphonies and quartets by Haydn and Mozart, *opera by Sarti, Piccini, Cimarosa, Gluck, Mozart, Méhul, and Cherubini are all classics*, just as are the fine overtures, duos and choruses that they contain.[28]

Castil-Blaze (François-Henri-Joseph Blaze) foregrounded vocal music, and especially opera, in his definition of 'classic' for the *Dictionnaire de musique moderne* (Paris, 1821). His list of composers looks familiar from previous chapters' listing of popular opera composers 1780–1800, mainly Italian, whose works were avidly arranged: Sarti, Piccini, Cimarosa, Gluck, Mozart, Méhul, and Cherubini. Castil-Blaze implies that items within these works – the 'fine overtures, duos, and choruses that they contain' – also attain this status of 'classic'. This definition of classic is similar to Weber's criteria for the 'pedagogical canon', with the prominence given to models for teaching. It is relevant to the Viennese salon context because of the focus there on *Bildung* – the pedagogical emphasis discussed above.

---

[26] On this subject see my 'Picturing Nineteenth-Century String Quartet Listeners', *Music in Art* 41/1–2 (2016), pp. 237–48; and my 'Theater Piece and *Cabinetstück*: Nineteenth-Century Visual Ideologies of the String Quartet', *Music in Art* 29/1–2 (2004), pp. 134–50.

[27] See Gradenwitz, *Literatur und Musik in geselligem Kreise*, p. 184.

[28] Castil-Blaze [François-Henri-Joseph Blaze], *Dictionnaire de musique moderne*, vol. 1 (Paris: Au magasin de musique de la Lyre moderne, 1821), p. 117 (my italics).

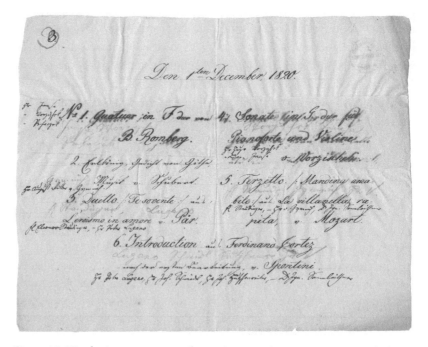

Figure 4.2 Handwritten programme for a private evening entertainment in the home of the Viennese lawyer Ignaz von Sonnleithner on 1 December 1820. Courtesy of Archiv, Bibliothek und Sammlungen der Gesellschaft der Musikfreunde in Wien, shelf mark 10520/133

Which genres of music were considered 'classics' in Vienna at this time, and by whom? And where did opera arrangements sit on the implied scale of musical status and value? The answers would have varied, depending on the gathering in question.[29] Otto Biba has published two contrasting programmes from Viennese salons of the era, one from 1819, held in the home of violinist Joseph Böhm; the other from 1820, from the salon of Sonnleithner. These programmes give a sense of the breadth of repertoire in Viennese musical salons, as well as the target audiences. The former showcased virtuoso violin music, evidently designed to show off Böhm as composer and performer, and offering what we might now call 'light' musical fare. This 'private musical entertainment' (*musikalisches Privat-Unterhaltung*) comprised two potpourris; an aria; a fantasie and variations for violin, clarinet, cello, and piano; and a polonaise. The Sonnleithner programme (see Figure 4.2) offered what we would now consider more 'serious' repertoire, opening with Bernard Romberg's String Quartet in

---

[29] This evidence is also discussed in my *Beethoven's Symphonies Arranged*, pp. 136–8.

F major, led by first violinist Leopold Jansa, followed by Schubert's 'Erlkönig'. There followed a duet by Paër ('Te sovente' from *L'eroismo in amore*), with tenor Peter Lugano and soprano Eleonore Staudinger; then a G major violin sonata by *Johann Hugo* Worzischek, Op. 5, played by Jansa; and vocal items by Mozart ('Mandina amabile', K. 480). The concert concluded with the Introduzione from Spontini's *Fernand Cortez*, played in a piano-vocal arrangement involving Lugano (as Alvaro) and pianist Johann Schmiedel.[30]

While the first programme celebrated virtuoso display and the second promoted connoisseurship and study, both potentially helped with canon formation by means of repeated reminders of preferred repertoire. It is striking that opera, in one form or another, pervades both these concerts, and this was typical of the Viennese salon. In the Böhm programme there is the potpourri, the aria, the *fantasie*, and the variations – any or all of which might be based on hits from operas. The Sonnleithner programme is more overtly connected to opera, with the striking excerpt from *Fernand Cortez*.

Class and gender were important determinants of the repertoire to be performed in a given salon. At one end of the size range and social spectrum was the elite quartet party. The diary of London visitor Sir George Thomas Smart gives evidence of such a party in the home of amateur Viennese cellist Ignaz Anton Aloys Dembscher on 8 September 1825. The music played at these gatherings was typically complex original chamber music, such as new string quartets by Beethoven; and the audience and performers consisted of wealthy, musical middle-class men. Of about twenty people present, only six or seven were women. The quartet players were professionals or advanced amateurs, as were those at the gatherings attended by Sonnleithner: Joseph Mayseder; Dembscher himself, who played the cello; and two other amateurs. The works were 'most difficult' and 'admirably played' – the parties offered occasions for musicians to develop musical professionalism.[31] Arrangements for strings alone might have been performed in such contexts, but they were more typical in smaller, closed gatherings of men, such as the male family members who got together for quartet playing in Schubert's and Sonnleithner's family circles around 1813, and in the larger gatherings involving singers that arose slightly later out of those occasions.[32]

The cellist Nikolaus von Zmeskall also held musical entertainments – similar to Dembscher's – for the preservation of string-quartet music,

---

[30] Biba, 'Public and Semi-Public Concerts', pp. 263–4.
[31] Hugh Bertram Cox and C. L. E. Cox (eds.), *Leaves from the Journals of Sir George Smart* (London: Longmans, Green & Co., 1907), p. 107.
[32] Hanslick, *Geschichte*, p. 202.

which were important in starting to establish a canon of chamber music. The exclusivity of these parties suggests that this repertoire was kept distinct from other chamber-music-making, including the performance of opera in string-quartet arrangements. These private string-quartet-only concerts were then taken into the public sphere by Schuppanzigh, who mounted 'all-string-quartet' concerts in the 1820s in Vienna, centred on the quartets of Haydn, Mozart, and Beethoven. A clearer instance of canon formation beginning in private and influencing public music-making would be hard to find. The music played in these concerts – and its performance there – attracted reviews that tended to seal its canonic status, with ascriptions of 'purity', 'homogeneity', and 'unity' understood as more or less overt statements of German nationalism, an important driver of German canon formation at this time.

'Domesticated' arrangements of public music found a more typical home in the more diverse, ad hoc private and semi-private musical gatherings of the early nineteenth century. Such was the musical party that Smart attended on 17 September 1821, at the house of Mr Kirchoffer, a 'friend of Ries'. Here the music 'was play'd by Amateurs, except the Leader, a young man, a Mr Feigerl – in the Conservatoire – taught the Violin by Böhm'.[33] This was a 'large Party' from the middle ranks of society: Smart was promptly introduced to several women, and also the head gardener at the Schönbrunn Palace. The music, like the society, was diverse. As in Sonnleithner's accounts cited above, the repertoire looked back to the eighteenth century, including one of Mozart's 'Haydn' quartets; some solo instrumental music and songs, and variations; and arrangements, including some works by Handel. There is no direct mention of opera arrangements, but they were typically included in such programmes.

Such arrangements were certainly part of the canon-forming process at this time. Parakilas gives the example of Lully's operas, which appeared in scores of various sorts in the eighteenth century: entire operas, single numbers, and arrangements, and contrafacta of those numbers. He explains the importance of arrangements for canon formation in terms of a broadening of audience base, via the sharing of memorable musical experiences:

These publications domesticated the music that people heard in the theatre, keeping alive the memory of what they heard and saw there, transforming it in their consciousness as they recreated it with their own voices and hands and imagined themselves in their favourite roles. Their domestic performances even

---

[33] Cox and Cox, *Leaves from the Journals of Sir George Smart*, pp. 125–6.

extended the audience of the music to include their friends and servants who never heard it in the theatre at all, so that it was described at the time as having entered the national consciousness[.][34]

The shared nature of the canon is underscored: sharing of the experience of music helps to build the canon once one has internalised the work. And, vice versa, the act of canon formation helps to build a community, even a nation: 'with these domestic performers returned to see the opera again, they were bonded with others like themselves and by a communal internalization of the individual roles'.[35]

Sonnleithner's account of the salons of Zizius, who held musical soirées in 1819–20, is one of several sources showing a growing awareness of 'classics' in Vienna at this time, but without necessarily taking an elitist approach to them.[36] According to Sonnleithner, Zizius' sister 'knew how to properly do the "honours" and was able to invite a grouping of attractive women to the evenings ... [and] the best dilettante and amateur circles, including some opera singers, felt so honoured to perform classic pieces and the newest piquant parlour music'.[37] The Zizius example is one of many indicating that gender mixing was common at these post-Congress salons, as were mixtures of dilettantes (understood then as semi-professionals) and amateurs (those involved in music for enjoyment and love). Most significantly, these were 'mixed' events musically, including both 'classic pieces' and 'parlour music'; and performers of various levels, including opera singers, were apparently happy with the diverse repertoire.

The Kirchoffer soirée offered exactly the easy mixture of 'classic pieces' and 'parlour music' described at the Zizius party – a blend of recent and older vocal and instrumental repertoire, and a medley of genres within these categories. Such an assortment was also typical of public concerts of the time.[38] The smaller-scale songs and variations probably counted then as 'parlour music'; larger-scale music from composers of the past, including the recent past, were coming to be considered 'classical pieces', even if not yet labelled as such. The definition of the two categories – 'parlour music'

---

[34] James Parakilas, 'The Operatic Canon', in Helen M. Greenwald (ed.), *The Oxford Handbook of Opera* (New York: Oxford University Press, 2014), p. 866.
[35] Ibid.
[36] Regarding Spohr's role in forming musical taste in the salons, mixing 'classics' with popular genres at this time: see my 'Die Streichquartette von Beethoven und Spohr: Ein Vergleich', *Spohr Jahrbuch* 3 (2019), pp. 37–56.
[37] Deutsch (ed.), 'Leopold von Sonnleithners Erinnerungen', p. 53.
[38] On this subject see William Weber, *The Great Transformation of Musical Taste: Concert Programming from Haydn to Brahms* (Cambridge: Cambridge University Press, 2008).

and 'classical pieces' – had more to do with the age of the music, and so whether it had withstood the test of time, than size. Mozart's 'Haydn' quartets, for example, would be counted as a prime example of small-scale 'classical pieces'.

Nor did it matter at this stage that the 'classical pieces' were often performed in arrangements in the private soirées. The original form of a work was not necessarily preferred in these contexts, as it was increasingly at the all-string-quartet events. Kerman finds that the idea of a canonic work 'has to imply the idea of a canonical performance', the performer 'representing the composer's inspiration and doing his best to convey this faithfully, "authentically"'.[39] But even though the idea was emerging of composer and work exerting 'authority', tied up with canon formation in Western music, it was still accepted that a particular work could be validly and effectively rendered in various kinds of performance, by various performers and instruments.[40]

In general, arrangement fostered rather than inhibited repetition and reverence at this time. Consider the case of Handel's oratorios, which received massive public performances in late-eighteenth-century Britain.[41] That music was transplanted to Germany, canonised in private performances by Gottfried van Swieten in the late eighteenth century and also through (public) emulation by Haydn in his own late oratorios (representing, in effect, pedagogical canon formation) around 1800. But the canonic status of Handel's oratorios was also perpetuated via domestic performance of excerpts in the nineteenth-century home. As Parakilas puts it, 'music was canonized as much by the private devotion of domestic performance as by public worship'.[42] Arrangements were celebrated for stimulating the listener's imagination, so that the original – and even its public premier – might be imagined from a private rendition.[43] The idea of a given composer and work exerting 'authority' via its 'original' form and genre – the term 'original' – came to be applied particularly to certain genres, especially symphonies and string quartets, which would take over as 'classics' in the 1830s and 1840s. But this idea remained largely irrelevant to opera, where singers exerted

---

[39] Joseph Kerman, 'A Few Canonic Variations', in Robert von Hallberg (ed.), *Canons* (Chicago: The University of Chicago Press, 1983), p. 183.

[40] On this topic see especially Mary Hunter, '"To Play as if from the Soul of the Composer": The Idea of the Performer in Early Romantic Aesthetics', *Journal of the American Musicological Society* 58/2 (2005), pp. 357–98.

[41] See Claudia L. Johnson, '"Giant HANDEL" and the Musical Sublime', *Eighteenth-Century Studies* 19/4 (1986), pp. 515–33.

[42] Parakilas, 'The Power of Domestication', p. 10.

[43] See my *Beethoven's Symphonies Arranged*, p. 168.

authority and 'the work' was understood as inherently mutable, and so not necessarily suitable for canonisation (see Chapter 5).

Cormac Newark and William Weber find that, historically, some operas have been held up as 'classics', but do not quite attain canonic status in the long run. They cite the example of Pergolesi's *La serva padrona* (1733), a major hit in its day and for long afterwards, and highly influential.[44] Pergolesi's *Stabat mater* makes it into Castil-Blaze's list, but not the opera. Indeed, the list of favoured composers was changing, and depended on where the list was made. Of Castil-Blaze's list, only operas by Mozart were frequently performed in Vienna into the mid-nineteenth century.

But works like Pergolesi's *La serva padrona* or Paisiello's *La molinara* were still in a sense canonised, even if they did not make it into the later nineteenth century's opera canon. Parakilas suggests that we think less about a developing list of canonic operas, and more about evolving systems of opera canon formation, leading to today's operatic canon. As Franco Pierperno has pointed out, systems of literary canons heavily influenced the formation of the operatic canon in the late eighteenth century, which was centred on Metastasio, Goldoni, and Da Ponte (who developed Goldoni's model), all of them Mozart's librettists.[45] In 1810s and 1820s Vienna, other operas were revered and repeated alongside the Mozart works, among them French grand opera, local *Singspiele*, and Italian opera, notably Rossini's: they, too, were celebrated and repeated in a complex process driven by economic, social, and cultural forces.

Parakilas takes a broad view of the operatic canon as an institution, a 'system of cultural upbringing'. He notes 'the entire system of production and consumption, not just the repertory, is canonic'.[46] With the term 'canonic' he seems to refer mainly to opera's 'larger than life' aura and effects, which apparently returns us to Kerman's 'canonical performance' in 'that oversized theatre with its oversized spaces … and oversized performing forces'. According to Parakilas, the canonic repertory 'demands and relies on a canonic style of vocal production'.[47] But he

---

[44] Cormac Newark and William Weber, 'General Introduction: Idiosyncrasies of the Operatic Canon', in Cormac Newark and William Weber (eds.), *The Oxford Handbook of the Operatic Canon* (Oxford: Oxford University Press, 2020), p. 10; see also Wolfgang Fuhrmann's concept of 'failed' canonisation, 'Gescheiterte Kanonisierungen: Drei Fallstudien zu Hasse, Paisiello und C. Ph. E. Bach', in Klaus Pietschmann and Melanie Wald-Fuhrmann (eds.), *Der Kanon der Musik: Theorie und Geschichte; Ein Handbuch* (Munich: Text+Kritik, 2013), pp. 160–9 ; see also Franco Piperno, 'Italian Opera and the Concept of "Canon" in the Late Eighteenth Century', in Newark and Weber, *The Oxford Handbook of the Operatic Canon*, p. 55.

[45] Piperno, 'Italian Opera and the Concept of "Canon"', p. 53.

[46] Parakilas, 'The Operatic Canon', p. 862.   [47] Ibid., pp. 862–3.

finds that arrangements are an integral part of the canonising systems at work in the first centuries of opera, including the nineteenth century. They are part of the systems that keep the works alive in performance and provide vehicles for canonic renewal.

Parakilas notes that aside from writing about the history of opera, all the crucial means of creating an operatic canon were in place by the beginning of the nineteenth century, even though many of the works that constitute the standard repertory of the operas houses today had not yet been composed. Opera houses (places where contemporary operas were performed) turned into repertory houses (places where canonic operas of the past were repeated) when two cultural forces were brought together. These 'forces' centrally involve middle-class people, such as those who were active in the early nineteenth-century Viennese salons. They are the often-ignored 'expert tastemakers, critics and educators, who campaigned for audiences to give serious attention to the work' and a 'middle class eager to earn a place for itself in the temples of cultural prestige' – to which people I now turn.[48]

Canon Formation and Politics in the Viennese Home

The most prominent agents of canon formation in Vienna at this time were men of the upper- and 'middle'-middle classes – those with the money for music and instruments, and leisure time in which to rehearse and perform. They, together with a small number of very talented women like Paradies, Hochenadl, and Arnstein, set in motion ideas of 'good taste', formed with respect to large-scale, often vocal repertoire of the past. These Viennese middle-class amateurs were to some extent reacting against, or modelling themselves on, aristocratic dominance and leadership in culture, asserting their own tastes in repertoire and standards of performance and listening. But they were also overcoming feelings of political powerlessness in the wake of Napoleonic invasions and under Francis I and the Metternich regime.

As Donald Daviau and Andrea Lindmayr-Brandl have observed, life in early nineteenth-century Vienna was double-faced.[49] In this era many Viennese strove to live innocuous lives, or at least lives that looked

---

[48] Ibid., p. 868.
[49] Daviau, 'Biedermeier: The Happy Face of the Vormärz Era'; Andrea Lindmayr-Brandl, 'Music and Culture in Schubert's Vienna', in Marjorie W. Hirsch and Lisa Feurzeig, *The Cambridge Companion to Schubert's 'Winterreise'* (Cambridge: Cambridge University Press, 2021), p. 21.

innocuous. Ordinary people were fearful of living authentically and in accordance with their opinions and morals. Outward appearances and behaviours needed to conform to the resolutions of the Congress of Vienna, which was concerned not only with revisionist ideas regarding the borders of Europe but also with a reversion to monarchical rule. Suspected insurrections were closely monitored and suppressed under the Metternich System, which was increasingly felt in Vienna. Meetings of groups were kept under surveillance; and police approval was required for all public concerts. Programmes, private letters, and published plays alike went first to the censor. Nestroy's plays, for example, were treated with suspicion because they represented a new liberal spirit spreading through Europe. Nestroy succeeded Ferdinand Raimund as the leading actor-dramatist at the Volkstheater. Raimund concentrated on romantic and magical fantasies, which were safely ambiguous. Nestroy used comedy for more overt parody and criticism, which got him into trouble with government officials. Literature had to be bland, dealing with anything but the social and political reality of everyday life.

This continual concealment of one's real opinions led to a psychological condition known as *Zerrissenheit*, a division between inner and outer lives. *Zerrissenheit* took an extreme toll on the nerves of some people, such as Schubert's poet friend Joseph Mayrhofer, who committed suicide. More generally, Daviau says, 'this same lack of basic freedoms caused widespread discontent among writers, journalists, intellectuals, university professors and students as well among the member nations of the Monarchy that wanted greater self-determination'.[50] Feelings of contentment, and importantly freedom (*Freiheit*), had as much to do with power and agency or self-determination as with wealth in *Vormärz* Vienna. Kiesewetter enjoyed a modest degree of agency within the Viennese government. He was a high-ranking official in the War Office, and after the Napoleonic Wars took leadership in the areas of the military concerned with education. As for the Jewish banker families, the salon hosts in question were certainly wealthy; however, they all lacked access to the top jobs and to the status afforded the 'old aristocracy'.

Daviau also finds that musical life suffered little as a result of the Metternich System: 'Because it was considered non-political, music could develop freely without the intrusion of censorship that restricted all written forms'.[51] This was not quite true of opera, whose libretti were closely

---

[50] Daviau, 'Biedermeier: The Happy Face of the Vormärz Era', p. 19. [51] Ibid., p. 24.

scrutinised for political content.[52] But it was nonetheless generally held to be true of music, provided it had no text. Grillparzer, who frequented the Sonnleithner salons, observed to Beethoven in a conversation book: 'The musician has no censor!'[53] And Christoph Kuffner, who probably provided the text for Beethoven's Choral Fantasy Op. 18, observed in Beethoven's conversation book: 'Today, the censor would not even allow a *Don Giovanni* opera if it were rewritten'.[54] To Ignaz Moscheles, Grillparzer wrote in verse about instrumental music's freedom:

> But music speaks a loftier tone
> To tyrant and to spy unknown,
> And free as angels walks with men
> Can pass unscathed the gaoler's ken.[55]

Many musicians were well aware that music-making was not always the non-political pursuit it was widely made out to be. It was used as a vehicle for political messages, overt in works such as the Marseillaise or Joseph Haydn's imperial anthem; and covert, as in magical and mythical operas among many other works.[56] The political situation in Vienna in the early nineteenth century had a significant impact on musical life not only because finances were tight and inflation was high. Small-scale, overtly non-political gatherings were the safest and therefore the most common for music-making, or for any other purpose among middle-class people. In the 1810s and 1820s, larger musical events could still take place with careful choice of activity and repertoire. This had important implications for canon formation. Certain works were more available and appealing for repeated performance in this climate of surveillance and censorship. Those with clear elements of political and social commentary would not pass muster with the censors.

---

[52] On this subject see R. J. Goldstein, 'Political Censorship of the Opera', in *Political Censorship of the Arts and the Press in Nineteenth-Century Europe* (London: Palgrave Macmillan, 1989), pp. 155–74; John A. Davis, 'Opera and Absolutism in Restoration Italy, 1815–1860', *The Journal of Interdisciplinary History* 36/4 (2006), pp. 569–94; Tamara Kamatovic, 'Censorship, Secrets, Correspondences, and Freedom: The Literary Public in the Viennese Biedermeier', PhD diss. (University of Chicago, 2020).

[53] Grita Herre (ed.), *Ludwig van Beethovens Konversationshefte*, vol. 9 (1988), p. 169.

[54] Ibid., p. 215.

[55] Charlotte Moscheles, *Life of Moschelese, with Selections from His Diaries and Correspondence* vol. 1, adapted from the original German by A. D. Coleridge (London: Hukst and Blackette, 1873), p. 207.

[56] See especially Lisa de Alwis, 'Censorship and Magical Opera in Early Nineteenth-Century Vienna', PhD diss. (University of Southern California, 2012); and W. E. Yates, *Theatre in Vienna: A Critical History, 1776–1995* (Cambridge: Cambridge University Press, 1996).

Charles Sealsfield (the pseudonym of Austrian-American journalist Karl Anton Postl), observed that the salons of the Viennese nobility and upper-middle classes were sites for covert political activity:

It is in the circles of the nobility, and the wealthier class of bankers, that you will find a certain degree of political freedom and liberty of speech, newspapers, and as they are called 'Verbotene Bücher', [prohibited books] in every tongue. There are no political saloons of liberals, as there are in Paris, except [in] the very highest families of the nobility ... but during a dancing, a dining, or whist party, some couples of gentlemen will loose themselves from the tables and step just occasionally into the next room; or a letter from Paris or London – of course not through the post – will glide from hand to hand, in that imperceptible way which Metternich has taught them.[57]

Sealsfield was an advocate for a German democracy, employing 'eyewitness' accounts, history, and anecdote to expose the oppressive Austrian regime under Emperor Francis I and his prime minister, Metternich. His writings need to be taken with a grain of salt, since they are deliberately polemical and somewhat unreliable; but he was widely travelled and had access to salons at various levels of society within Vienna; he published from London, then moved to Switzerland, a place where he was free to speak his opinions.

Some of the key agents in establishing public musical life and musical canons in early-nineteenth-century Vienna were the upwardly mobile intelligentsia: the bankers, lawyers, and government officials to whom Sealsfield refers – among them a number of Jews. Culturally, if not directly in politics, they were becoming leaders, and could champion the repertoire that would suit their cause, first of all in their semi-private salons. Stephen Rumph makes a similar argument regarding E. T. A. Hoffmann's championing of Beethoven's Fifth Symphony from Leipzig in 1810. For Hoffmann, Rumph argues, music was a medium of revelation, and would combat French elegance and sensualism with German profundity, spirituality, and intuition. Here his writings sat alongside those of political Romantics such as Kleist, Adam Müller, and Brentano.[58] In Vienna, salons, frequented by distinguished middle-class intellectuals such as Wilhelm von Humboldt, August Wilhelm Schlegel, and Friedrich Schlegel, had a broadly

---

[57] Charles Sealsfield [Karl Postl], *Austria As It Is: or Sketches of Continental Courts, by an Eye-Witness* (London: Hurst and Chance, 1828), p. 187.
[58] On E. T. A. Hoffmann's canonisation of Beethoven's symphonies, see Stephen Rumph, 'A Kingdom Not of This World: The Political Context of E. T. A. Hoffmann's Beethoven Criticism', *19th-Century Music* 19/1 (1995), pp. 50–67.

similar cultural-political agenda, aimed if not directly at French sensualists, then certainly at establishing educated German middle-class amateur listeners and performers as leaders and arbiters of taste.

But composers and publishers also wanted to become arbiters of taste. An example of an attempt at this is an 1816 decision by Viennese publisher Sigmund Anton Steiner to issue three of Beethoven's newest orchestral works – *Wellington's Victory*, and the Seventh and Eight Symphonies, Opp. 91–3 – in arrangements for various combinations of chamber group, simultaneously, and concurrently with the original orchestral edition, which was issued in parts and full score.[59] In total, seven versions were published at once of the symphonies, and eight of *Wellington's Victory*. The arrangements ranged from solo piano to wind nonet (*Harmonie*), and *Wellington's Victory* was also released in a version for a nine-part ensemble of 'Turkish' instruments. Steiner and his team clearly considered arrangements to be appropriate vehicles for this music (as probably did Hoffmann, whose 1810 review of Beethoven's Fifth was based on a piano reduction); and he did not focus on the idea of the 'original', except to claim (probably fallaciously) that Beethoven himself had overseen the arrangements.[60]

Steiner's advertisement clearly appeals to the middle-class intelligentsia, and tries to shape taste by pushing forward a comparative newcomer, Beethoven, as the German genius to watch:

The name of the ingenious Ludwig van Beethoven as it were guarantees the high value of the two grand symphonies announced here. But even without mentioning his name, everyone well informed in the field of musical art would recognise the creator of these masterworks. Just as Mr van Beethoven is acknowledged to be the greatest composer of our times, these symphonies – which were performed here in Vienna under the direction of this famous composer to the benefit of charity with extraordinary acclaim – belong to the most successful creations of his profound, fecund genius. … Often even the expert ear is astonished by the profound mysteries of their peculiar fantasies, but [the expert ear] is seized by enthusiastic exaltation when, hearing them repeatedly, the part writing unfolds in heavenly lucidity.[61]

---

[59] 'Pränumerations-Anzeige auf zwey neue grosse Sinfonien (in A. und F. dur) von Ludwig van Beethoven', in Ludwig van Beethoven, *Wellingtons Sieg* [arranged for Turkish music ensemble] (Vienna: Steiner & Co., 1816). The advertisement is found in all of Steiner's original editions of *Wellington's Victory*, on page 1, with the exception of the Turkish music and version for two pianos; the advertisement also appeared in the *Wiener Zeitung*, on 6 March 1816.

[60] Discussed further in my *Beethoven's Symphonies Arranged*, pp. 116–52; see also Hoffmann, 'Recension'.

[61] Beethoven, *Wellingtons Sieg* [arranged for Turkish music ensemble], preface.

German profundity, spirituality, and intuition are celebrated here; and, just as in the Hoffmann review of Beethoven's Fifth, Steiner confers canonic status on Beethoven and at the same time tells the reader how to listen and what to listen for to appreciate this. This advertisement is canon-forming rhetoric par excellence, creating and setting the parameters of agreement.

This example shows how publishers, in commissioning and marketing arrangements, could try to further canon formation. But despite the overt appeal of their lengthy advertisement to the educated middle-class amateur, such arrangements represent only a small part of what the Viennese enjoyed in their home concerts, and just one facet of canon formation. As we have seen, talented Viennese amateurs like Kiesewetter and Zmeskall, and professionals like Pössinger, were well able to produce their own arrangements of music from scores or instrumental parts. So published arrangements do not tell the whole story. Then, as a wider consideration of Steiner's publishing catalogues for these years will demonstrate, arrangements of orchestral music, aside from opera overtures, were the exception rather than the rule. In particular, Steiner and Haslinger's catalogues reveal a substantial taste for French grand opera in the 1810s. For example, Spontini's *Fernand Cortez* appears there in numerous different arrangements: the overture arranged for flute, violin or guitar, and selected pieces for piano solo (without voice), piano and voice, guitar, six- and nine-part *Harmonie*, two flutes, two violins, and guitar and voice. A potpourri for guitar by Diabelli based on the work was also published.

Towards Operatic Canon Formation

The case of *Fernand Cortez* helps to show how the Viennese populace could champion their own repertoire, engage systems of opera canon formation, and use the opera to covert political ends. First of all, a glance through the arrangements of *Fernand Cortez* from this time reveals that firms other than Steiner got on the bandwagon: Artaria released a piano arrangement of the opera's introduction, as well as separate piano arrangements of the choruses and marches (see Example 4.1).[62] These were part of an anthology of music for piano, to which people like Sonnleithner, with an interest in domestic performance, might subscribe. But there was also a four-hand

---

[62] See Gaspare Spontini, 'Le commencement de l'Ouverture de l'Opera: Fernand Cortez', *Anthologie musicale ou Recueil périodique pour le Forte-Piano/Musikalischer-Sammler für das Forte-Piano* (Vienna: Artaria & Co., n.d.), Österreichische Nationalbibliothek shelf mark: MS36373-4°/3.

version of the entire opera for piano, carried out by the arranger Johann Phillipp Samuel Schmidt (1779–1853) in Berlin, published by Böhm around this date, probably reflecting the favour in which the work was then held by the Prussian king. Schmidt was a composer and was closely associated with Carl Friedrich Zelter's Singakademie and Liedertafel in Berlin. In addition to his compositions, he completed thirty-eight piano reductions for symphonies, quintets, and quartets, as well as one of Anton Radziwiłł's *Faust*. A string-quartet arrangement would also have been entirely in keeping with the Sonnleithner music parties, where original works for string quartet were central repertoire. Earlier, an arrangement of *Fernand Cortez* by Viennese violinist Anton Wranitzky (1761–1820) had been published by the Bureau de Musique des Theatres (see Example 4.2, below). Wranitzky, a composer of chamber music in his own right, had distinguished himself as an arranger with his 1799 string-quintet version of Haydn's *Creation* (Bonn: Simrock).[63]

These arrangements all appeared after the work was performed at the Theater am Kärntnertor in 1812, with the role of Télasco taken by tenor Johann Michael Vogl – a professional singer who performed at the soirées and salons of Kiesewetter and Schubert. He appeared in 'redface', that is, pseudo-Indigenous costuming of a white person as part of their depiction of a character in an artwork, which might appear offensively stereotypical today.[64] Indeed, the Aztecs are typecast as the primitive, unenlightened 'other' in this opera. This is reinforced by the music. Early critics complained about the adventurous harmony and the loudness of the music, which contributes to the othering of the Aztecs. But the setting, in a culture of the distant past (the conquest of Mexico took place 1519–21) made it possible to transfer the allusion to the othered culture (supposedly in this instance more primitive and menacing) to refer to any other culture, as circumstances might indicate. The numerous arrangements of *Fernand Cortez* are a good example of how the Viennese 'domesticated' a work, in the sense of making it their own, and ascribed to it their own meanings.

As to these meanings, *Fernand Cortez* was originally intended as political propaganda to support Napoleon's invasion of Spain in 1808. Cortez symbolises Napoleon, while the bloodthirsty Aztec priests are meant to represent the Spanish Inquisition (the French aimed to civilise the Spanish, as the *conquistadores* had the Aztecs). But in the end, the political message

---

[63] See Thormählen, 'Playing with Art', pp. 348–60.
[64] The original costume can be viewed at www.wikiwand.com/en/Fernand_Cortez#Media/File: Telasco_in_Fernand_Cortez_(Vienne).png.

Example 4.1 From Spontini's *Fernand Cortez*, in *Anthologie musicale ou Recueil périodique pour le Forte-Piano / Musikalischer-Sammler für das Forte-Piano* (Vienna: Artaria & Co., n.d.): (a) Introduction, bars 1–24

probably worked rather in reverse, the work appealing more to Napoleon's detractors. The popularity of the piece declined in France with the waning of the French army's fortunes in Spain and Portugal, but not in Vienna and the German lands, which were now subject to Napoleonic invasions. King Wilhelm Friedrich III of Prussia ordered a performance of *Fernand Cortez* in Berlin in 1814, and he subsequently sought to engage Spontini at the Berlin opera, being even more impressed with the revised version of 1817. In 1819, Spontini was appointed General-Musik-Director at the Berlin opera for ten years, against the will of Count Brühl, who wanted a composer more familiar with the German language and theatre.[65]

---

[65] See Francien Markx, *E. T. A. Hoffmann, Cosmopolitanism, and the Struggle for German Opera* (Leiden: Brill Rodopi, 2016), pp. 329–30.

Example 4.1 (b) Allegro vivace, bars 1–22

So a concluding performance of the opening of *Fernand Cortez* was an appropriate choice in 1820 for a Viennese salon host like Sonnleithner, who supported the general aspiration to Enlightenment without a one-sided commitment to German art. The choice also reflects an aesthetic stance, one that comprehends rather than eschews the modern soundscape. The stage direction for the Introduzione in the original score invokes the sublime, involving a great storm and vast underground vaults, incommensurable forces, and prostration before great power:

> The first enclosure of the great temple of Mexico, illuminated by fires on a stormy night. The idol of Talepulchra, God of Evil, supported by two golden tiers, rises up at the bottom of the hall; the doors leading to the underground vaults are opened, where the prisoners of war destined for sacrifice are kept. As the curtain rises, the Priestesses and the Wizards stand prostrate with their faces to the ground; only the High Priest stands, facing the idol, on a small scaffold.

Example 4.2 Anton Wranitzky's string-quartet arrangement of Spontini's *Fernand Cortez* (Vienna: Bureau de Musique des Theatre, n.d.), Overture, bars 1–22

Figure 4.3 Set design by Maler Militz for *Fernand Cortez* by Gaspare Spontini, staged at the Vienna State Opera in 1893. Historisches Museum der Stadt Wien. Courtesy of Di Agostini Editore/agefotostock

The 1809 premiere had been famous for its spectacular effects, including the appearance of seventeen real horses on stage. The work's striking theatrics and sheer noise must have been difficult to capture in the salon. But the increasingly sturdy Viennese pianos of the time would help to render the fluctuating dynamics, sforzando chords, and sharp accents of the opening (see Example 4.1). Such arrangements would capture something of the sonic world that now formed part of the salon-attendee's recently lived experience – the noise and chaos, vividly described by Beethoven, of the Napoleonic invasions of Vienna in 1809 – now, at a safe distance, felt and heard as 'sublime'.[66] After the entrance of Alvaro, a chorus of prisoners (tenors and basses) enters. In the 1820 Sonnleithner salon performance, this 'chorus' seems to have been sung by tenor Johann Hutschenreiter and bass Ignaz von Sonnleithner, according to almost illegible annotations on the programme.

Domesticated versions disseminated *Fernand Cortez*, and many other operas, to people who might otherwise not have heard them. Arrangements like these helped people to make opera in some sense their own, and make

---

[66] The Napoleonic invasion of Vienna was captured by Beethoven in 1809 in a letter of 26 July to his publisher Breitkopf, where he complains of the disruption and noise caused by the French troops.

it memorable because it is experienced in and as performance; they also imbued it with new meanings via the new contexts of performance. Most importantly, such arrangements allowed ordinary people to exercise their own choice and taste in art, and to play an important role in deciding which operas stood the test of time and made it into public performing canons. So later 'canonic' performances of *Fernand Cortez*, such as one involving an elaborate set by Maler Militz at the Vienna State Opera in 1893 (Figure 4.3), depended to an appreciable extent on earlier small-scale repetitions – even those on solo guitar or piano – from the earlier nineteenth century.

A Split in the Musical Canon?

> Whatever family of the middle class you enter, the pianoforte is the first object which strikes your eyes; you are hardly seated, and a flaggon filled with wine, another with water, and Presburgh [sic] biscuit placed before you, when the host will tell Caroline to play a tune to the gentleman. To play is their pride, and in that consists chiefly the education of the middle classes.[67]

Parakilas observes that canon formation is not a simple matter of authorities making the decisions and imposing their own tastes and values on consumers. Consumers' processes of 'domestication' (by which Parakilas means 'making the music their own') show their power and agency.[68] This understanding of consumer power in canon formation would seem to apply neatly in early nineteenth-century Vienna. Homes, and salons within them along with other private, mostly familial gatherings, became centres of musical activity, and the 'domestication' of music frequently took the quite literal form of creating musical arrangements, tailored to the tastes, standards, and needs of those present there.

In seeking to define the larger roles and status of opera in Vienna at this time, we need to think outside the walls of the more elite salons. The *silence* of many contemporary verbal accounts of domestic life on the subject of opera arrangements is striking: it seems that the performance of opera arrangements in the home was so common as to go mostly without mention, except in publisher's catalogues, and places like Sealsfield's account cited at the beginning of this section, which documents the ubiquity of music-making in Vienna. Elsewhere, this silence also has to

---

[67] Sealsfield, *Austria As It Is*, p. 202.
[68] Parakilas, 'The Power of Domestication', especially pp. 6–7.

do with the people who were performing opera arrangements – the ubiquitous Miss Carolines at the piano – who went largely unobserved except by admiring friends and family members. There are two layers of middle-class music-making to be distinguished: among the upper echelons of the middle class, who had the time, money, and influence to put on lavish musical salons; and among the many more musical amateurs who could afford music-making in the home, but not on a large scale or via regular salons.

It might seem that the many amateur female pianists were often merely the vehicles for disseminating works already widely embraced as canonic. But this group actually exercised some power in the process of canon formation. Women were seen as the ideal interpreters of music,[69] and publishers quickly got on the bandwagon, arranging and anthologising the 'most beloved' repertoire, new and old, for female amateur pianists. Publishers packaged and marketed these choices in ways that promoted the repeated performance of this repertoire and helped to confirm its value. One of the best known of these publications in Vienna around 1820 was the *Musikalische Damen-Journal* of the multifaceted composer, publisher, and teacher Maximilian Joseph Leidesdorf for the publishing house of Sigmund Anton Steiner. The advertisement announces the canon-forming function of the publication, its selection and sharing of excellent music of the past and present: 'This journal will contain in a tasteful compilation all the beautiful things with which the most popular composers enrich the world from time to time, together with the latest and most interesting pieces of music, which are performed in all local and foreign theatres.'[70]

More than twenty volumes of the *Journal* each offered a varied collection of original pieces and piano arrangements of vocal or instrumental music for these people. Opera was everywhere in evidence, especially that of Rossini and Mozart, in various forms ranging from entire transcriptions to potpourris on favourite themes. The first volume included short excerpts from Mozart's *Die Zauberflöte* and also Franz Danzi's *Der Berggeist*, a Spanish dance, the Polonaise from Rossini's *L'italiana in Algeri*, and a potpourri based on the Finale from *Die Entführung aus dem Serail*, 'for easy performance at the piano' ('leicht für Klavier gesetzt'). Several volumes included potpourris from a single work; but volume 14 included the entirety of Carl Blum's *Rosenhütchen* and all of Rossini's *Richard und*

---

[69] Kordula Knaus, 'Fantasie, Virtuosität und die Performanz musikalischer Inspiration: Pianistinnen und Pianisten in Wien um 1800', in Patrick Boenke and Cornelia Szabó-Knotik (eds.), *Virtuosität*, Anklaenge: Wiener Jahrbuch für Musikwissenschaft (Vienna: Mille-Tre, 2013), pp. 57-73.
[70] *Musikalische Damen-Journal* (Vienna: Steiner & Co., 1820), prefatory advertisement.

Zoraide; volume 16, arrangements from *Emma von Leicester* by Meyerbeer; and volume 17, arrangements from Rossini's *Der Türke in Italien*. Building on the success of this journal, in 1829 Tobias Haslinger published the *Hommage aux Dames. R[é]pertoire des nouvelles Compositions brillantes pour le Pianoforte*. These enterprises celebrated female performance as much as they did the works of major opera composers of the day. Johann André in Offenbach also had a *Journal de musique pour les Dames*, chiefly offering arrangements of chamber music for piano.

Back in Vienna, Czerny in particular dedicated himself to women pianists, observing how piano playing allowed dilettantes to make their way in the world:

Fortepiano playing, although suitable for everyone, is one of the most beautiful and honourable activities, especially for women and ladies. With it, one can provide not only oneself, but also many others with a noble and decent pleasure, and with great progress, also achieve a distinction in the world, which is certainly as pleasant for the dilettante as for the real artist.[71]

Czerny's words may sound condescending today. But in practice, as explained in Chapter 6, this meant that in the early nineteenth century, piano-playing female amateurs could attain a modest share of agency in determining and perpetuating the performance canon. After all, they often determined when, how often, and exactly how a given arrangement was performed – and even whether a given work was performed at all, in times when public concerts were in short supply.

Women also supervised the formation of young talent and taste, contributing in another way to canon formation. The Viennese firm Diabelli, together with Schott and Simrock, rearranged *Don Giovanni* and other operas into pedagogical versions that are specifically reduced in scale and difficulty to cater to beginners. Further examples include publications like Diabelli's *Little Pieces* (*Kleinigkeiten*) and the *Selection of Beloved Melodies for the Pianoforte with Attention to Little Hands* (*Auswahl beliebter Melodien für das Piano-Forte mit Berücksichtigung kleiner Hände*). This sharing of 'choice' repertoire that would otherwise go out of active performance was helping to create the pedagogical and performing canons. By choosing to buy, perform, and teach this music, many female amateurs played a role, alongside other agents, in canon formation in early nineteenth-century Vienna.

---

[71] Carl Czerny, *Briefe über den Unterricht auf dem Pianoforte vom Anfange bis zur Ausbildung als Anhang zu jeder Clavierschule* (Vienna: Diabelli & Co., 1839), p. 2.

Table 4.1 Michele Clark's list of the total number of pieces arranged from Rossini's operas and advertised as available for sale from 1815 to 1830 from Viennese publishers

Publisher	Number of Rossini opera arrangements for sale in Vienna from 1815 to 1830
Sauer, Leidesdorf, and Berka	360
Weigl	269
Senefelder, Steiner, and Haslinger	247
Mechetti	139
Mollo	89
Hoftheater Verlag	86
Cappi, Witzendorf	74
Artaria and Co.	69
Diabelli and Co.	54
Maisch-Sprenger-Artaria	16
Paterno	10

Evidence of these amateurs' tastes can be found in publisher's catalogues. In particular, they proclaimed a voracious appetite for Rossini opera. Michele Clark gives general information on the popularity of Rossini arrangements at this time.[72] Her Table 2.7, reproduced above, lists the combined total of arrangements of Rossini's music that was advertised for sale by Viennese publishing firms in the period 1816–30 (Table 4.1). Although this already seems like a vast number of arrangements, in comparison with the figures considered in Chapters 1 and 2, the total count of Rossini opera arrangements represented in Viennese catalogues, but not necessarily advertised for sale in newspapers and including reprints, is much higher. In other words, Clark's evidential focus results in an undercount. To take Diabelli and Co. alone, their publishing catalogues in the period 1816–24 include 471 entries related to Rossini, most of them for arrangements of his operas, and quite a few for arrangements of individual numbers. For example, the collection of arrangements for piano *Euterpe für Pianoforte 2-händig* contains twenty-nine items, twenty-five of which are arrangements from Rossini operas. No. 25 is the ever popular 'Di tanti palpiti' from *Tancredi*, which opera appears thirty-six times in Diabelli and Co.'s catalogues from 1816 to 1824 – it was a terrific hit with the Viennese, for reasons to be discussed in Chapter 5. There are a mere eleven entries on Beethoven. These include an

---

[72] Michele Leigh Clark, 'The Performance and Reception of Rossini's Operas in Vienna, 1822–1825', PhD diss. (University of North Carolina at Chapel Hill, 2005), pp. 102ff.

arrangement of his overtures and incidental music: *Creatures of Prometheus*, *Coriolan*, and *Egmont*; and, more tellingly, his own arrangement of the still popular *La molinara* by Paisiello. There are no arrangements of symphonies at all. Clearly the emphasis was on theatrical works, and opera in particular.

Opera's champions were starting to follow a different path in canon formation from champions of instrumental music. In contrast to Castil-Blaze, with his eye on opera, Kiesewetter, in his *History of European-Western Music* (1834), styles 1780–1800 'The age of Haydn and Mozart. Vienna School' and finds that instrumental music reached perfection in that period.[73] This influential view persists to the present day.[74] The symphonies and especially string quartets that came to be performed by professional ensembles, by the 'great' composers (chiefly Haydn, Mozart, and Beethoven), were being chosen by a specialised and educated public from this time onwards, and later labelled as *the* paradigmatic works of Viennese Classicism.

Weber finds that by the 1840s the term 'classic' was irrelevant in the opera world.[75] In the later nineteenth century, opera, and specifically Italian opera, did not form a well-defined body of canonic works for public presentation and reverence in concert halls. But Parakilas says that, on the contrary, opera was being canonised in parallel, and opera theatres were starting to become repertory theatres.[76] What happens at this time is not so much a split in the canon as a divergence in canon-formation processes. This has to do with the different social roles and ontological status of opera as against, say, symphonies and string quartets, which were becoming more clearly delineated.

Newark and Weber talk about event-oriented interpretational frameworks as the most relevant for opera.[77] More broadly, the process of performance is a much stronger determinant of canon formation for opera than for those other largely instrumental genres of Western classical music – as it is for the jazz and popular music canons, for example; and so

---

[73] Raphael Georg Kiesewetter, *Geschichte der europaeisch-abendlaendischen oder unsrer heutigen Musik* (Leipzig: Breitkopf & Härtel, 1834), pp. 95–6.
[74] On this subject see James Webster, *Haydn's 'Farewell' Symphony and the Idea of Classical Style: Through-Composition and Cyclic Integration in His Instrumental Music* (Cambridge: Cambridge University Press, 1991), pp. 350–1.
[75] William Weber, 'Redefining the Status of Opera: London and Leipzig, 1800–1848', *The Journal of Interdisciplinary History* 36/3 (2006), p. 513.
[76] Parakilas, 'The Operatic Canon', pp. 867–8.
[77] Weber and Newark, 'General Introduction', p. 16.

mutability, as it occurs through performance, is part and parcel of 'the work' of opera, and a central way in which large and diverse communities of operatic canon-forming practice are built up. Italian opera, in particular, became something of a soundtrack to everyday nineteenth-century lives, banged out chiefly on pianos, but also on any other instruments that were handy, and sung in the streets. These social and communal processes involving arrangement and domestication were not peripheral, but rather central to the creation of the operatic canon.

5 | Rossini 'As the Viennese Liked It'

> Gioachino Rossini . . . belonged among the shining examples that appeared at that time, but the German judges of art of that time deemed him to be an ignorant schoolboy, because he had more genius than counterpoint in him. But even before one of his operas was publicly performed in Vienna [*L'inganno felice* on 26 November 1816; *Tancredi* on 15 February 1817], one had already heard the great alto aria from *L'italiana in Algieri* performed by Miss Sofie von Wertheimstein, and the cavatina: 'Di tanti palpiti' from *Tancredi* performed by a son of the house, and the melodic charm as well as the harmonic turns of these pieces, which were not yet worn out at that time, immediately found decisive recognition.[1]

The period 1816–28 was the heyday of Rossini opera in Vienna. *Tancredi*, for instance, was the fourth most popular opera performed at the Kärntnertortheater in that period, with around 134 performances; and Rossini was the second most popular opera composer there, with around 778 performances of his works. This chapter will explore why, in an era so strongly associated with Beethoven and Schubert, Rossini was such a hit in Vienna, looking at the contribution of opera in the home to this popularity. The quotation from Sonnleithner's *Memoirs* above hints at part of the answer: opera arrangements spread Rossini's music around a wide public even before public performances were staged. Hit numbers such as 'Di tanti palpiti' from *Tancredi* were performed over and over, with various combinations of instruments and voices. The 'judges of German art' decried his work in newspaper reviews; but this did little or nothing to dampen the market's enthusiasm. Sales of Rossini's operas rocketed, as publishing catalogues from the era will be used to demonstrate.

The Rage for Rossini

Opera in the Viennese home in this era (1816–28) can be situated in the context of a developing market economy. An active theatrical and musical

---

[1] Deutsch (ed.), 'Leopold von Sonnleithners Erinnerungen', p. 146.

life, strengthened by Joseph II in the late eighteenth century, supported the emergence of this economy. The Viennese theatres came to depend on a public eager to attend opera, ballet, and spoken drama, and were kept afloat by subscriptions and ticket sales rather than court patronage. During Joseph II's reign (1765–80) the social classes affluent and educated enough to appreciate opera and drama grew, leading to a need for permanent theatres supported by the public. Commercial, subsidised theatres furthered the Enlightenment aim of cultural education and nurtured German nationalism by promoting German plays and operas and by training actors and singers. They differed from the private court theatres, which excluded most of the public, and also from the touring theatrical companies. Three theatres were built outside the city walls in the late eighteenth century: the Theater an der Wien (completed 1801), the Theater in der Josefstadt (founded 1788), and the Theater in der Leopoldstadt (opened 1781).

Clark describes Vienna as 'a center of the thespian world for German-speaking countries throughout the first half of the nineteenth century'.[2] Five theatres operated in Vienna: the three outside the city walls, and the two public court theatres (Hoftheater) in the central district, the Burgtheater (opened 1741) and the Kärntnertortheater (built 1709). Until 1811, both the Burgtheater and Kärntnertortheater presented drama and opera, but after this point the Burgtheater presented plays and the Kärntnertortheater opera. In the 1820s the Kärntnertortheater came to have a monopoly on performances of Italian opera; earlier it was the only theatre in Vienna to employ a permanent German troupe, as well as an Italian troupe on an ad hoc basis. Many French and Italian operas were performed there in translation.

This lively theatrical life persisted in – and perhaps partly because of – the oppressive political climate. Under Metternich, the police and other judicial forces maintained the strictest system of censorship in all of Europe. Numerous playbills indicate that 'Gott erhalte Franz den Kaiser' was to be sung before a performance in a Viennese theatre, attesting to the tense political climate persisting after the Napoleonic Wars, and the perceived need to remind people of their patriotic duty. German opera was marginally safer than other kinds, from a political perspective, at least with the right libretto. It had its staunch advocates in 1810s Vienna, including vociferous critics of Italian opera who would soon speak out against

---

[2] Clark, 'The Performance and Reception of Rossini's Operas', p. 21.

Rossini.[3] In the previous decade, German opera had been well represented in the twenty-four volumes of the *Journal für Quartetten Liebhaber*, published by Chemische Druckerei, from 1807 to 1810.[4] The opera composers this journal featured most in excerpted arrangements were, in descending order, Weigl, Ignaz von Seyfried, Cherubini, Joseph Vogler, Umlauf, Anton Fischer, Gyrowetz, Mozart, Hummel, and Catel. Most of the names are wholly forgotten today as composers of opera (see Table 5.1).

Table 5.1 *Journal für Quartetten Liebhaber*, published by Chemische Druckerei, opera arrangements in the first three volumes, 1807

Vol no. (pl. no.)	Composer	Title (translated)	Österreichische Nationalbibliothek shelf mark
1 (593)	Mozart	Overture from the opera *Idomeneo*	A-Wn MS12665–4°/1,1
	Cherubini	Pantomime March from the opera *Faniska*	A-Wn MS12665–4°/1,2
	Gyrowetz	March from *Agnes Sorel*	A-Wn MS12665–4°/1,3
	Paër	Duet from *Sargino*	A-Wn MS12665–4°/1,4
	Umlauf	March from *Die Volksstämme*	A-Wn MS12665–4°/1,5
	Gluck	The Scythian Ballet from *Iphigenia auf Tauris* (*Iphigénie en Tauride*)	A-Wn MS12665–4°/1,6
2 (601)	Paër	Overture from the opera *Sargino*	A-Wn MS12665–4°/2,1
	Boieldieu	Romance from the opera *Der Kaliph von Bagdad* (*Le calife de Bagdad*)	A-Wn MS12665–4°/2,2
	Gyrowetz	March from the opera *Ida*	A-Wn MS12665–4°/2,3
	Cherubini	Hymn from the opera *Medea* (*Médée*)	A-Wn MS12665–4°/2,4
	Weigl	March from the opera *Vestas Feuer*	A-Wn MS12665–4°/2,5
	Gluck	Sacrificial March from *Alceste*	A-Wn MS12665–4°/2,6
3 (607)	Weigl	Overture from the opera *Vestas Feuer*	A-Wn MS12665–4°/3,1
	Paër	March from the opera *Sargino*	A-Wn MS12665–4°/3,2
	Cherubini	Ballet from the opera *Anacreon*	A-Wn MS12665–4°/3,3
	Dalayrac	Romance from the opera *Nina*	A-Wn MS12665–4°/3,4
	Seyfried	March of the Moors from the opera *Alamar*	A-Wn MS12665–4°/3,5
	Johann Gallus = Mederitsch	Priest's March from the opera *Babylons Pyramiden*	A-Wn MS12665–4°/3,6

---

[3] See Christoph-Hellmut Mahling, 'Zur Beurteilung der italienischen Oper in der deutschsprachigen Presse zwischen 1815 und 1825', *Periodica Musica* 6 (1988), pp. 11–15.

[4] Full list of contents is given in Imogen Fellinger, *Periodica Musicalia (1789–1830)* (Regensburg: Bosse, 1986), pp. 254–60.

In public, Mozart's later operas, and especially *Die Zauberflöte*, occupied pride of place and were staged frequently in 1810s Vienna. Private musical salons followed suit, as Chapter 4 has shown. *Singspiele* and ballets popular at this time included works by Adalbert Gyrowetz (especially), Josef Kinsky, Johann Baptist Schenk, and Wenzel Robert von Gallenberg. When Beethoven's *Fidelio* started to attract success in 1815, it was championed as specifically German theatre. However, much of the German-language repertoire was based on French stories – for instance, Beethoven's *Fidelio* and Weber's *Der Freischütz* derived their plotlines from French *opéra comique*. Both works were much admired and often repeated, especially *Der Freischütz*.

Before 1816, when Rossini's works reached Vienna with a visiting Italian theatre troupe at the Kärntnertortheater, translations of French opera into German dominated in the theatres, with works by Auber, Boieldieu, Dalayrac, Herold, Isouard, Méhul, Spontini, and Cherubini among others. They were heard along with occasional revivals of older Italian operas by Cimarosa, Paër, Mayr, and Paisiello, maintaining the pre-1800 pattern. Gradually, though, Italian opera began to increase in popularity. A rage for Rossini's operas, in particular, is clear from the evidence of published arrangements for domestic use. But first we need to know what was performed in the public theatres.

Clark has traced the repertoire at the various Viennese theatres, especially the Kärntnertor, where many of the playbills have survived.[5] The repertoire performed in the Kärntnertortheater from 1811 to 1830 is shown in the graph below (Figure 5.1). Following the first public staging of Rossini's works in Vienna in 1816 and their popular reception by the public, performances of Italian operas started to increase, rising to a peak in 1824. They did not eclipse French opera and *Singspiele*. But there was marked displacement of these genres by Rossini's operas in 1822–1825. In this period, the number of Italian opera performances at the Kärntnertortheater (including German translations) exceeds those of either French or German opera. But the graph alone does not give the full picture, because many of the works categorised under 'Italian opera' in Figure 5.1 were in fact by Rossini. Rossini's operas make up 80 per cent of the combined Italian opera categories in 1822 and 1823, 60 per cent in 1824, and 44 per cent in 1825.

---

[5] Clark, 'The Performance and Reception of Rossini's Operas', especially Appendices F and G, pp. 347–419.

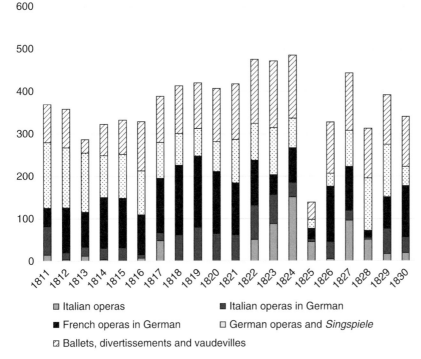

Figure 5.1 Bar graph showing Repertoire performed at the Kärntnertortheater, 1811–30, by genre

Table 5.2 lists the ten most popular opera composers at the Theater am Kärntnertor, 1811–1830. Here Rossini, with diverse operas, takes second place only to Adalbert Gyrowetz, who supplied the public with an abundance of very popular *Singspiele*, ballets, and divertissements throughout the period. However, Clark notes that Rossini's works, including parodies, were the most performed or imitated in every theatre in the city.[6] This meant a relatively wider audience for Rossini's operas than for other dramatic works – and it was widened yet further by means of arrangements.

Table 5.3 lists the ten most popular operas at the Kärntnertor, 1811–30, with *Tancredi* in fourth place. Michael Jahn traces the origins of the Viennese 'Rossini frenzy' to this opera.[7] Looking at reviews of the Vienna premier of *Tancredi* in 1817, it might seem that it was the Italian singers

---

[6] Ibid., p. 2.
[7] Michael Jahn, *Di tanti palpiti . . . : Italiener in Wien*, Schriften zur Wiener Operngeschichte 3 (Vienna: Der Apfel, 2006), p. 67.

Table 5.2 Most popular opera composers at the Kärntnertortheater, 1811–30[*]

Gyrowetz (number of works presented: 810)
Rossini (778)
Weigl (495)
Boieldieu (413)
Mozart (315)
Spontini (297)
Wenzel Robert Graf Gallenberg (289)
Isouard (239)
Méhul (210)
Josef Kinsky (194)

[*] Figures obtained from Clark, 'The Performance and Reception of Rossini's Operas', Appendix G, pp. 378–419.

Table 5.3 Most popular operas at the Kärntnertortheater, 1811–30

Weigl	*Die Schweizerfamilie* (performed 174 times)
Spontini	*Die Vestalin* (141)
Weber	*Der Freischütz* (127)
Rossini	*Tancredi* (in German and Italian 106)
Boieldieu	*Der Neue Gutsherr* (113)
Boieldieu	*Johann von Paris* (113)
Schenk	*Der Dorfbarbier* (130)
Méhul	*Joseph und seine Brüder* (111)
Mozart	*Die Zauberflöte* (98)
Gyrowetz	*Der Augenarzt* (95; French text freely adapted by Emanuel Veith)

who captured the audience's imagination. Their excellent interpretation was certainly part of the magic. In particular, mezzo Gentile Borgondio came to Vienna in 1816 and enjoyed great success in the role of Amenaide in *Tancredi*, having to repeat 'Di tanti palpiti' (soon to become a hit) numerous times. But reviews also speak of the music, insofar as it could be separated from its vocal performance, and it becomes clear that listeners appreciated the music itself, partly because it foregrounded singing. One Viennese reviewer applauded '[the] beautiful music of Mr Rossini, his masterly art of orchestration and thereby making the singing predominant'.[8]

The peak of public interest in Italian opera occurred in 1822–5, not coincidentally. It was partly due to the impresario Domenico Barbaia, who brought the composer and some other Neapolitan musicians from Teatro

[8] *Wiener Theater-Zeitung* 9/102 (21 December 1816), p. 405f.

San Carlo in Naples to visit the Kärntnertortheater in the spring and summer of 1822.[9] Around the same time, the Viennese increasingly seemed to prefer their Italian opera in Italian. Reviews suggest that this had to do with a preference for Italian singers over Germans.[10] But earlier German singers had also enjoyed considerable success in translated Rossini operas, which suggests that Rossini's music itself spoke eloquently to audiences, and that its spellbinding effect was invariant in translation, the fan following of particular fine singers notwithstanding. In the quotation from Sonnleithner's *Memoirs* at the beginning of the chapter, the 'melodic charm and harmonic turns' are specified as the main features that made Rossini's music so popular with the Viennese.

The intense Viennese interest in Italian opera was also partly due to the first work that was performed by the Neapolitan visitors, *Zelmira* (1822), which was, unusually, a very big success with the Viennese critics as well as the public. Critics tended to praise its special suitability for German audiences. It seemed to them that Rossini had made a concession to German aesthetics and tastes, which was especially gratifying. One reviewer noted:

Zelmira has played at the Italian theatre [Kärntnerthor] and always to a full house, a proof of the public's liking and of the value that must be inherent in the performances, since the Viennese public belongs to the most musically educated of all Europe and to which the performance of music must be suitable.[11]

Critical Dissent

Of opera composers still well known today, Mozart and Weber were highly popular in this era (see Table 5.3), and Mozart's operas, in particular, were canonised. The Viennese held up works by Weber, Mozart, and Beethoven as yardsticks against which other German-speaking composers should measure themselves – this was part of scholarly canon formation with a view to establishing a German operatic tradition.[12] They used journalistic means to generate interest in German composers

---

[9] On Barbaia in Vienna, see Henry Raynor, *Music and Society Since 1815* (London: Barrie and Jenkins, 1976), pp. 67–8.
[10] See Jahn, *Di tanti palpiti*, pp. 76–7; and Clark, 'The Performance and Reception of Rossini's Operas', pp. 259–60.
[11] Anon., *Wiener Zeitschrift für Kunst, Literatur, Theater und Mode* 53 (2 May 1822), p. 430.
[12] Ibid., p. 253.

and to manipulate Viennese opinion in favour of German music and against Italian opera. Their primary target was Rossini, whose works usually found at best a mixed reception – as seen from the Sonnleithner's observations quoted at the beginning of this chapter. This led to critical dissent about Rossini's operas, which (other than *Zelmira*) apparently did not measure up to German critical standards; but this did not seem to dampen the general public's appetite for them. Indeed, *Tancredi* was the fourth most popular opera performed in the Kärntnertortheater in the period 1811–30. This critical dissent hindered the development of a scholarly canon of Rossini and other Italian composers' operas, at least for the time being.

Like other German critics of the time, the Viennese critics were bothered by the lack of specifically Germanic traits in Rossini's music, and in general by the 'many violations against harmony and counterpoint' that Sonnleithner cites. As Emmanuele Senici has shown, the problems that early critics had with Rossini's music extend more broadly.[13] At root were issues with the dramaturgy. They claimed that Rossini's music was not good at characterising individual people and generally failed as textual interpretation through music.[14] The general thrust of the criticism is caught by one critic's pithy phrase: 'Rossini's music has exquisitely sweet, and exquisitely flat moments'; the implication is that the melodies were beautiful but the teleological drive of, say, a Beethoven symphony was lacking.[15] Not all moments were found to be either flat or exquisite. Some were just plain loud. Complaints about noise surfaced in connection with *La gazza ladra*, especially the overture; but this accusation was more general. The year 1821 was 'Rossini Year' in the Viennese theatres, with six Rossini premiers, including *L'italiana in Algeri* and *Mosè in Egitto*. The introduction to *Mosè* was particularly admired (Rossini was criticised heavily in other works for jumping in almost *in medias res*, without the accustomed working up of suspense and anticipation through a well-argued overture); but some found the instrumentation too much for the Viennese theatres. Again, the work was deemed noisy.[16]

Of all the criticisms of Rossini, concerns about originality were the most frequent. The critics latched on to the way Rossini reuses themes and

---

[13] Emanuele Senici, *Music in the Present Tense: Rossini's Italian Operas in Their Time* (Chicago, IL: University of Chicago Press, 2019).
[14] Jahn, *Di tanti palpiti*, pp. 61–8. [15] Ibid., p. 81. [16] Ibid., p. 103.

melodies in his operas as evidence that he lacked originality. One writer complained of *La pièlra del paragone*:

> The overture is written by Mr Stunz and shows little originality .... An aria by Caraffa [Michele Carafa] is also inserted. Some pieces of music have, despite their freshness and liveliness, a rather superficial character and do not provoke further consideration, because everything is already exposed at first sight, that is, on the surface.[17]

Senici observes that these writers may have been confusing lack of originality with the fact that Rossini's music is inherently and internally repetitive, from the level of the phrase to that of the work.[18] More generally, the non-specific and even anti-mimetic character of the music bothered critics, especially when they could not immediately attach the music to Rossini as author.

But all these criticisms could be turned on their head when the commentator understood the dramaturgical reasoning behind the noise, repetition, and loose relationship between character and representation. The occasional reviewer seemed to almost get what Rossini was about. It was said, for example, that Rossini's music moved towards 'a more secure attitude as a colourist, correct perception of the passions, and to a high degree all those eminent merits, which, with more solidity, would stamp him in the eyes of the connoisseur as the celebrated hero'.[19] The funeral march at the beginning of the overture to *Armida* was particularly acclaimed, along with numerous arias. These numbers, along with many more that the critics did not like, were rapidly excerpted, translated for solo piano or instrumental ensemble, packaged as 'favourite pieces' (*Beliebte Stücke*) and turned over as arrangements to a market hungry for Italian opera.

Rossini Arrangements

Not only staged productions, but also spin-offs in the form of take-home opera arrangements, from publishers including those affiliated with the Hoftheater, contributed to a burgeoning market economy. Sheet music was becoming cheaper to produce, especially with the advent of lithographic

---

[17] Anon., *Allgemeine musikalische Zeitung mit besonderer Rücksicht auf den österreichischen Kaiserstaat* 37 (9 May 1821), col. 293.
[18] Senici, *Music in the Present Tense*, pp. 57–61.
[19] Anon., *Allgemeine musikalische Zeitung* 24/4 (23 January 1822), col. 60.

editions, but it was still expensive. Publishers were dependent on sales to keep them afloat. Like the theatre managers, they needed to tune in to market sentiment to decide what to produce. Chapter 4 shows that *Tancredi*, which premiered in Vienna in December 1816, features thirty-six times in Diabelli and Co.'s catalogues from 1816 to 1824, and is the most arranged work issued by this publisher in this period. The success of *Zelmira* in 1822 was assisted by the dissemination of Rossini's works before and during that year. Arrangements in various forms, for different functions, locations, and consumers, of works including *Tancredi*, paved the way for this success. Then, following the Viennese premier of *Zelmira* on 13 April 1822, Diabelli and Cappi cashed in on its success straight away, publishing several variations by Czerny on popular themes from the work, advertised in the *Wiener Zeitung* on 22 July:

Variations brillantes pour le Pianoforte sur la Cavatine favorite: Ah se e verdi quell ch'io sento (Zelmira)
Variations pour le Pianoforte sur le Terzetto favorite: Soave conforto dans l'Op[é]ra Zelmira
Variations pour le Pianoforte seul sur la Cavatine finale (Deh circondatemi) dans l'Op[é]ra Zelmira

Not wanting to restrict the fun to pianists, on 5 August Diabelli advertised two books of arrangements involving csakan and guitar (ad lib): *Thèmes favoris de l'Op[é]ra: Zelmira, de Rossini, vari[é]s pour le Csakan seul avec accomp: de Guitarre [sic] ad libitum*. These volumes were advertised at the same time as arrangements from *Tancredi*, *La donna del lago*, *Matilde di Shabran*, and also Weber's extremely popular *Freischütz*. The creation and dissemination of these arrangements formed a significant part of the process of textualising Rossini's operas and the various kinds of arrangements, a process to which we now turn.

It is difficult to generalise about opera arrangements published in Vienna at this time. The performing medium is not always specified in publishers' catalogues; nor do they always make it clear whether a given item in a set or series is available separately. Sometimes the source opera is not specified, and often dates are not provided. The best way to date undated publications is by searching out the corresponding advertisements in the *Wiener Zeitung*, which give an approximate date by which an item would be newly available for sale, but this does not help to determine how long an item remained on sale, nor how well it sold.

What evidence there is suggests that publishers timed the release of opera arrangements to coincide with, or sometimes anticipate, the

Rossini Arrangements 147

Figure 5.2 Title-page engraving of a solo piano arrangement of excerpts from *Il barbiere di Seviglia* (Vienna: Sauer & Leidesdorf, 1823). Courtesy of Österreichische Nationalbibliothek Musiksammlung, shelf mark MS8875-qu.4°/4

corresponding premier at the Theater an der Wien or the Kärntnertortheater. Figure 5.2 shows the enticing title-page engraving of an arrangement of *Il barbiere di Seviglia* (Sauer & Leidesdorf, 1823).[20] Such vignettes (also used in London publications) remind the potential buyers of the opera production, and tempt them to turn the page to re-experience the work, or to acquaint themselves with it before seeing a staged performance. So this was another way publishers sought to build on or extend the public theatre-going experience. Often the language of the first local performance influenced whether selections from the same opera were printed in Italian or German. In succeeding years, German became the main language for

---

[20] See my 'Marketing Ploys, Monuments, and Music Paratexts: Reading the Title Pages of Early Mozart Editions', in Eisen and Davison (eds.), *Late Eighteenth-Century Music and Visual Culture*, pp. 155–72.

some publishers regardless of this consideration, such as the influential German publisher and inventor of lithography Johann Alois Senefelder.[21]

Which operas were the most popular, on the evidence of arrangements? *Tancredi*'s success in 1816 launched a series of varied instrumental and vocal arrangements of his operas in Vienna. Best liked were Rossini's *opere serie* or *semi-serie*: *Tancredi*, *Otello*, *La gazza ladra*, *La donna del lago*, and *Armida*; although *Il barbiere di Seviglia*, *L'italiana in Algeri*, and *La Cenerentola* also sold well in arrangements. Reprints like that shown in Figure 5.2 for *Il barbiere di Seviglia*, announcing on the title page that they are 'new and improved', witness the popularity of a given arrangement. Others of his *opere buffe* were less popular with the Viennese.

Certain publishers, such as Diabelli, Leidesdorf and Sauer, and Artaria, made a specialty of Rossini arrangements. The scores of *Zelmira*, *Semiramide*, and *Maometto II* were supposed to be sold only by Artaria, who had obtained exclusive rights to these works. But this did not stop other publishers, especially Diabelli, from producing their own arrangements. In general, all Viennese publishers of music got on the Rossini bandwagon. This was a time, post-Congress of Vienna, of even higher inflation, when extravagant spending had taken its toll on the economy. So publishers were listening very carefully to market cues, and not doing anything too risky. The Steiner/Beethoven symphony arrangements scheme discussed in Chapter 4 was something of a risk, but Steiner had an economic safety net: Rossini arrangements. Early-nineteenth-century Viennese publishers stayed with a safe brand name (Rossini) and product type (piano arrangements), but diversified the product in smart ways to capture new buyers and maximise profits. Consumers (mainly Viennese amateurs) exerted their power by various means, and it was in publishers' interests to maximise consumers' choice, providing them with 'Rossini as you like it'.

Ensemble Choices

Published Rossini arrangements were geared towards preferred instruments. Piano arrangements had been plentiful in the late eighteenth century and were now even more abundant. But we also find quite a few arrangements involving flute, guitar, and csakan in particular. Flute playing had also always been strong in Vienna, where the tradition of wind playing was reinforced by military bands; and flute could be readily exchanged with violin. The guitar

---

[21] On this topic see Klitzing, *Don Giovanni unter Druck*, p. 235.

Example 5.1 Cavatina 'Di tanti palpiti' from Rossini's *Tancredi*, arranged by Diabelli for voice and guitar in *Philomele: eine Sammlung der beliebtesten Gesänge mit Begleitung der Guitare [sic]* (Vienna: Diabelli, 1819), bars 1–10[22]

Anmerkung
Diese Cavatina mit den Manieren der Mad: Borgondio, muss, wie sie hier steht, in der Fistl gesungen werden, für jene aber, welche selbe mit der natürlichen Stimme singen wollen, nimmt man zum accompagniren eine Terz-Guitarre, und der Gesang ist dann um zwey Töne erhöht.

was also a very popular instrument around 1800. Guitar arrangements went two ways at this time. On the one hand, the guitar was an ideal instrument to diversify women's participation beyond voice or piano. Among the most popular arrangements, Diabelli's of 'Di tanti palpiti' from *Tancredi* (1819) would have figured. It appeared in a published collection of opera excerpts for guitar, *Philomele: eine Sammlung der beliebtesten Gesänge mit Begleitung der Guitare [sic]* (Example 5.1). The guitar variations by Friedrich Joseph Spina in Artaria's *Zelmira* series (1822) were also, like those in the *Philomele* collection, geared to amateurs.

But the guitar occupied an ambivalent position in musical culture in early nineteenth-century Vienna, regarded by some as the instrument of

---

[22] This Cavatina, with the ornaments of Madame Borgondio, must, as it stands here, be sung in falsetto, but, for those who want to sing it with the natural voice, one takes a Terz guitar [small guitar tuned a minor third higher] for accompaniment, and the vocal line is then raised by two notes.

dandies. Virtuosos, especially Giuliani, had an influence on markets at this time and raised the status of the instrument. His performances during the Congress of Vienna, in particular, led to the guitar being accepted as a virtuoso instrument in Vienna. This did not mean that only the more difficult arrangements were for public consumption: dilettantes were of a potentially high calibre, and were becoming more so with access to better training. Publishers made considerable efforts to supply the more advanced guitar players with Rossini opera arrangements. An example is *L'italiana in Algeri. Opera von G. Rossini, für Flöte oder Violin und Guitar[r]e Eingerichtet von Anton Diabelli* (Mechetti, 1819). This publication contains just six numbers, drawn from early in the opera; the flute or violin part is relatively simple, the guitar part relatively complex.

The csakan was a Viennese speciality and gentleman's instrument. It could double as a walking stick, a feature associated with recreational use and outdoor performance. Diabelli produced a set of 'favourite themes' from *Zelmira* for csakan and guitar, in two books: *Thèmes Favoris de l'Op[é]ra: Zelmira, de Rossini, Variés pour le csakan seul avec accomp. de guitarre [sic] ad libitum*. But the firm also produced an entire periodical devoted to music for csakan alone, entitled *Mon Plaisir*. Rossini numbers appear frequently in its pages. Book four, for instance, contains 'Tancred, Oper von Rossini', but as usual the opera has been 'cherry-picked' and is represented by just a few choice numbers.

As for ensemble arrangements, string quartets were still popular in Vienna post-1816, for men to perform, but they were well outnumbered by piano arrangements. Pössinger specialised in string-quartet arrangements of operas in this time, but even he made concessions to the flute performers, for example in his arrangement of *Zelmira* published by Artaria: *Zelmira, Grand Opera dal Maestro Rossini Ridotta in Quartetti per Flauto, Violino, Viola e Violoncello da F. A. Pössinger* (no date).[23] It becomes apparent that arrangers made different selections of 'favourite pieces' depending on the ensemble. For example, an arrangement of *Pi[è]ces Favorites de l'Op[é]ra Zelmire [sic]* for violin or flute with accompaniment of guitar by Frederic Spina, published by Artaria, can be compared with Friedrich Starke's arrangement of *Zelmira* for 'military music' (two clarinets, two oboes, two bassoons, contrabassoon, and two trombones; ad lib.). Both collections include the duet No. 6 and the march-like cavatina 'Terra amica'. But not surprisingly, the flute (violin) and guitar version mainly has arias, whereas

---

[23] A copy is available in the Österreichische Nationalbibliothek, shelf mark MS10681-4°. On this topic see also Clark, 'The Performance and Reception of Rossini's Operas', p. 112.

the arrangement for military music version provides arrangements of some larger numbers and those of more military character, like marches.

Opera Arrangement Contents

By far the most common arrangement is for piano, either two hands or four. Many of them came in large sets of arrangements from the same work, but not amounting to a complete set. Such is the case with Artaria's 1822 piano arrangement of *Zelmira*, which bore the title-page claim: 'only legitimate edition of the full piano/vocal score of the opera, *Zelmira*, under the direction of the composer' ('Einzig rechtmässige Ausgabe des vollständigen Clavierauszugs der Oper: Zelmira, unter Leitung des Compositeurs'). The claim to completeness turns out to be wide of the mark. It can be seen as a symptom of the emerging market economy. On 3 May 1822, Artaria & Co. had advertised for the first time the availability of 'most of the vocal pieces' from Rossini's opera *Zelmira*, with piano accompaniment, in the music advertisements section of the *Wiener Zeitung*. The month before, Rossini had publicly announced that Artaria would be the exclusive outlet for arrangements of this new opera in Vienna, and Artaria made much of this. As we have seen, other publishers like Diabelli issued their own versions of *Zelmira*; but only Artaria could claim theirs to be 'genuine', because they were based on autograph scores that Rossini himself had brought with him. Such claims of proximity to the author amounted to little more than an advertising ploy to impart a sense of exclusivity. Artaria was also the only printer to advertise his products on the court theatres' playbills, usually with the tagline: 'The complete piano edition of this opera, with or without text, will appear shortly, courtesy of Artaria and Comp.' But this was a time when anyone could produce an arrangement and get it published if they could attract a publisher's interest. Artaria's actions speak to the fiercely competitive nature of the music-publishing business, with many competitors for the same consumers.

The claim to be authorised and indeed supervised by the composer appeared not only on the piano arrangement of *Zelmira*, but all other Artaria versions. So, for example, the arrangement of *Zelmira* for military ensemble by Starke was allegedly carried out 'according to the original score for the sole rightful publisher and owner of the same, under the supervision of the composer himself' ('nach der Original Partitur für einzig rechtmässigen Verleger und Eigenthümer derselben, unter Ansicht des Compositeurs selbst'). As for completeness, it is noted: 'The musical pieces of the opera

Figure 5.3 Leidesdorf & Sauer's 'Collection of Complete Operas' series title page (Collection des Operas completes de Rossini, 1820s). Courtesy of Österreichische Nationalbibliothek Musiksammlung, shelf mark MS70339-qu.4°/4

Zelmira that do not appear in this volume are also available arranged and written for *Harmonie* according to the original score from the undersigned dealer' ('Die in diesem Hefte nicht vorkommenden Musikstücke der Oper Zelmira sind ebenfalls nach der Original Partitur für Harmonie bearbeitet und geschrieben in unterzeichneter Handlung zu haben'). This was another sales ploy in a marketing strategy of delivering music 'as you like it'.

Title pages of opera arrangements from this time often describe their contents as 'complete'. Just how 'complete' can we expect them to be? The Leidesdorf and Sauer series title page shown in Figure 5.3 is notable in this respect. The publisher advertises this publication as a 'collection of complete operas'. This common claim on the title pages of opera arrangements at this time is misleading in two ways. First of all, most of these 'complete' sets are far from complete accounts of the operas, because they consist of selected favourites, often including the overture where there was one, arias, and chosen ensembles. Rarely were recitatives and choruses included. Then, the 'complete' sets were often arranged so that the buyer could pick and choose – each item having the name of the composer, work, and number at the top, and separate pagination. Each item was thus ready to be sold separately as sheet music. These publications foster a habit of thinking of Rossini's operas as isolated numbers rather than as a coherent narrative. Or if there were to be a narrative, in the sense of a sequence of individual operatic numbers, it could be one chosen by the consumer. So, even 'complete' works in arrangements were weighted towards the buyer's choice.

Even if an opera was less well represented in public performances, like, for example, *Le siège de Corinthe*, firms like Artaria, Diabelli, and Leidesdorf and Sauer still considered it expedient to put together large and expensive 'complete' editions of it. In the case of Artaria's *Collection complète des Opéras de Rossini pour le Pianoforte seul* (1826), part of the marketing strategy may have been to include the name of the arranger on the title page. In this case, Viennese-born Franz Schoberlechner (1797–1843) was a prominent musician on the Viennese scene (see also Example 5.5a). A pianist and dramatic composer, Schoberlechner was a child prodigy and pupil of Hummel. Hummel composed his second concerto for Schoberlechner, who played it in public when he was ten years old. Precisely this kind of precocious talent drew the interest of the Viennese concert- and opera-going public.

A related publication type demonstrates the popularity of overtures. Another collected (but not complete) edition by Leidesdorf is of Rossini opera overtures only, arranged for the piano, each sold separately. The set includes the overtures to *Armida*, *Mosè in Egitto*, *Il Turco in Italia*, *Il barbiere di Seviglia*, *Mathilde*, *Eduardo e Cristina*, *L'inganno felice*, *Otello*, *Adelaide e Borgogna*, *Riccardo e Zoraide*, *La donna del lago*, *Il signor Bruschino*, *La scala di seta*, *L'italiana in Algeri*, *Aureliano in Palmira*, *Demetrio e Polibio*, *Bianca e Falliero*, and *Elisabetta*. Overtures, individual arias, and sets of 'favorite pieces' were the most commonly sold arrangements from his operas, although popular choruses and marches were also available. These items were not just public favourites and comparatively easy to perform, but also relatively easy to arrange.

Jean Herbert Schneider has made a study of Rossini opera arrangements for string quartets from this era, considering what was arranged, how complete a given arrangement was, and what kinds of modifications were made.[24] Most of the recitatives are omitted, and vocal parts are also omitted or dramatically altered. For example, in Pössinger's transcription of *La gazza ladra*, he deleted seven pieces, reducing sixteen numbers to nine – the

---

[24] Schneider, 'L'arrangement d'opéras pour quatuor à cordes', pp. 229–40.

Sinfonia and Introduzione, four arias, and a duet – and reduced the Finale II to a single section. Pössinger is also very liberal with the tempo indications in five of the numbers, modifying them and shortening larger sections in Finale I, the aria Podesta No. 11, and the duet No. 12.

The *Tancredi* manuscript arrangement, also by Pössinger, listed in Table 5.4, shows a few other types of modification. The manuscript version of this does not include all the numbers, and they are out of order relative to the original arrangement (which itself has some clear differences from the critical edition).[25] Occasionally, too, arrangements include numbers that were not in the original edition. Such is the case, for example, with Pössinger's string-quartet arrangement of *Armida*.

Table 5.4 Manuscript arrangement by Franz Alexander Pössinger of Rossini's *Tancredi*, compared to the original score (Österreichische Nationalbibliothek Musiksammlung shelf mark Mus.Hs.2991)

Arr. no., title	No. in MS copy of arr.	Original	Scene
Overture	Overture	Sinfonia	
		Act I	
No. 1 Allegro	No. I	No. 2 Coro ('Più dolci, e placide'; arr. uses Coro for No. 1, Cavatina for No. 2)	3
No. 2 Allegro	No. II	No. 2 Cavatina Amenaide ('Come dolce all'alma mia')	3
No. 3 Andante sostenuto		No. 3 Cavatina Tancredi ('Tu che accendi questo core')	5
		Begins from bar 65 of original (Maestoso) after 3½ bar intro (before bar 65 there is recitative)	
No. 4 Allegro giusto	No. V	Act II, No. 14 Duetto [Amenaide, Tancredi] ('Lasciami: non t'ascolto')	(13)
		Follows Ferrara 1813 version: in the first act the Duetto for Amenaide and Tancredi (No. 5) was deleted and the Duetto originally in Act II (No. 14) was inserted	
No. 5 Finale	No. III	No. 6 Coro (bars 51–66, tempo di marcia)	10, 13
		Andante to end taken from No. 7, Finale Primo, bar 135 (to end)	
		Act II	
No. 1 Andante		Not included in the original	
No. 2 Andante		No. 11 Duetto [Tancredi, Argirio] ('Ah se de' mali miei')	8

[25] The viola part of the printed arrangement is available digitally from the Österreichische Nationalbibliothek: https://digital.onb.ac.at/RepViewer/viewer.faces?doc=DOD%5F51857%26order=1%26view=SINGLE.

Table 5.4 (cont.)

Arr. no., title	No. in MS copy of arr.	Original	Scene
No. 3 Andante		The opening Andante is not in the original. No. 12 in the original begins with an Andante, but is in a different time signature with some divergent material Allegro to end comes from No. 12 [Aria Amenaide], allegro onwards (bar 49)	10?
No. 4 Allo. mod.		No. 13 Coro ('Plaudite, o popoli')	12
No. 5 Allegro		N. 16 ii Coro di Saraceni ('Regna il terror nella Città')	16
No. 6 Andante		Appendix III: Ferrara 1813 No. 16 iiia [Rondò Tancredi] ('Perché turbar la calma')	15
No. 7 Finale	Finale	No. 17 Secondo Finale ('Fra quai soavi palpiti')	Ultima (20)
(Additional material)			
No. AA Allegro	No. IV	Act I No. 1 Introduzione	1–2
No. BB Allegro maest.		Not in the original	
No. CC Andante sost.		Act I Finale Primo (covers bars 1–134, then 'attacca Marcia')	13
No. DD Allegro		Act I No. 6 Coro (bars 1–50, from bar 51 is part of No. 5 in the arrangement)	10

Works Based on Rossini's Operas

Works based on themes from selected operas, another very common publication type at this time, involved more intervention to reconfigure operatic numbers as sets. They included rondos, variations, 'Bouquets des mélodies', duos 'on themes from', sonatas 'on a theme from', potpourris, and many other types. The implication of the titles is often that the choice of elements within the arrangement was dictated by the buyer. Many of these pieces were based on a single favourite theme. But they could also combine 'favourite themes' (*beliebte Themen*) from one or more operas of a given composer, or include themes by various composers, as in a potpourri. In general, as critics pointed out disparagingly, potpourris were put together with little regard for semantics or coherence of musical form. Some potpourris, especially those of Spohr, showed regard for musical values; and in other cases there are also dramatic connections to be made between the elements.[26] But even if these works are not the finest music by modern standards of coherence and logic, they are nonetheless an important index of 'opera as you like it' in this era for reception historians.

So what do these publication types tell us? They show us Spontini, Rossini, Mozart as highly popular composers of opera whose works were deemed eminently repeatable; and they show us how the Viennese wanted their Rossini – how people wanted to listen to and interact with his music. One important category of arrangements is dances drawn from operas. Musicians often took themes from Rossini's music and used them as the basis for new dances. Josef Wilde, for example, composed twelve waltzes based on excerpts from *La gazza ladra*, as part of a larger series of waltzes. Diabelli cashed in on the rage for dance music, coupled with the rage for Rossini, with his 1819 arrangement *Rossini Waltzes with Trios and Coda for the Piano Forte after the Most Popular Motifs from the Operas: Otello and La gazza ladra* (*Rossini-Walzer mit Trios und Coda für das Piano-Forte nach den beliebtesten Motiven der Opern: Othello und La Gazza Ladra*).[27] This was a terrific money-spinner, as evidenced by three sequel volumes that followed from Diabelli in 1820, all arranged for piano by Diabelli, containing 'Rossini's Waltzes with Trios and Coda'. Two were based on popular motifs from *Il barbiere di Siviglia* and *Riccardo e Zoraide*; the third was based on *La Cenerentola*.

Rossini opera excerpts were also turned into or reproduced as dances, especially from the late 1810s into the 1820s. There are printed and handwritten examples of waltzes arranged from Rossini's operas. For example, the Preghiera from *Mosè in Egitto* appears in Joseph Lanner et al.'s *Walzer mit Klavierbegleitung*, a collection of waltzes.[28] These arrangements turned opera (in this case a solemn prayer from an opera) into what might be termed functional music for entertainment. This was perhaps more easily done with Rossini's melodies than those of many others of the time, owing to his manifold repetitions. And in this way the arrangers created yet more opportunity for memorable repetition.

How else, on the evidence of the publications, did people want to hear their Rossini? Variations were very popular, as they had been since the late eighteenth century.[29] But variations now become a distinct category in

---

[26] Till Gerrit Waidelich, 'Das Opern-Potpourri: Musikalisches Kaleidoskop, ars combinatoria oder musikimmanente Pornographie?', in Hinrichsen and Pietschmann (eds.), *Jenseits der Bühne*, pp. 127–39.

[27] A digital reproduction is available at: https://digital.onb.ac.at/RepViewer/viewer.faces?doc=DTL_8793408&order=1&view=SINGLE.

[28] See also Clark, 'The Performance and Reception of Rossini's Operas', p. 103.

[29] On this topic see Christine Siegert, 'Semantische Aspekte instrumentaler Opernbearbeitung', in Hinrichsen and Pietschmann (eds.), *Jenseits der Bühne*, pp. 13–17.

publication catalogues. This form is something that could fall into amateurs' hands, especially those of advanced amateurs, but also tended in the semi-professional direction; again, such publication accords with the contemporary salon culture, which sits on the cusp of the public and private spheres. Variations represent a 'have-it-your-way' gesture directed at virtuosi, but, from a marketing point of view, were also an effective way of getting the themes into the Viennese listener's ears with manifold enticing repetitions.

Sets of variations from Rossini's music were extremely popular, as one might expect. People like Diabelli and Czerny were arranging music so that the amateur could play it their way; but virtuosos like Joseph Mayseder, Giuliani, and Sigismond Thalberg (respectively a violinist, a guitarist, and pianist), who were also influencing the styles and types of arrangement, often arranged music so that it was both playable by a professional and delightful to the amateur listener. A prime example is Mayseder's arrangement *Variations Concertantes pour le Piano-Forte et Violon sur la Cavatine 'Di tanti palpiti'* (published 1820), which is his Op. 16 and so taken into Mayseder's own creative output as both violinist and composer. Until variation six, the set is not far beyond the reach of an advanced amateur, despite some tricky string crossing, double- and triple-stopping and high-register passagework. But variation six does all of this and adds frequent trills (see Example 5.2). The piano part is also quite difficult. This was music for performance in public, or by virtuosi in salons. Mayseder performed in salons that Sonnleithner attended, as well as publicly. He played second violin in Schuppanzigh's quartet; and in 1815 (during the Congress of Vienna) he, Hummel, and Giuliani gave the Dukaten Konzerte – a concert series in the botanical gardens of the Schönbrunn Palace, for which each entry cost one Ducat.[30] So, with variations, potpourris, and also some of the more challenging solo piano arrangements, in the 1810s and 1820s one starts to see a clear split emerging between arrangements for the amateur and those for the professional. Giuliani's variations on 'Di tanti palpiti' for two guitars are difficult from the outset, already reaching great intricacy by the third variation (Example 5.3).

Typical and popular as these variations and potpourris were, they were eclipsed by vast numbers of arrangements of single operatic numbers, often collected into sets and series, which were dedicated to amateurs and gave them hands-on experience of Rossini's operas. An example is Diabelli's series *Euterpe*, subtitled 'a series of modern and exquisitely popular compositions

---

[30] On the Dukaten Konzerte, see Jones, 'Music by the Ducat: Giuliani's Guitar and Vienna's Musical Markets, 1806–1819', PhD diss. (University of Toronto, 2020).

Example 5.2 Joseph Mayseder, *Variations Concertantes pour le Piano-Forte et Violon: Sur la Cavatine 'Di tanti palpiti'*, Op. 16 (Vienna: Artaria, c.1820), variation six, bars 1–24

for amusement in hours of leisure' ('eine Reihe moderner und vorzüglich beliebter Tonstücke zur Erheiterung in Stunden der Musse'; see Figure 5.4). Rossini featured extensively in these volumes, which were for piano, four hands. The duetting pair could pick and choose among numbers and order them at will, or play through the snapshots from a given opera in the order given them by Diabelli. Example 5.4 shows a wordless version of a cavatina from *Otello*, 'Deh calma oh ciel'/'O Gott, hab' Mitleid'; followed by one of the aria 'Ah si per voi gia sento/Ich fühl von heisser Liebe'. Text incipits are given in Italian and German, and on the inside title above the music is inscribed 'with the vocal part left out' ('mit Hinweglassung der Singstimme'). Of course, someone could conceivably sing along; but with piano four-hand performance the emphasis is on the two interacting pianists, who need to concentrate hard on coordination. So in this case, 'as you like it' probably amounted to 'as instrumental music, performed for fun with another pianist'.

Example 5.3 Mauro Giuliani, variations for two guitars on 'Di tanti palpiti' from *Tancredi* (Vienna: Weigl, n.d.), opening of third variation, guitar 1, bars 1–7

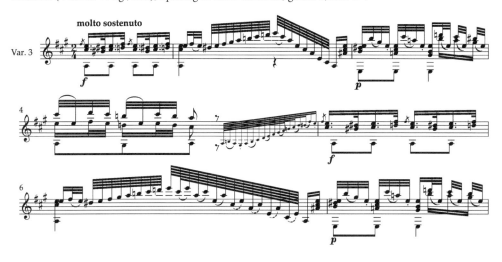

Figure 5.4 Title page of *Euterpe: eine Reihe moderner und vorzüglich beliebter Tonstücke zur Erheiterung in Stunden der Musse* (Anton Diabelli & Comp., 1818–45). Courtesy of Österreichische Nationalbibliothek Musiksammlung, shelf mark MS1117-qu.4°/10

Example 5.4 Excerpts from Rossini's *Otello* for piano four hands, in *Euterpe: eine Reihe moderner und vorzüglich beliebter Tonstücke zur Erheiterung in Stunden der Musse* (Vienna: Cappi and Diabelli, 1819), Österreichische Nationalbibliothek shelf mark MS1117-qu.4°/10: (a) Andante sostenuto

Euterpe was a long-lived double series from the firm Cappi & Diabelli (1818–45; see Table 5.5), featuring mostly opera arrangements for four-handed and two-handed performance. Rossini figured extensively, especially at first – see Table 5.4, which shows the first publications in the series. An advertisement for these volumes (reproduced in Table 5.6) sets this publishing endeavour in the

Example 5.4 (a) Andante sostenuto (cont.)

economic context of the time, translating 'Viennese currency' (*Wiener Wahrung* or W. W.) into the new coins (*Conventions Münzen* or C. M.; see columns 5 and 6). To reform Austria's monetary system, which had been heavily inflated as a result of the Napoleonic Wars, the Imperial Patent of 20 February 1811 decreed that the banco bills then in circulation were to be exchanged for redemption certificates at 20 per cent of their nominal value, which were referred to as Viennese currency. On 1 February 1812, Viennese currency became valid, and, with the patent of 30 March 1812, new copper coins were issued. The patent of 1 June 1816 (Austrian National Bank) initiated the voluntary redemption of paper money for Viennese currency. But by now a marked distrust of paper money had grown, since the massive wartime needs of the Habsburg Empire had led to the issue of 'anticipatory bills' (*Antizipationsscheine*), a considerable increase in the amount of money in circulation, and a corresponding fall in the exchange rate for Viennese currency. Most of the new banknotes received for redemption were immediately exchanged for coins, and the National bank's cash reserves shrank to an extent that threatened to jeopardise the stabilisation of the financial system. So although the initial exchange rate for W. W. into C. M. was 0.4, in 1819

Example 5.4 (b) Vivace marziale (bars 1–9), Österreichische Nationalbibliothek shelf mark MS1117-qu.4°/10

Table 5.5 *Euterpe für das Pianoforte*, first volumes (Vienna: Cappi & Diabelli, 1819)

Plate no.	Composer	Title
237	Felice Blangini	No. 1 Favourite boleros (*Son Gelsomino*)
238	Boieldieu	No. 2 Two romances from the opera *Rothkäppchen* [*Le petit chaperon rouge*]
239	Boieldieu	No. 3 Chorus of the Woodcutters and Nanette's aria from the opera *Rothkäppchen*
240	Rossini	No. 4 Three marches from the opera *Elisabetta, regina d'Inghilterra*
241	Rossini	No. 5 Three marches from the opera *Tancredi*
242	Rossini	No. 6 Three marches from the opera *Otello*
243	Rossini	No. 7 Three marches from the opera *Die diebische Elster* [*La gazza ladra*]
244	Rossini	No. 8 Aria ('Che ascolto') from the opera *Otello*
245	Rossini	No. 9 Duettino and Canzonette from *Otello*
246	Rossini	No. 10 Desdemona's Cavatina and Otello's Aria
247	Rossini	No. 11 Cavatina ('Di piacer mi balza') from *Die diebische Elster*
248	Rossini	No. 12 Cavatina ('Vien fra queste') from *Die diebische Elster*

Works Based on Rossini's Operas   163

Table 5.6 Advertisement for *Euterpe*, translating 'Viennese currency' (*Wiener Wahrung* or W. W.) into the new coins (*Conventions Münzen* or C. M.)

		Euterpe					
		A Series of Modern and Exquisitely Popular Compositions for Amusement in Hours of Leisure		W. W.		C. M.	
No.	Author	For Solo Piano	Key	f	x	f	x
220	Diabelli	No. 1. Favourite boleros with the vocal part left out	D	–	45	–	24
221		No. 2. Two romances from the opera *Rothkäppchen* by Boieldieu with the vocal part left out	B, C	–	45	–	24
222		No. 3. Chorus of the Woodcutters and Nanette's Aria from *Rothkäppchen* with the vocal part left out	E, D	–	45	–	24
223		No. 4. Three marches from the opera *Elisabetta, regina d'Inghilterra*, by Rossini	D, G, C	–	45	–	24
224		No. 5. Three marches from the opera *Tancredi*, by Rossini	D, C, C	–	45	–	24
225		No. 6. Three marches from the opera *Otello*, by Rossini	B, F, D	–	45	–	24
226		No. 7. Three marches from the opera *La gazza ladra* or *Die diebische Elster* by Rossini	D, A, Cm	–	45	–	24
227		No. 8. Aria 'Che ascolto'/'Was hör ich' from the opera *Otello* by Rossini with the vocal part left out	Es	–	45	–	24
228		No. 9. Duettino and Canzonette from *Otello* by Rossini with the vocal part left out	G, Gm	–	45	–	24
229		No. 10. Desdemona's Cavatina and Otello's aria from *Otello*	G, D	–	45	–	24
230		No. 11. Cavatina 'Di piacer mi'/'Was ich oft im Traume sah' from the opera *Die diebische Elster* by Rossini with the vocal part left out	E	–	45	–	24
231		No. 12. Cavatina 'Vieni fra'/'Komm in die offnen Arme' from *Die diebische Elster* with the vocal part left out	D	–	45	–	24
489		No. 13. *Der Abschied der Troubadour*, melody by Blangini with the vocal part left out	F	–	45	–	24
490		No. 14. Introduction and Cavatina 'Sieh schon der Morgenröthe' from the opera *Der Barbier von Sevilla* [*Il Barbiere di Siviglia*] by Rossini, with the vocal part left out	G, C	–	45	–	24
491		No. 15. Cavatina 'Un voce poco fa'/'Frag ich mein beklo[m]men Herz' from *Der Barbier von Sevilla* with the vocal part left out	E	–	45	–	24
492		No. 16. Final Polacca from *Der Barbier von Sevilla* with the vocal part left out	G	–	45	–	24
493		No. 17. Three Marches from *Der Barbier von Sevilla*	C	–	45	–	24
494		No. 18. Cavatina 'S'ella m['e] ognor'/'Wird sie getreu' from the Opera: *Richard und Zoraide* [*Ricciardo e Zoraide*] by Rossini with the vocal part left out	[C]	–	45	–	24
495		No. 19. Three Marches from *Richard und Zoraide*	C	–	45	–	24

Table 5.6 (cont.)

		Euterpe A Series of Modern and Exquisitely Popular Compositions for Amusement in Hours of Leisure		W. W.		C. M.	
No.	Author	For Solo Piano	Key	f	x	f	x
496		No. 20. Aria with Chorus 'Ja hoffe Kunigunde' from the Opera *Faust* by Spohr with the vocal part left out	D	–	45	–	24
497		No. 21. Cavatina 'Il mio piano'/'Dieser Plan ist unvergleichlich' from the opera *Die diebische Elster*, by Rossini with the vocal part left out	A	–	45	–	24
498		No. 22. Aria 'Si per voi pupille amate'/'Dich zu retten' from *Die diebische Elster* with the vocal part left out	C	–	45	–	24
499		No. 23. Finale from *Die diebische Elster* with the vocal part left out	G	–	45	–	24
500		No. 24. Three Romances 'La sentinelle', 'Partant pou[r] la Syrie', 'Vous me quittez' with the vocal part left out	C, D, F	–	45	–	24

Diabelli used the higher rate of 0.53 for his sheet music sales: people were keen to use their W. W. and the risk to Diabelli was, as it turned out, well calculated. The bank's cash reserves were righted in 1820.

Comparative prices put the cost of this sheet music in perspective, keeping in mind that inflation was still relatively high after the Congress of Vienna.[31] In 1824, Beethoven could dine very cheaply for 24 kreuzer (kr., C. M.), or the cost of one volume from Diabelli's *Euterpe*. In 1820, an expensive suit could cost 100 silver florins (fl.), or 6,000 kreuzer (250 volumes from Diabelli's *Euterpe*). In 1823, Beethoven paid 1 fl. 30 kr., or 90 kr., for a wood cutter and hauler to bring him firewood. In 1825, the secretary of the Hoftheater, Joseph Schreyvogel, earned 2,000 fl. per annum, or 120,000 kr., and in 1828 Sealsfield remarked in *Austria As It Is* that a gentlemen needed to earn such a salary to live comfortably in Vienna. So this sheet music was well affordable for the average middle-class family.

The titles of other extensive series from Diabelli, in Table 5.7, show an orientation towards the preferred instruments and towards opera. The emphasis on Rossini opera is seen in two of the titles, and is in fact present throughout these volumes. Diabelli and other Viennese publishers also issued numerous less extensive sets and series that equally targeted opera-loving amateurs. Of particular note are the volumes intended for women and

---

[31] On this subject see Alice M. Hanson, 'Incomes and Outgoings in the Vienna of Beethoven and Schubert', *Music & Letters* 64/3–4 (1983), pp. 173–82.

Table 5.7 Other series from Diabelli in the 1820s, featuring opera arrangements

Philomele für die Guitarre [sic], started 1819

Philomele für das Pianoforte, started 1819

Der musikalische Gesellschafter in einsamen Stunden, started 1819

Abendunterhaltungen für Flöte oder Violine und Guitarre, started 1818

Auserlesene Sammlung für eine Baßstimme, started 1819

Euterpe [two hands], started 1819

Euterpe [four hands], started 1819

Favorit-Duetten, started 1820

Apollo am Damen-Toilette, started 1820

Orpheus für 2 Guitarren, started 1821

Rossini's Opern-Repertorium für die Jugend, started 1821[*]

Mon plaisir (für Csakan solo), started 1821

Rossini's Ouverturen, started 1821

Productionen im häuslichen Freundschafts-Zirkel f.d. Flöte m. Begleitung das Pianoforte, started 1822

Neueste Sammlung komischer Theater-gesänge, started 1823

[*] The first volumes (all 1821) contained music by Rossini; thereafter the series ran as *Opern-Repertorium für die Jugend* with music by other composers.

children. These publications speak to the centrality of music education and canon formation in the home. Figure 5.5 shows the title page of Diabelli's *Trifles: Arranged for Piano-Forte with Consideration of Small Hands* (*Kleinigkeiten für Piano-Forte mit Berücksichtigung kleiner Hände eingerichtet*), a series geared specifically to children; there is a lot of Rossini in this set, which might have to do not only with popularity but also with the ease with which numbers could be arranged for children, especially overtures and arias. Repetition makes for ease and enjoyment of learning, as do melodies without complex contrapuntal accompaniment. For women there was the *Musikalische Damen-Journal*, in which Rossini is one of the names most represented.

Many of these Rossini arrangements were well within the reach of amateur musicians of modest skill. As for the string-quartet arrangements, Schneider finds them technically demanding, especially for the first violin. They would probably have been performed in private, led by a professional; and they served a pedagogical function – the lower parts being taken by lesser-skilled amateurs who could learn from the practical experience of ensemble playing.[32]

---

[32] Schneider, 'L'arrangement d'opéras pour quatuor à cordes', p. 238.

166 Rossini 'As the Viennese Liked It'

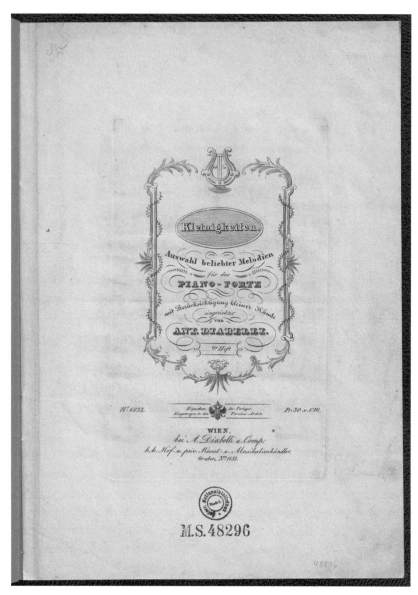

Figure 5.5 Title page from *Trifles: Arranged for Piano-Forte with Consideration of Small Hands* (*Kleinigkeiten für Piano-Forte mit Berücksichtigung kleiner Hände eingerichtet*), vol. 2 (Vienna: Diabelli, 1830). Courtesy of Österreichische Nationalbibliothek Musiksammlung, shelf mark MS48.296-4°

One possible reason for publishers selling 'complete' opera arrangements in separable parts was to allow the buyer to pick out numbers that were within their abilities. Take, for example, the second number (trio)

Example 5.5 (a) Trio, No. 2 from *Le siège de Corinthe* in Franz Schoberlechner (Vienna: Artaria and Haslinger, 1826) piano reduction, bars 1–19

from *Le siège de Corinthe* in Schoberlechner's (Vienna: Artaria and Haslinger) piano reduction (Example 5.5a). This music is arranged using thick textures and octaves, not suitable for little hands. Elsewhere, runs and high-register trills are used to realise orchestral timbres and textures, and the penultimate number, Marche: Allegro Brillante, even has some printed fingering. Example 5.5 compares the trio, No. 2 in this 'adult' version with a youth-oriented version, in Haslinger and Artaria's *Le siège de Corinthe, zweckmässig bearbeitet für die Jugend* (Example 5.5b). Many concessions

Example 5.5 (b) Trio, No. 2 in Haslinger and Artaria's Le siège de Corinthe, zweckmässig bearbeitet für die Jugend, bars 1–35

are made in the latter to the smaller hands and lesser skills of young pianists. The long and difficult introduction is wholly omitted; the key is changed from E major to C major, and the accompaniment is simplified to avoid thick textures and wide leaps or hand stretches. But there are still tricky runs, rhythmic complexity, and registral shifts to contend with.

Clearly it was not always easy to make Rossini's music simple, although many critics of the time faulted his music for its simplicity.

The publishers of *Le siège de Corinthe ... für die Jugend* say it is 'suitably arranged' (*zweckmässig bearbeitet*). But the phrase is more or less redundant, regardless of whether this publication really was suitable for young players in all its parts. All arrangements aimed to be 'suitable' – they imply an addressee, a buyer/performer with a particular level of skill and other requirements such as preferred instrumentation and degree of compositional intervention. This is more clearly apparent if we compare the final number in the arrangement 'für die Jugend' with the finale of Sigismund Thalberg's Op. 3, *Impromptu pour le piano-forte sur les thêmes favoris de l'opéra: Le siège de Corinthe de Rossini Composé et Dedié à Madame La Comtesse Gabrielle de Dietrichstein née Comtesse de Wratislaw par Sigismond Thalberg* (Example 5.6) The youth version takes simplification a little too far, introducing voice-leading errors in the opening and closing prayer in an effort to avoid hand stretches. Thalberg's arrangement might equally be qualified as 'suitably arranged': from a 25-bar prayer that opens and closes with homophony and has an easy lilting melody with gentle accompaniment, he generates a massive 149-bar bravura showpiece for himself and other piano virtuosi.

In our context, the quality or 'correctness' of these arrangements is not the focus (in Example 5.6a there is overlapping between parts, incorrect voice doubling and so forth); rather, we are concerned with what these arrangements say about reception. In summary, the arrangements listed above show a purposeful effort by publishers to cater to diverse performers within the market; they also show publishers catering to cultural reorganisation of the market, with amateurs developing into professionals, and concert life emerging from the salons. Publishers were clearly working with, and as, arrangers in their efforts to meet the changing market. It was good for sales to get a respected musician to do the arranging, in response to customers' expectation of idiomatic arrangements, well suited to a given instrument or voice. There were many anonymous arrangers in this era; but, especially as arrangements became increasingly virtuosic, it was becoming common to specify the arranger on the title page.

Named arrangers at this time fell into two main categories. First there were known musician arrangers, some of them publishers themselves, some of them hired by publishers – the era of regular 'house' arrangers had not yet begun. It would arrive in the mid-to-late nineteenth century in connection with the large, long-established publishing houses like Peters and Breitkopf & Härtel. Diabelli is an example of a respected musician and

Example 5.6 (a) Preghiera finale in Haslinger and Artaria's *Le siège de Corinthe, zweckmässig bearbeitet für die Jugend* (Vienna: Artaria and Haslinger, 1827)

publisher who became known as an arranger. Sedlack and Pössinger have already been mentioned, and by the late 1810s and 1820s they had become quite literally household names in Vienna, as arrangers.

Then, arrangements by professional musicians could also attract buyers, including amateurs. Mayseder's *Bouquet Musical/composé des plus beaux morceaux de l'opéra Guillaume Tell de J. Rossini pour violon et pianoforte* might be considered a showpiece more for the virtuoso in the salon or

Example 5.6 (b) Finale based on the Preghiera in Thalberg's Op. 3, Impromptu pour le piano-forte sur les thèmes favoris de l'opéra: Le siège de Corinthe (Vienna: Artaria, c.1828), bars 1–22 and 144–9

concert hall than for the amateur in the home. On the other hand, the violin part is not all that difficult. The 'concertante' element seems to apply more to the pianist than the violinist – perhaps taking account of the many talented amateur pianists in Vienna at this time. The violin part contains some *spiccato* (off-string bowing), a little cadenza flourish and a few slightly tricky double stops. The piece would have been within reach of a talented pianist and a violinist of modest skill. Instrumental arrangements were also made by singers, for example Benedict Randhartinger's *Le Comte Ory: Opéra en deux actes. Musique de G. Rossini. Réduit pour le piano-forte seul* (Artaria & Co., 1829). Randhartinger was a well-known tenor in Vienna, a friend of Schubert, and would become a singer and Kapellmeister at the Imperial Court in the 1830s and 1840s.

Another form of title-page branding to appeal to the wider market was reference to singers' interpretations, for example in *Recitativ, Canzonette und Cavatina der Desdemona 'Ah Come Infino Al Cuore'. Aus der Oper: Othello. Gesungen von Mad: Fodor* (Artaria, 1823). This title page specifies numerous agreeable terms of 'arrangement', calculated to appeal to 1810s and 1820s Viennese markets: a popular arranger and well-known publisher who specialised in opera arrangements (Diabelli), a favoured origin genre and composer (Italian opera and Rossini), and the most favoured instrumentation (solo piano). To top it off, the piece that was arranged so congenially was (it is claimed) reproduced in the interpretation sung by the favourite soprano of the day, which, a contemporary reviewer reported, had been heard by a massive audience with rapt attention:

At last the eager expectation of the audience was satisfied, as the first performance of the opera: 'Othello' by Rossini by the Italian singers took place. . . . the following trio with Siga. Fodor caused a furore, but this singer celebrated her greatest triumph with her vocal pieces in the third act, especially with the Preghiera [following 'Ah Come Infino Al Cuore']. Flexible, attractive voice, bravura, pure intonation, tasteful, appropriate performance . . .[33]

Josephine Fordo was in Vienna in 1823. Fresh from Teatro San Carlo in Naples, she created the role of Desdemona in the Viennese premier of Rossini's *Otello*, and also sang in his *Il barbiere di Siviglia* and *La gazza ladra* – all of them great favourites. Publishing excerpts that she had sung, as she had sung them, was truly publishing opera as the Viennese liked it.

---

[33] Anon., *Allgemeine Theaterzeitung und Unterhaltungsblatt für Freunde der Kunst, Literatur und des geselligen Lebens* [formerly: *Wiener Theater-Zeitung*] 16/34 (20 March 1823), p. 135; see also p. 23.

Why Rossini?

Returning to Figure 5.1, showing repertoire performed at the Kärntnertortheater in the years 1811–30 by genre, we see that this graph only shows the tip of the iceberg. An enumeration of public performances of Rossini operas does not represent the terrific resonance of his works with a broad public, and the reverberations of extensive repeated performance in the home. This resonance is more apparent when we look at the publishers' catalogues and consider the lengths to which they went to meet the market. Savvy publishers were capitalising on market preference in ingenious ways, devising new products (different instrumentation, combinations, formats), clever packaging (title-page wording and design, bundling in sets and series), and clever advertising. Rossini opera arrangements were helping to establish a market for musical works: the nature of the product was being shaped by the market's tastes, needs, and demands, rather than being imposed, for example, by critics. Indeed, we have seen that the critics were largely hostile to Rossini's opera at this time.

Why was there a Rossini rage in Vienna in this era? We could look further at plots. *Tancredi* was very popular in arrangements, and certain of its plot elements aligned neatly with the political situation in Vienna. There are internal conflicts, which are apparently abated, and there is apparent unity, comparable with that brought about by the Congress of Vienna. Tancredi, although treated badly and banished, exhibits patriotism, rather like some of the prominent Viennese *salonnières* of the day, who were under surveillance, or (in the case of the Jews) felt the threat of expulsion. The opera also talks about divisions among the nobility; and of people of lower class, like Tancredi, who are honourable – another relevant theme in early nineteenth-century Vienna. Rossini's *Il barbiere di Seviglia* also has a class-based plot. But the rage for Rossini extends well beyond these two hits. We need to look at plot delivery or dramaturgy, rather than themes. It is worth noting the ways that the arrangements, which are such a good index of the Viennese popularity of Rossini's opera, actually amplified certain aspects of Rossini opera that the critics found objectionable. Senici has broadly categorised the criticisms levelled at Rossini's operas at this time. These classes of criticism can be aligned usefully to the various types of arrangement that have been distinguished.

Critics found fault with the anti-mimetic aspect of Rossini's operas – the lack of direct imitation in the musical text, and the apparently separate course that the music takes from that of the drama. Senici cites Giuseppe

Carpani, who finds that the music follows its own logic, rather than that of the text; and Senici concludes on the basis of analysis as well as criticism that the link between reality and musical representation on stage is looser in Rossini's operas than in those of his predecessors and contemporaries.[34] The process of excerpting, in removing text and rearranging numbers, loosened this connection still further in opera arrangements. Most arrangements at this time are untexted and were performed off stage. The emphasis was on their hands-on enjoyment by amateurs in the home. Where the amateurs, or the arrangers or publishers, created a narrative out of arrangements, it was often one with its own musical logic, as in a set of variations; or no other logic than maximising pleasure, as in the sequence of hits strung together in a potpourri.

The repetitive nature of Rossini's operas is a particular target of critics from this time, including Viennese critics. His music is constructed from the repetition of a small number of musical ideas. Phrases, numbers, and aspects of entire works are echoed; and critics also deplored the larger-scale repetition they heard – Rossini borrowing from one opera in another (and sometimes even from another composer's work). All these kinds of repetition were greatly amplified by the performance of arrangements – often a single arrangement of a particular hit, like 'Di tanti palpiti' from *Tancredi* – over and over again in the home. This mimicked on-the-spot encores of hit numbers on the operatic stage, but went much further in creating 'earworms' from Rossini's arias, overtures, and ensemble numbers. The ever-popular variations created out of Rossini's themes redoubled the repetition, the hit tunes now performed over again in public by Giuliani, Mayseder, and other stars, then repeated at home, talent permitting. Rossini's manifold repetitions were also mercilessly (and enjoyably) lampooned in various parodies such as Moscheles' piano parody on 'Di tanti palpiti', which was first released by Steiner in 1817, and makes much of the repetition of motivic fragments (Example 5.7).

Looseness regarding genre was another fault the critics found with Rossini opera, especially the blurring of the distinction between *opera seria* and *opera buffa*.[35] This distinction is perhaps most attenuated by arrangement, which translates the music into various 'destination genres' and chops up works into numbers or recombines them in other configurations; a potpourri, or a wind-up finale added onto the end of a set of 'favourite melodies' takes little account of the generic boundary. The use of

---

[34] Senici, *Music in the Present Tense*, p. 30.   [35] Ibid., pp. 97–102.

Example 5.7 Ignaz Moscheles' piano parody on 'Di tanti palpiti' from *Tancredi* (Vienna: Steiner, 1817), bars 1–64

contrafacta (different texts from the original libretto) also muddied the waters of genre, though more prominently in England than in Vienna at this time; we have seen prayers, for example, turned into waltzes. In general, arrangement ran roughshod over genre in the interests of feasibility and performability, and with the end goal of pleasure in the act of performance.

Noisiness was a common criticism of Rossini's operas: this might seem to be easily mitigated by chamber arrangement.[36] But even in a domestic

---

[36] See especially Melina Esse, 'Rossini's Noisy Bodies', *Cambridge Opera Journal* 21/1 (2009), pp. 27–64.

setting the reverse could also easily apply. Noisiness could be amplified through the mechanics of the instrument, such as triple-strung bass strings on pianos, pedals, even special stops, reverberating through the drawing room and into the rest of the house; also through thickened textures heard in the small-scale acoustics of the salon. The choice of ensemble might also amplify noise: a setting for *Harmonie* would emphasise loudness, as could four-hand piano music with plenty of action in the bass register. These were two of the more prominent ensembles for arrangement.

This takes us to theatricality, which can be particularly heightened by ensemble arrangements. Senici finds theatricality to be fundamental to Rossini's operas. Rossini often makes one aware of the staged nature of the art: for example hearing and viewing a stage song.[37] In Rossini's case, theatricality is so prevalent as to become an integral part of the aesthetics and dramaturgical mode of his operas.[38] It can arise from stage songs or performative moments, such as an apostrophe to a distant beloved including the throbs of a wounded heart in the 'tanti palpiti'. But it is also intimated in the sum total of many elements (repetition, borrowing, noise, genre mixing) that lend a detached, anti-mimetic character to entire operas, not just particular numbers. Carl Dahlhaus, speaking of the mixing of comic and serious genres in Rossini's operas, argues that the listener is set at a remove by this element of theatricality:

The extremes meet: the farcical takes on catastrophic proportions in the frenzy of the music; the tragic, in its moments of greatest despair, exposes the marionette strings from which the characters are dangling.[39]

Rossini's brand of theatricality might be difficult to connect with the non-staged, excerpted numbers that we find in arrangements; on the face of it there is no direct frame of reference to the rest of the source operas. But as we have seen, the publishers supplied such a frame: title pages and packaging emphasised the relationship of the excerpted songs to their operas, and to opera as a genre, inherently theatrical. The arrangement itself then prompted the consumer to refer back to the absent 'original' and fill in the gaps imaginatively. But I would argue not only that arrangements heightened people's sense of the theatricality of Rossini's works', something that can be inferred from the negative criticism. Arrangements of Rossini operas also compounded the sense in which amateurs, at home,

---

[37] Senici, *Music in the Present Tense*, pp. 141–59.
[38] Extensively discussed by Senici, ibid., pp. 153–7.
[39] Carl Dahlhaus, *Nineteenth-Century Music* (Berkeley, CA: University of California Press, 1989), p. 64.

performing and listening, felt that they were *taking part in theatre* – performing, trying on roles, and being observed doing so – engendering a heightened awareness of self and others in relation to the highly problematic reality of the time.

That Rossini's operas heightened the sense of engagement in theatricality is suggested by the eyewitness accounts of salons and publishers' catalogues. We have seen that from the late eighteenth century onwards the Viennese upper and upper-middle classes showed a great thirst for things theatrical in their home entertainments – not only via play readings and the actual staging of plays, but also in a preference for theatrical games and, of course, opera arrangements. Now an expanded consumer base could buy, relatively cheaply, products that their own feedback and choices had ensured were precisely geared to satisfying this thirst; and overwhelmingly, on the evidence, they did buy them.

But why this engagement in theatricality would become so desirable, even necessary, at this time and in this place remains to be explained. This takes us to the effects of Rossini's dramaturgy. Senici argues that by loosening the connection between operatic representation and the lived experience of spectators, Rossini made an opening for various political imaginings in response to the broad suggestions of the plots.[40] This imaginative space was particularly appealing and necessary for the Italian-opera-going classes at this point in history. Viennese arrangements, as we have seen, loosened the connection between operatic representation and reality still further, opening up space for imaginative hearings and enactments that might bring theatre into even closer alignment with lived experience than would a seat (or standing room) at the opera.

As to why it might it be necessary or desirable to engage so often and enthusiastically in home theatrics, various answers present themselves, and some we have already explored. Education and entertainment come up repeatedly as motives, as does self-actualisation – being allowed to 'have it your way' and try out new roles (including leadership of musical ensembles). *Bildung* was extremely important to the upwardly mobile middle classes. Escape from political repression and social restrictions was also particularly important to the Viennese at this point in history. Theatrics allowed people not only to imagine other realities by trying on new roles, but also to forget the climate of repression and surveillance. This was

---

[40] Senici, *Music in the Present Tense*, especially pp. 154–5; and Senici, '"An Atrocious Indifference": Rossini's Operas and the Politics of Musical Representation in Early-Nineteenth-Century Italy', *Journal of Modern Italian Studies* 17/4 (2012), especially p. 424.

especially so for the upper- and middle-class opera-going, salon-holding public, who could see potential power in society and politics for themselves, attainable were it not for the government.

Mozart opera arrangements potentially fulfilled this public's desire for all of these things, and were accordingly still enormously popular. Weber's *Der Freischütz*, in particular, offered an outlet for nationalism.[41] But Rossini opera arrangements offered something more. Perhaps there was more room for sheer pleasure and fun from the beautiful melodies and the overtly theatrical high jinks, for more people, including children. But there was also more room for covert subversion of the status quo of Viennese society and politics, and therefore for empowering feelings of agency. On one level, any degree of amateur theatrics was somewhat risqué.

Theatricality had, after all, a long history of being perceived as problematic, starting with Plato. Its detractors were many in the 1810s, when novels by Jane Austen, among others, used theatrical activity as a sign of trouble for the social order. In *Mansfield Park*, for instance, theatre spills over into life and upsets the 'correct' pairing of couples in the plot.[42] The effects of the theatricality are felt through Maria and Henry Crawford's disruption of the local social order, which we see through the eyes of Fanny, who disapproves of the amateur theatrics. Austen thus sets the reader at a critical distance from the performance depicted in the story. In the eighteenth century the expressive actor was seen as a problematic figure, who is supposedly 'true to life' but dissembles all the same, by definition. Diderot addressed this problem in his *Paradoxe sur le comédien* (1770). Here he raised the question of whether the most expressive actors felt or in fact feigned the sentiments that they acted. The problematic 'forgetting of self' expected of consummate actors raises questions about dissimulation in social circles, and perhaps especially in the salon, where one might present oneself under false pretences.[43] But in early nineteenth-century Viennese homes, amateur

---

[41] See Margaret King, 'Opera and the Imagined Nation: Weber's *Der Freischütz*, Schinkel's Neues Schauspielhaus and the Politics of German National Identity', in Suzanne M. Lodato, Suzanne Aspden, and Walter Bernhart (eds.), *Word and Music Studies: Essays in Honor of Steven Paul Scher and on Cultural Identity and the Musical Stage* (Amsterdam: Rodopi, 2002), pp. 217–28.

[42] Senici refers to this example, *Music in the Present Tense*, pp. 146–7; see also Philippa Jane Kennerley, '"We always know when we are acting wrong": Performance and Theatricality in Jane Austen's Works', MA thesis (University of Otago, 2013), https://ourarchive.otago.ac.nz/handle/10523/3961.

[43] See especially Michael Fried, *Absorption and Theatricality: Painting and Beholder in the Age of Diderot* (Berkeley, CA: University of California Press, 1980); see also David Marshall, *The Surprising Effects of Sympathy: Marivaux, Diderot, Rousseau, and Mary Shelley* (Chicago, IL: University of Chicago Press, 1988), especially pp. 105–34.

theatrics could be delightfully and usefully risqué. They provided freedom through play in a time of repressive surveillance, when potentially every social occasion had spectators who were government spies.

Daviau finds that the wealthy classes of Metternich's Vienna fared much better than most, and did not experience the debilitating *Zerrissenheit* (division of self), described in Chapter 4, that afflicted members of lower classes:

> Those financially able to enjoy the benefits of a wealthy lifestyle did not chafe under the restrictive Metternich system of government and did not suffer from the spirit of resignation and the division between their inner and outer lives which are inseparably associated in the literature about the Vormärz.[44]

But in *Austria As It Is*, Sealsfield spoke of reactions to repression in all levels of Viennese society:

> The tide runs in Vienna towards gross sensuality in the people; – mute obedience in the public officers; – gloom or dissoluteness among the high nobility, and towards the most complete despotism in the Government, which grasps with the iron claw of its emblem – the double eagle – the whole empire, and keeps it in its baneful embraces.[45]

The 'baneful embraces' of the double-headed eagle's claw are served by the government officials' ears (and eyes), which are apparently everywhere:

> There is scarcely a word spoken in Vienna which they [the government] do not hear … As the Government has taken every care to debar them from serious or intellectual occupation, the Prater, the Glacis, the coffee-houses, the Leopoldstadt theatre, are the only objects of their thoughts and desires.[46]

Sealsfield repeatedly overstates his case in advocating democracy. In this way he underplays some efforts by the government to improve literacy at this time; some significant strides in concert life despite government restrictions; and also the power of theatres and coffee houses to foster serious and intellectual discourse.[47] This sets up later music historians like

---

[44] Daviau, 'Biedermeier: The Happy Face of the Vormärz Era', p. 25.
[45] Sealsfield, *Austria As It Is*, p. 215.   [46] Ibid., p. 194.
[47] On developments in literacy and *Bildung* in this era see Franz L. Fillafer, *Aufklärung habsburgisch: Staatsbildung, Wissenskultur und Geschichtspolitik in Zentraleuropa, 1750–1850* (Göttingen: Wallstein, 2021); on concert life in this era see especially Alice M. Hanson, *Die zensurierte Muse: Musikleben im Wiener Biedermeier* (Vienna: Böhlau, 1987), pp. 100–30; on coffee houses as sites for intellectual discourse (taking over from salons) in Vienna see Sonnleitner, 'Vom Salon zum Kaffeehaus. Zur literarischen Öffentlichkeit im österreichischen Biedermeier', especially p. 82.

Hanslick to discover the 'gross sensuality' of the Viennese people of this era (in Sealsfield's terms), which would imply indulgence in theatrical works and little appetite for 'serious' music. Sealsfield writes:

> A new opera of Rossini in the Karthnerthor theatre [sic] will, with these good people, produce quite as much and even more excitement than the opening of the Parliament in London. Their opera is, however, splendid and Mozart's Zauberflote [sic] (magic flute) or Don Juan, heard in the Karthnerthor [sic] theatre, is a delicious enjoyment. The ballets in the same are inferior to the Parisian. How little propensity the Viennese have even to serious music, Haydn's Creation performed in the Imperial riding-school by 350 musicians sufficiently proved. Though the grandest performance I ever witnessed, yet it was but thinly attended.[48]

Sealsfield does not grasp the larger meanings of and reasons behind the apparent 'gross sensuality' and lack of propensity for 'serious' music, although he rightly draws attention to the constant surveillance, especially of middle- and upper-class people. So the *Biedermeierzeit* he describes has been understood in pejorative terms as designating a time when these classes lived in self-indulgent happy ignorance. Rossini opera and the wide popularity of dancing are taken as harbingers of this trend; or they are ignored, for example when Rossini and Lanner get supplanted by Beethoven (and sometimes Schubert) as representing Viennese music of the period.[49]

But the musical vogues for Italian opera and dancing do not have to be minimised as symptoms of a base retreat into pleasure. They can be understood as expressions of the darker side of *Biedermeierzeit*, and especially of the Metternich system, of an intelligent and talented public seizing one of the few sources of real freedom within their grasp: the freedom to watch and listen how they wanted, and to a music that expressed something of the condition of constant spectatorship and constant play-acting that they knew in their daily lives. In this time of problematic social voyeurism, this meant Mozart, in *Figaro*, where Cherubino hides under a dress to avoid being seen by Susanna; or *Don Giovanni*, where Don Giovanni dissembles by singing a seductive song beneath Donna Anna's window, in disguise, and hoping to be overheard.

---

[48] Ibid., p. 203.
[49] Corrected in books like Nicholas Mathew and Benjamin Walton (eds.), *The Invention of Beethoven and Rossini: Historiography, Analysis, Criticism* (Cambridge: Cambridge University Press, 2013); and Erica Buurman, *The Viennese Ballroom in the Age of Beethoven* (Cambridge: Cambridge University Press, 2022).

But most of all it was Rossini's operas, with their 'melodic charm' and 'harmonic turns', that immediately found decisive recognition precisely for their ability to reposition Viennese musical amateurs vis-à-vis 'judges of German art' and other watchdogs of the repressive Austrian society of the time.

6 | Industry, Agency, and Opera Arrangements in Czerny's Vienna

After Rossini's visit to Vienna in 1822, no Italian troupes visited the Kärntnertortheater for four years. It was closed twice for extended periods in the 1820s because of financial and organisational problems. But public demand for Rossini's operas remained, and Barbaia sponsored three more years of Italian opera at the Kärntnertortheater, consisting largely of Rossini's works. After Barbaia's departure in 1828, Rossini's operas were still staged, but now the repertoire settled back into the previously popular standards – translations of French and Italian operas into German, *Singspiele*, and ballets. Donizetti's success in Vienna, notably including a visit in 1842, was, like the Rossini rage, related to Habsburg cultural politics in the 1830s – particularly an assertion of the supranational identity of the Austrian Empire.[1] Donizetti and other opera composers (Auber, Bellini, Boieldieu, Cherubini, Mozart, and Müller, for instance) never reached the heights of popularity attained by Rossini, but the rage for opera in Vienna was still in full swing.

This was still the Age of Metternich, and Austria maintained a repressive police state, which in turn encouraged music-making in the home. Viennese publishers continued to build an industry on arrangements for home performance of works by the favoured composers from public performances of opera in Vienna. The catalogues of Diabelli, Haslinger, K. K. Hoftheater, Mollo, and Senefelder, which extend into the 1830s and 1840s, reflected these preferences: they include vast numbers of opera arrangements of numerous kinds, mainly for piano.[2] K. K. Hoftheater's thirty-volume *Die musikalische Biene: Ein Unterhaltungs Blatt für das Piano Forte* (1819–20), whose title page is depicted in Figure 6.1, is typical and apt with its 'busy' bee. It was among the first of many extended series

---

[1] Claudio Vellutini, 'Italian Opera in *Vormärz* Vienna: Gaetano Donizetti, Bartolomeo Merelli and Habsburg Cultural Policies in the Mid-1830s', in Axel Körner and Paulo M. Kühl (eds.), *Italian Opera in Global and Transnational Perspective: Reimagining Italianità in the Long Nineteenth Century* (Cambridge: Cambridge University Press, 2022), pp. 96–112.

[2] In 1826 Haslinger took over the publishing house of Steiner, and in 1832 the publishing house of Mollo, becoming one of the most important music publishers of the era.

Figure 6.1 Title page from *Die musikalische Biene: Ein Unterhaltungs Blatt für das Piano Forte* (1819–20), volume 3 (Vienna: K. K. Hoftheater, 1819), with close-ups showing the names of composers on flowers and leaves (left to right: (a) Paër, Haydn, Mozart; (b) Spontini, Rossini, Salieri, Paisiello, Weigl, Cherubini, Boieldieu. Courtesy of Österreichische Nationalbibliothek Musiksammlung, shelf mark MS9687-qu.4°/3

devoted to piano arrangements from Viennese publishing houses in this era. These series were chiefly destined for use by amateurs in the home. They featured favoured composers of German, French, and Italian operas of the day and recent past. For example, volume three of *Die musikalische Biene* contains variations on a theme from the *Nachtlager in Granada* by Ferdinand Stegmayer; a duet (Damon and Philis) 'Wir eilig weg' from *Nachtigal und Rabe* by Weigl; a duet (Count and Susanne) from *Le nozze di Figaro* by Mozart; and a duet (Desdemonda and Emilia) from *Otello* by Rossini – all for solo piano and well within the reach of the amateur.

But mass production for an amateur market has only just come to interest historians. Most scholars of this period in Viennese history, including cultural historians, ignore or denigrate the manifold published arrangements from this industry. Daviau, discussing the label *Biedermeier*, passes over arrangements and points instead to the original works of canonic composers – Gluck, Haydn, Mozart, Beethoven, and Schubert. He finds that 'Music played an important role in this family-oriented lifestyle, but the music itself displays no qualities that can be called Biedermeier'.[3] The canonic works rise above their time in his account and the music that is 'of' the time on the evidence of popularity seems to be unworthy of mention. Ruth Solie seeks to recover Schubert as a *Biedermeier* composer, but likewise distances his music from this term, which she appropriates 'not to describe any category or style of music but to characterise a coherent system of values associated with domesticity and with the activities, including the music, found in the home'.[4] The door is left open for discussing ways in which music of the time might reinforce or deny these values. Robert Waissenberger finds arrangements to be characteristic of this era, even naming this phenomenon 'the flowering of musical arrangements' ('Die Blütezeit des musikalischen Arrangements').[5] But, like the other scholars, he suggests that Viennese music designed specifically for the market is necessarily of low quality, or at least simple. He sees the flourishing of arrangements in the hands of publishers as a symptom of decline, assuming that small-scale music-making within the average Viennese home leads to small-minded artworks and inferior taste. Regarding publications like *Die musikalische Biene* he writes: 'Of musical "classics", of works that made spiritual claims on the performer, one was hardly interested, and when one offered reprints of Mozart or compositions of Beethoven, these only counted as an occasional beautifying or cleaning up of the publishing programme'.[6]

---

[3] Daviau, 'Biedermeier: The Happy Face of the Vormärz Era', p. 23.
[4] Solie, 'Biedermeier Domesticity and the Schubert Circle', p. 126.
[5] Robert Waissenberger, *Wien 1815–1848: Bürgersinn und Aufbegehren; die Zeit des Biedermeier und Vormärz* (Vienna: Überreuter, 1986), p. 260.
[6] Ibid., p. 262.

These scholars' accounts distort the history in several ways. We need to look in more detail at the publishers' programmes and into the arrangements themselves to see the useful cultural work they did – and not only because Beethoven and especially Mozart serve more than to merely beautify or 'clean up' publications like *Die musikalische Biene*.[7] Mozart's name is very prominent in Viennese opera arrangement publications in this era, especially those of Carl Czerny (1791–1857), one of the foremost Viennese arrangers of the time. For instance, Czerny's Op. 797, *Ten grand concertante fantasies for two pianos on selected motifs from classical and modern operas* (*Dix grandes fantasies concertantes pour deux pianos sur des motifs choisis des opéras classiques et modernes*), from the end of the period in question, samples 'nectar' (motifs) from the operas of Handel, Haydn, Beethoven, Mozart, integrated with motifs from Bellini, Auber, Donizetti, and more recent composers (Figure 6.2). The title-page illustration likewise shows classical and modern motifs. By this stage (*c*.1840) there were numerous piano arrangements like this one, dedicated to advanced performers playing in more public contexts than envisioned in *Die musikalische Biene*.

We also need to re-examine two historiographical barriers to our seeing these extensive sets of arrangements, along with massive numbers and many varieties of isolated opera arrangements, as anything more than busywork, or worse, the production of inadequate copies. First, the views of the scholars cited here reflect a larger historiographical problem in connection with the term *Biedermeier*. It was coined after the era to which it refers, in relation to a fictional schoolmaster, Gottlieb Biedermeier (a God-loving common man, literally), who figures in a satirical Viennese newspaper around 1857. The label is ripe for review regarding Viennese musical culture.[8] The word *Biedermeier* invokes a skewed interpretation of German cultural history *c*.1815–48, according to which the smug, self-satisfied middle classes seek out lightweight art that mirrors their small-mindedness and has no real value.

Perceived problems with the quality of this music (which is re-examined later in this chapter) are surely compounded by the sheer quantity of arrangements, especially for piano, that poured from Viennese arrangers and publishers of the period. K. K. Hoftheater makes a sales point of this industry with the figure of the busy bee on the title page of *Die musikalische Biene*. The bee (arranger) sucks nectar (musical essence?) from choice flowers. The leaves and flowers are labelled Händel (Handel), Haydn, Mozart, Salieri, Cherubini,

---

[7] Hannah Lindmaier, 'Ortswechsel: Oper im Salon musizieren; Bearbeitungen als Teil der frühen *Fidelio*-Rezeption in Wien', in Melanie Unseld and Julia Ackermann (eds.), *Beethoven.An. Denken: Das Theater an der Wien als Erinnerungsort* (Vienna: Böhlau, 2020), pp. 165–85.

[8] See Vago, 'Musical Life of Amateur Musicians in Vienna', p. 1.

Boieldieu, Weigl, Paisiello, Spontini, Rossini, Beethoven, Gyrowetz, Pär (Paër), Gluck, Zingarelli – some of the most popular opera composers of the time and of the recent past (see Figure 6.1a and 6.1b). The bee takes this nectar back to the hive (the publishing house or the home) for transformation into honey (money for publisher and arranger; musical riches for the home). The metaphor is appropriate for publishers, arrangers, and Viennese musical amateurs. Arrangers were indeed industrious; they and their publishers reaped profits, while the music-buying public gained products of great use and value to them.

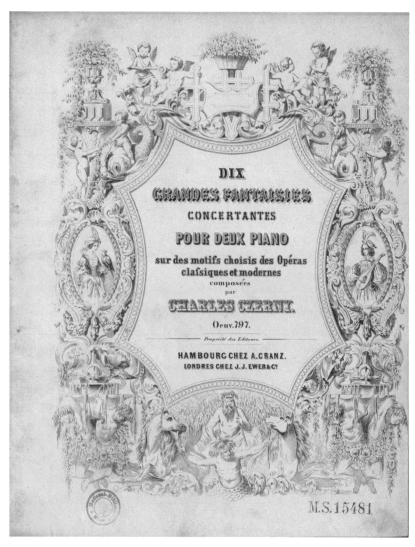

Figure 6.2 Title page from Carl Czerny's *Dix grandes fantasies concertantes pour deux pianos sur des motifs choisis des opéras classiques et modernes*, Op. 797 (Hamburg: Cranz, *c.*1840), Courtesy of Österreichische Nationalbibliothek Musiksammlung, shelf mark MS15.481–4°/1

But this economic model is sorely at odds with the economics of musical genius, which developed through the nineteenth century in step with the concept of autonomous musical 'works', and still stands in the way of a sound appraisal of this music. In the economics of musical genius, as it is virtually defined by the nineteenth-century reception of Beethoven, the (male, German) composer labours intensively to produce compositions – not too many of any one kind, since each must be original – which are complete, coherent, and perfect as they stand. These musical works need, and indeed admit, no further work by other hands, so as to possess a value that stands above money and commodity, as 'art for art's sake'.

Czerny violated this model – unwittingly of course, the model being essentially anachronistic – by engaging heavily in arrangement and spending a good deal of his time teaching Viennese women to play the piano well. He is a prime example of a Viennese 'busy bee' of his era, who would be derided by music historians from Hanslick to the present as merely 'industrious' (*fleissig*).[9] At stake in both historiographical problems is agency, and who is allowed to have it. The anachronistic model of *Biedermeier Hausmusik* as trivial music protects canonic musical works and the economy of genius by constructing aligned partitions between public and private, male and female, and 'high' and 'low' forms of music and music-making. The contemporary musical-bee model, on the other hand, moves between these domains and assigns agency to potentially disruptive figures, as far as the economy of musical genius is concerned – to arrangers, the market, and women.

This chapter will recover the benefits – the proverbial musical honey, and the wider cultural importance – of the musical bee. I step away from the foregone value judgements associated with the terms *Biedermeier*, domestic music, and mass production – all encapsulated in the pejorative use of the word *Hausmusik* during the nineteenth century.[10] Like Solie, I wish to uncover 'the varieties of musicking or the range of meanings of music as a human experience' connected with the domestic music of this era – which, she notes, are invariably left behind by modern musicologists in favour of a focus on individual, canonic (and, I would add, original) compositions.

To understand opera in the Viennese home, it is helpful to consider, with Solie, the values that became attached to *Biedermeier* domesticity, especially social formation, domestic stability, and wholistic education. In revaluing Viennese opera arrangements of this era, it is also worth

---

[9] Hanslick, *Geschichte*, p. 221.
[10] Nicolai Petrat, 'Musizierpraxis und Ideologie. Zur Hausmusik im 19. Jahrhundert', *Das Orchester: Zeitschrift für Orchesterkultur und Rundfunk-Chorwesen* 38/5 (1990), pp. 494–500; and Petrat, *Hausmusik des Biedermeier*, especially pp. 81–96.

considering how they inspired public-sphere agency extending beyond domesticity. I discuss quantitative aspects of piano-opera arrangement culture in Czerny's Vienna and reasons for the boom in pianos, pianists, and associated publications. Then I turn to qualitative considerations, looking at the ways in which these piano-opera arrangements promoted the agency of listeners, arrangers, performers (advanced and amateur), and women in particular.

The Piano as Opera Orchestra

> If it were only possible to hear the productions of the great composers by means of a full orchestra they would be very little known; the taste for music would be less common, and the progress of this art would be significantly slower.[11]

Fétis wrote these words in his 1829 treatise on the art of producing a piano reduction at the keyboard. The treatise itself was a sign of the times. By the end of the eighteenth century, the piano had become the only solo instrument that was regularly played in public concerts. With the advent of mass production in the nineteenth century, it was marketed to the ascendant bourgeoisie, and became a symbol of cultivation and modernity. With the hardware there came the appropriate software: in the 1820s and 1830s, piano transcriptions (for two hands, four hands, and two pianos) became ever more prominent throughout Europe, almost completely taking over the field of arrangements during this time.

Piano transcriptions were among the first to bring opera into the home for amateur performance in the eighteenth century, and in the 1820s and 1830s their popularity soared. This trend was closely related to developments in the piano itself – its expanding range, greater power, and thus increased capacity to reproduce orchestral textures.[12] Pianos developed through a symbiotic relationship between instrument makers, performers, and composers.[13] But the instruments were also developing in step with

---

[11] François-Joseph Fétis, *Traité de l'accompagnement de la partition sur le piano ou l'orgue* (Paris: Pleyel et Cie, 1829), p. 1; translated and discussed in Jonathan Kregor, 'Franz Liszt and the Vocabularies of Transcription, 1833–1865', PhD diss. (Harvard University, 2007), p. 7.

[12] Edwin M. Good and Cynthia Adams Hoover, 'Designing, Making, and Selling Pianos', in James Parakilas (ed.), *Piano Roles: Three Hundred Years of Life with the Piano* (New Haven, CT: Yale University Press, 1999), pp. 31–71; see also Marlise Hansemann, *Der Klavier-Auszug: von den Anfängen bis Weber* (Leipzig: Mayen, 1843), pp. 102–15.

[13] Alan Davison, 'Franz Liszt and the Development of 19th-Century Pianism: A Re-Reading of the Evidence', *The Musical Times* 147/1896 (2006), p. 34.

concert and opera repertoire, becoming more and more suited for the rendering of increasingly complex operatic scores.[14] Over the course of the eighteenth and early nineteenth centuries, the piano's four-octave range expanded to reach over six-and-a-half octaves by the middle of the nineteenth century. Piano-making received a decided impetus in the 1770s from John Broadwood in London and Johann Andreas Stein in Vienna. Vienna temporarily led the piano-making industry around 1800: new piano factories were built in Vienna by Johann Andreas Streicher (1794) and Conrad Graf (1804). Carl Maria von Weber purchased a Streicher piano in 1813. Graf's attempt in 1821 to produce quadruple-strung pianos, rather than triple stringing the bass, did not prove successful, but Streicher's hammer action from above (1825) proved a more durable innovation. A particular milestone was Sébastien Érard's invention of the piano's double-escapement action in 1822, which allowed the rapid repetition of a tone without lifting the finger from the key, and a more sensitive response to touch.

Changes in materials and stringing also expanded the pianist's capacity for power, velocity, and expressive range, making the piano an ideal instrument for transcriptions of orchestral music. In 1839, Liszt expressed his desire to push the instrument's limits yet further in this direction:

But the extension of capabilities acquired by the piano in recent times as a result of the progress made in execution and the refinements introduced in the mechanism make it possible to do more, and better, than has been done up till now. Through the indefinite development of its harmonic power, the piano is tending to assimilate all orchestral compositions to itself. In the space of its seven octaves it can produce, with few exceptions, all the characteristics, all the combinations, all the figures of the most scholarly composition, and leaves the orchestra with no other advantages (though they are indeed immense) but those of diversity of timbres and of mass effects.[15]

Liszt and others spoke of the piano's new-found capacity to reproduce orchestral music. This included not just purely orchestral music, but also opera, which Liszt himself transcribed. Indeed Arthur Loesser, who charts the rise of the piano in Western culture, considers the piano music of 1825–75 as a 'dependency' of opera, because operatic transcriptions, fantasies,

---

[14] Thomas Christensen, 'Public Music in Private Spaces: Piano-Vocal Scores and the Domestication of Opera', in Kate van Orden (ed.), *Music and the Cultures of Print*, Critical and Cultural Musicology (New York: Garland Publishing, 2000), p. 76.
[15] Liszt's Preface to the Beethoven Symphonies, 1st ed. (Rome, 1839), in Van Dine, 'Musical Arrangements and Questions of Genre', p. 12.

and variations formed the largest portion of music for the keyboard.[16] Loesser cites the newer Parisian piano variations, which responded to the demands of an 'assertive moneyed crowd' by theatrically introducing the main theme (often derived from opera) after a flourish and a suspenseful leading chord, rather than clearly stating that theme.[17] As we have seen, piano variations on themes from operas had been well established since the days of Mozart and Traeg; they retained their popularity, as a glance through publishing catalogues of the period reveals.

The following table (Table 6.1) shows the Mozart-opera-related publications that appeared in the publishing catalogue of Senefelder, Steiner, and Haslinger in the 1830s and 1840s, including three sets of variations, demonstrating the popularity of this kind of arrangement at this point and the continuing vogue for Mozart opera. The variations on Mozart's 'Voi che sapete' from *Le nozze di Figaro* by Bohemian-Viennese violinist Leopold Jansa are a case in point. Starting with a recitative-like flourish for violin and ending on a suspenseful dominant seventh, they do not reveal their thematic origins until the first variation (Example 6.1). Not even the title page gives away the popular stage song sung by Cherubino in Act 1, but any opera-going listener of the time would have immediately recognised it.

As Hanslick observes, developments in the piano went together with the development of virtuoso piano playing.[18] But they also afforded new possibilities for amateur performers. Piano arrangements needed to respond to the demands of an increasingly broad market, of which the amateur pianist held the lion's share. In Vienna, this principal market included some highly talented dilettantes.

The Pianists

The boom in piano arrangements needs to be set in the context not only of developments in the instrument itself, and in concert life, but of a burgeoning consumer base of amateurs who attended the opera and concerts, bought pianos, played arrangements, and fed back into the cycle of production and reception. In his *Geschichte des Concertwesens in Wien* (1860), Hanslick points to the leadership of Vienna in pianism in the

---

[16] Arthur Loesser, *Men, Women and Pianos: A Social History* (New York, NY: Dover Publications, 1990), p. 596.
[17] Ibid., p. 595.   [18] Hanslick, *Geschichte*, p. 225.

Table 6.1 Mozart-opera-related publications that appeared in the publishing catalogue of Senefelder, Steiner, and Haslinger in the 1830s and 1840s

Composer	Op., translated title, instrumentation, format (Q = landscape; H = portrait), price, edition/publisher (when specified)	Advertisement date (*Wiener Zeitung*)
Johann Baptist Cramer	Fantasia on a Theme from the Opera: *Don Giovanni*, piano and flute, H, 1fl., London, J. B. Cramer & Co.	WZ No. 32; 10.2.1831
Johann Nepomuk Hummel	Op. 124, Fantasia on a Theme from Mozart's *Le nozze di Figaro*, piano, Q, 1fl.	WZ No. 203; 4.9.1833
Frédéric Chopin	Op. 2, Variations on 'La ci darem la mano', piano, H, 2fl., Nouvelle edition	WZ No. 252; 31.10.1839
Sigismund Thalberg	Op. 14, Grand Fantasia and Variations on Two Motifs from the Opera *Don Giovanni* by Mozart, piano 4 hands by C. Czerny, H, 2fl.	WZ No. 293; 22.10.1840
Leopold Jansa	Op. 58, Homage to Mozart. Introduction and Variations on a Theme by Mozart, violin and piano, H, 1fl. [Based on 'Voi che sapete' from *Le nozze di Figaro*]	WZ No. 263; 23.9.1842
Josef Lanner	Op. 196, The Mozartists [Die Mozartisten], Waltz, violin and piano, H, 1fl.15x, [Various Mozart opera themes, concluding with a 'waltz' on Overture to *Die Zauberflöte*]	WZ No. 194; 16.7.1842

Example 6.1 Introduction, Leopold Jansa, *Hommage à Mozart: Introduction et Variations sur un thême de Mozart* (Vienna: Senefelder, Steiner, and Haslinger, 1842), bars 1–6 and 21–3

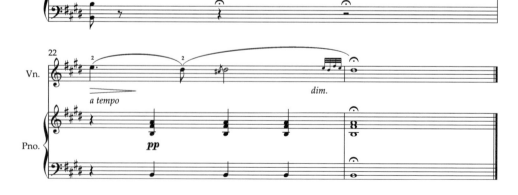

period 1815–30, and to increasing numbers of women and child pianists in public concert life.[19] But he disparages Czerny for spending so much time on teaching. Hanslick's focus was on public music-making and so he was not seeing, or rather not wanting to see, how private-sphere music-making bore directly on the development of public concert life. Although Hanslick recognised that the 'stately image' of public music-making had its roots in the people (*das Volk*), he saw it as necessarily developing through the great German composers of the recent past: Gluck, Haydn, Mozart, and Beethoven.[20] Other evidence, apparently not consulted by Hanslick, suggests that private-sphere music-making and piano arrangements were a much greater force on, and much more entangled in, public music-making.

One such source is an *Addressen-Buch* compiled by Anton Ziegler, listing musicians, institutions, instrument makers, and composers in Vienna at the start of the era of interest in this chapter, and published in 1823.[21] It shows increasing numbers of musicians compared with the earlier lists of Schönfeld (1797) and Mösel (1808), and a major involvement of women in musical life, especially as pianists. The bulk of the book is a sixty-page listing of composers and *Dilettanten* in Vienna at the time, with their addresses. There are separate lists of performers in the Gesellschaft der Musikfreunde, from which we can see that performers like Katherine Hochenadl, who developed as a musician by organising and performing in private-sphere concerts featuring arrangements, now entered the more public arena as leading pianists of the day. But the *Addressen-Buch* is not neatly divided into 'professionals' and 'amateurs', any more than it cleanly separates public- and private-sphere musical activities. For instance, three of the women listed separately under *Dilettanten* are also noted as virtuosos, including child prodigy Leopoldine Blahetka (then fourteen years old). Two other female prodigies are listed with their ages: Louise Ehler (ten years old) and Fanny Sallamon (eleven years old). The list of *Dilettanten* is remarkable for the many family groupings, especially of female pianists. Table 6.2 shows an excerpt from the *Addressen-Buch*, showing the Clary family pianists (and one singer).[22] The list is mixed with regard to class. Blahetka was the daughter of a factory

---

[19] Ibid., p. 223. [20] Ibid., pp. x–xi.
[21] Anton Ziegler, *Addressen-Buch von Tonkünstlern, Dilettanten, Hof- Kammer- Theater- und Kirchen-Musikern, Vereinen, Lehr- und Pensions-Instituten, Bibliotheken zum Behufe der Tonkunst; k.k. privil. Kunst- und Musikalien-Handlungen, Instrumentenmachern, Geburts- und Sterbtagen vorzüglicher Tonkünstler &c. in Wien* (Vienna: Strauß, 1823).
[22] Ibid., p. 7.

Table 6.2 Excerpt from Anton Ziegler's *Addressen-Buch*, showing the Clary family pianists (and one singer) in Vienna in 1823

Clary Aldringen, Hr. Gr. v., Imperial and Royal Chamberlain (pianoforte), lives in the city, Herrngasse No. 28

Clary, Her Highness Frau Christine Fürst. von (pianoforte), as above

Clary, Comtesse Mathilde von (pianoforte), as above

Clary, Comtesse Euphemia von (pianoforte), as above

Clary, Leontine Comtesse v. (pianoforte), as above

Clary, Frau Louise Gr. v., born Gräfinn von Chotek, Sternkreutz: Order: Lady, Lady of the Palace (pianoforte), as above

Clary, Frau Jenni Gr. v., born Gräfinn von Dietrichstein (pianoforte), lives in the city, Kohlmarkt No. 257

Clary, Fräulein Julie (singer), suburb of Weißgärber, Hauptstraße, No.19

---

inspector, and lived in Josefstadt (close to the centre, and with a theatre), whereas the listed Clary family women all lived in the inner city. Czerny was, by this time, upwardly mobile thanks to his extensive teaching, and lived in Krugerstrasse in the central district.

In the list of composers and *Dilettanten*, female pianists (168) outnumber male pianists (147), and are slightly fewer in number than male violinists (171).[23] Men outnumber the women in this list of *Dilettanten* as a whole, almost 2:1 (480 to 250). The piano is very clearly the preferred instrument among the women, with voice taking second place. Among the male pianists, there is a sizable number (twenty-three) of piano teachers ('Clavier-Meister'), including Czerny. This needs to be borne in mind in assessing the standards of the men and women who would have performed the arrangements discussed later in this chapter.

These figures were obtained by sampling rather than census, and were largely put together from responses to newspaper advertisements. Ziegler himself points to the great difficulty he had compiling the publication, and notes that it is to be considered a general overview of the foremost people and institutions of music in Vienna at that time.[24] He aimed at an approximate mapping of musical Vienna, and the resulting figures probably represent only a small sample. They may give an indication of relative proportions – especially gender proportions – among the musicians then in

---

[23] This list includes men who are listed as 'Clavier-Meister', and the numbers for male pianists and violinists overlap somewhat, since the most popular combination of two or more instruments for men in this list is violin and piano. Two female violinists are listed.

[24] Ziegler, *Addressen-Buch*, Vorrede.

Vienna. Grete Wehmeyer reports that around 1847, so towards the end of Czerny's life, there were around 2,000 piano-playing amateurs in Vienna, whose population had grown from around 35,000 in the early 1820s to around 50,000.[25] If we assume that piano-playing amateurs made up roughly 4 per cent of the Viennese population in the early 1820s, extrapolating from Wehmeyer's figures for 1847, then this suggests around 1,400 amateur pianists in 1820s Vienna – of which Ziegler managed to sample possibly the top one quarter. The figures are high, but not unlikely: Mozart had already dubbed Vienna 'Klavierland' in a letter to his father of 1781.[26]

The Repertoire: Mass Production

Scholars seeking to characterise musical culture in German-speaking lands in this era are right to focus on quantity. There was a booming piano-music industry and we can start to speak of mass production. By 1844 Adolf Hofmeister's catalogue of printed music published in German-speaking lands lists over 5,000 items of four-hand piano music, some 50 pages from 320 pages of piano music in total, including 59 entries for Rossini's operas and 16 entries for Mozart's.[27] The catalogue also offers much two-hand piano music, including two-hand transcriptions and duets with other instruments, to complement a wide range of solo music, leaving no doubt as to the popularity of the piano in general. In these two-hand piano categories (solo and ensemble) there are 111 entries related to Rossini's operas and 50 for Mozart's. But the piano-based arrangements did not completely eclipse other kinds of arrangements that had been popular earlier in the century, and were still popular, for example, among the largely male string-quartet players. Twenty-two arrangements are listed at the end of the Mozart quartets category in this catalogue, twenty of which are opera arrangements, some in several versions (for example, there are four different versions of *Die Zauberflöte*). This, together with sources

---

[25] See Grete Wehmeyer, 'Czerny, Carl', in Ludwig Finscher (ed.), *Die Musik in Geschichte und Gegenwart: allgemeine Enzyklopädie der Musik*, 2nd ed., Personenteil vol. 5 (Kassel: Bärenreiter, 2001), col. 222.
[26] Letter of 2 June 1781, in Anderson, *The Letters of Mozart and His Family*, p. 739; see also Bauer et al., *Mozart: Briefe und Aufzeichnungen*, vol. 3, pp. 124–5.
[27] Carl Friedrich Whistling, *Handbuch der musikalischen Literatur oder allgemeines systematisch-geordnetes Verzeichniss der in Deutschland und in den angrenzenden Ländern gedruckten Musikalien auch musikalischen Schriften und Abbildungen mit Anzeige der Verleger und Preise*, vol. 1 (Leipzig: Hofmeister, 1844–5), https://babel.hathitrust.org/cgi/pt?id=umn.31951002245016j;view=1up;seq=5.

such as the long list of Viennese violinists cited in the previous section, suggests that the string quartet remained in vogue as a medium for opera arrangements, despite the boom in piano-opera arrangements. A reviewer for the *Allgemeine Wiener Musik-Zeitung* in 1841, for instance, found piano transcriptions to be the most useful, but confirmed that arrangements for string quartet were also worthy.[28]

The changing layout of Hofmeister's catalogue is instructive regarding the piano music boom in general. When it was first published in 1817, by Carl Friedrich Whistling, the catalogue was a single volume grouped into three sections. The first listed instrumental music in alphabetical order according to genre, followed by a section devoted to vocal works, and an appendix comprising collections, theoretical works, and portraits. This grouping already suggests a departure from the locational thinking about genre seen in Traeg, who divided his catalogue into music for chamber, theatre, and church respectively. But by 1844–5, when the third edition was released by Hoffmeister (it subsequently spilled over into twelve supplements), the grouping needed to be altered again. The catalogue was now issued in two volumes; the first of music for strings and wind instruments, the second devoted to music for piano, organ, harp, and harmonica. This second volume was more than twice the size of the first, and was very largely taken up with piano music. In 1817, the bulging piano category was already taking up 40 per cent of the volume. But four-hand piano music, representing 7 per cent of the piano music, would double as a proportion of the 1844 catalogue.

These trends concern the German-speaking lands more generally. What were the Viennese amateurs playing and learning in this era? On the evidence of Viennese publishers' lists and catalogues, they were performing much piano music, including plenty of opera arrangements. We have already seen that there were many piano arrangements of opera on sale in Vienna in preceding periods – for example in Traeg's catalogue, where they make up a significant portion of a vast self-contained category of 'Clavier-Music', under 'Cammer-Music'. The numerous opera arrangements in Diabelli's second publishing catalogue for the period 1816–24 are discussed in Chapter 5. It is instructive to compare this second catalogue with his third, for the period 1824–40. This third catalogue covers twice as many years as the second one, but is more than twice as large. Czerny is the most frequent arranger represented, followed by Diabelli himself in close second place.

---

[28] *Allgemeine Wiener Musik-Zeitung* 97 (14 August 1841), p. 405.

Diabelli's third publishing catalogue is representative of the time and place in its heavy emphasis on piano arrangements, chiefly of opera. Among the composers of the operas that were arranged, Mozart figures prominently, Beethoven hardly at all. The main composers represented are Auber, Bellini, Boieldieu, Cherubini, Müller, and Mozart; and there is a continued emphasis on composers of French opera, including Dalayrac, Grétry, Méhul, and Isouard. Rossini's popularity continued through the 1820s (his last opera was *William Tell* in 1829), but then declined. Piano works of all kinds are prominent, but especially dances (waltzes), and also variations and Lieder. And collections of opera arrangements also became very popular and typical of the era, following the Hoftheater's example with *Die musikalische Biene*. Diabelli issued extensive sets and many series (volumes of printed music containing groups of pieces), devoted largely to opera arrangements: *Philomele: eine Sammlung der beliebtesten Gesänge mit Begleitung der Pianoforte eingerichtet und herausgegeben von Anton Diabelli für das Pianoforte*; *Euterpe*; and Czerny's *Bijoux théâtrales, ou Collection des Rondeaux, Variations et Impromptus sur les Motifs les plus favoris des nouveaux Opéras p[our] P[iano]f[or]te*. All brought opera to the amateur in the home on a regular basis until the middle of the nineteenth century. These series often include words such as 'journal', 'magazine', or 'periodical' (or variants) in their titles, but they refer to published music, not text.

An overview of the very successful printed music series *Philomele* indicates how tastes were changing in opera as well as in Lieder, and generally helps demonstrate how central vocal music was in this era, despite the heavy emphasis on the piano. *Philomele* started in 1819 and continued through the 1830s; in between, the two- and four-hand series of *Euterpe* were also released. Schubert Lieder are well represented in *Philomele*, reflecting the close relationship between Diabelli and Schubert. Of opera composers, Mozart is the most popular, with forty-nine items scattered through the series. Donizetti comes next, with thirty-three items, appearing mainly towards the end of the series; then Auber, a French composer of opera, comes a close third, with thirty-two items, mainly in the middle of the series. Bellini also figures regularly in the 1830s, with twenty-three items in the middle of the series; while Rossini, with only thirteen items, appears around the start of the series in the 1820s. Rossini's declining popularity with the Viennese is neatly illustrated by these figures, as is the enduring appeal of French grand opera (seen also in Figure 5.1).

Imogen Fellinger lists twenty music series of this kind (volumes of printed arrangements) from Vienna in the era examined in this chapter, most of which comprise mainly opera arrangements for piano. An early example is

Steiner & Comp.'s *Musikalisches Damen-Journal*, published in twenty-three volumes between 1818 and 1824. It is clear from this list that Vienna was leading the way in such publications. For example, the musical journal *Amphion* and its follow-on *Der neue Amphion* (from 1824) gave rise to copycat volumes in Stockholm (starting in 1824), Meissen, and Brussels (both commencing in 1825). The enduring significance of transverse flute and csakan repertoires in Vienna is signalled by several extensive Viennese series devoted mainly to opera arrangements for these instruments, notably *Mon Plaisir* (for csakan) and *Der musikalische Gesellschafter* (for flute) – all of this music primarily for men. But most of these series are for piano and voice, and are aimed at women. Some of these volumes are specifically designed to facilitate the performance of opera in the home, such as *Polyhymnia: A Guide for Private Stages and Joy in Singing from the Year 1825* (*Polyhymnia: Ein Taschenbuch für Privatbühnen und Freude des Gesanges auf das Jahr 1825*), which appeared in Dresden, Leipzig, and Vienna in 1825 and in a second edition in 1829; but it is mainly dedicated to Heinrich Marschner's *Singspiel*, *Der Holzdieb*. More wide-ranging and more typical is a journal of excerpts from recent operas for voice and piano: *Journal musical périodique pour le chant avec accompagnement de pianoforte ou répertoire de plus intéressantes compositions extraites des nouveaux opéras* (c.1830).

Czerny took considerable initiative in publishing series of arrangements, such as the extensive *Wiener Musikalisches Pfennig-Magazin für das Piano-Forte allein*, beginning in 1834. The contents of the first fifty volumes of this weekly publication are shown in Figure 6.3. Czerny's own short pieces (rondolettos, waltzes, variations) are interleaved with his arrangements of various works by contemporary and past composers, chiefly of opera. In keeping with the nationalistic sentiments of the time, there are several national airs interleaved as well; but Czerny, with his overall aim of broadening the repertoire of the amateur pianist, and assisting with the challenge of playing at sight, includes a broad repertoire, not just local or Austro-German. An advertisement in the *Pfennig-Magazin*, series two, reads:

There has always been a lack of short, yet brilliant and tasteful piano pieces that can be used to amuse oneself and others in the space of a few minutes. Here, too, the *Pfennig-Magazin* offers a selection that has not been available until now. So many talented students can only make little progress in speed reading and playing at sight because they lack the necessary variety of pieces to be studied.[29]

---

[29] *Wiener musikalisches Pfennig-Magazin für das Piano-Forte allein*, series two (Vienna: Haslinger, 1835), prefatory advertisement.

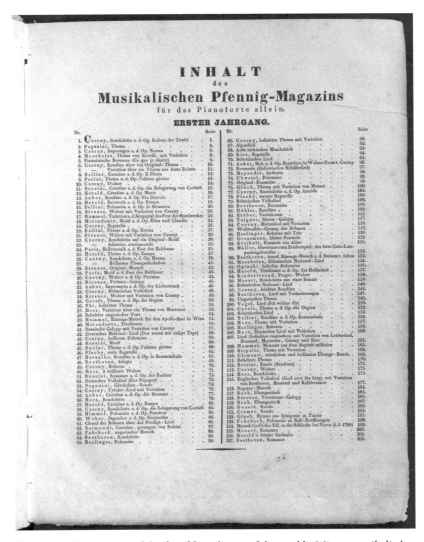

Figure 6.3 The contents of the first fifty volumes of the weekly *Wiener musikalisches Pfennig-Magazin für das Piano-Forte allein*, edited by Czerny, series 2 (Vienna: Haslinger, 1835), dedicated to broadening the repertoire of amateur pianists. Courtesy of Österreichische Nationalbibliothek Musiksammlung, shelf mark MS26.641-4°/1

The advertisement goes on to point out that the volumes are a cheap way to fulfil this function, which is also a great help to the (usually male) teacher.

Opera-specific collections were changing in this era, giving more attention to the arranger as author, and they were increasingly geared to more advanced performers. A prime example is Czerny's *Souvenir théâtral: Collection périodique de fantaisies élégantes sur les motifs les plus favoris des nouveaux opéras*, Op. 747. This opus contains opera paraphrases intended primarily for the virtuoso performer, which he also published in a variety of other series for various publishers.[30] In between these two levels of difficulty (represented by the *Pfennig-Magazin* on the one hand and *Souvenir théâtral* on the other) were many other sets designed to develop the pianist, broadening her skills and repertoire and providing entertainment in the process. There were also various types of arrangement in these series, ranging from the more literal transcription to the paraphrase, with much looser links to the original work.

So much for the *quantity* of opera arrangements that were then available to meet the needs of the plethora of those who had newly taken up the piano, due to increasing access to that instrument. In what follows, I consider the *quality* of these arrangements, to counter the idea that this small-scale art was necessarily small-minded. I discuss quality in terms of cultural value: the way arrangements of opera afforded agency in musical life, particularly that of listeners, arrangers, and performers – the people we tend to ignore when we foreground composers and original works. The emphasis is on several interrelated trends in Diabelli's third catalogue and other Viennese publishing catalogues of the era: the presence of more textless ('ohne Worte') arrangements of opera; the growing variety of individual pieces inspired by opera; and the more frequent explicit reference to arrangers. These are all trends seen in the previous era, but they now become increasingly marked.

Opera 'ohne Worte' and the Agency of the Listener

Items in the *Pfennig-Magazin*, and many other piano arrangements of this era, were issued without words. Sometimes this was announced ('ohne Worte' or 'mit Hinweglassung der Worte') on the title page, or in an advertisement – such as that inside the front cover of the *Pfennig-Magazin*, reproduced in Figure 6.4. More often by the 1830s, the appearance of piano arrangements of opera without the vocal text went unannounced. Originally, piano arrangements of opera were published with text, often both German and Italian for Italian opera, while all other chamber arrangements of opera had, almost invariably, no text. But by

---

[30] Grete Wehmeyer, *Carl Czerny und die Einzelhaft am Klavier, oder, Die Kunst der Fingerfertigkeit und die industrielle Arbeitsideologie* (Zurich: Atlantis, 1983), p. 71.

Figure 6.4 Title page of a collection of operas arranged for piano 'mit Hinweglassung der Worte', published by Haslinger and advertised in Czerny's *Pfennig-Magazin*, series 2 (1835). Courtesy of Österreichische Nationalbibliothek Musiksammlung, shelf mark MS26.641-4°/1A

1811, this dual approach to printing opera arrangements (piano arrangements with text, other arrangements without) could no longer be taken for granted. The presence of text was not usually announced on the title pages of piano arrangements of opera. But now Artaria released *Die Entführung*,

Così, and *Tito* in editions for solo piano 'mit Text'; and in 1814 *Fidelio* 'mit Text'.[31] By 1819, piano arrangements of opera start to appear in Vienna with no text and instead 'mit Hinweglassung der Worte' ('leaving out the words') on the title page. This change did not affect other instrumental arrangements of operas, which remained largely without text, vocal incipits aside. Beethoven's incidental music to *Egmont* arranged in full for string quartet by Alexander Brand for Simrock in 1826 was most unusual in having text underlay. The original string-quartet parts include the original text in all parts so that all the players can follow the vocal cues. The reason for this exceptional provision of text is quite clear: *Egmont* is a melodrama, combining spoken recitation with short pieces of accompanying music; both verbal text and musical text are required for the publication to make sense dramatically and musically. Such publications, together with arrangements with text incipits, and moreover the vocal and theatrical basis of many arrangements for chamber ensembles of this era, might well have inspired Beethoven in adding textual clues and cues in several of his late quartets.

There are many *ohne Worte* arrangements of operas for piano, string quartet, and other ensembles in the early nineteenth century. Most of them were produced mainly for two pragmatic reasons: to provide even more chamber music (especially string quartets) for opera fans and musical amateurs; and to provide a small-scale accompaniment for domestic singing parties. A home opera might be produced, as in the salons Sonnleithner attended, using printed or memorised text. Thus we read in an advertisement from 1800 for *Figaro* arranged for string quartet:

This opera is here completely transcribed into quartets, which combine the double advantage that they 1. satisfy the admirers of Mozart's music as quartets by themselves; but also 2. can be used as accompaniment to the singing instead of the instrumental parts, either alone, or with the piano reduction. Transcribed in this way, the following have already been issued by this publisher: DON JUAN, TITUS, DIE ENTFÜHRUNG and so forth.[32]

What about the new 'ohne Worte' piano arrangements that started to appear around 1819 in Vienna and elsewhere? Andrea Klitzing suggests that Mozart's operas, and *Don Giovanni* in particular, were so well known by this

---

[31] For a full scan of Artaria's 1814 solo piano arrangement of *Fidelio* with text, see www.beethoven.de/en/media/view/4529268960788480/scan/0.

[32] Mozart, *Le nozze di Figaro (Die Hochzeit des Figaro), Opera de W. A. Mozart arrangée en Quatuor à deux Violons, Alto & Violoncelle, Livere I u. II* (Bonn: Simrock, 1800).

time from repeated public and private performance that text or plot reminders were no longer needed.[33] The first *Don Giovanni* piano reduction with the text 'mit Hinweglassung der Worte' appeared in Vienna in 1819 as a lithograph done by Steiner in collaboration with Leidesdorf, and also by Thade Weigl in collaboration with Joseph Huglmann. But 'Hinweglassung der Worte' was also applied to new works like Rossini's operas, which did not have a comparably extensive performance history. The reason for the appearance of these editions is nonetheless probably partly pragmatic, in the same way as the preceding ensemble arrangements of opera. The 'ohne Worte' piano transcriptions could be played as they were published, without words, saving space and money; and the lovers of opera, who were often already familiar with the original, could hear yet more piano music related to works of their favourite composers. Or the arrangements could serve as accompaniment for amateur singers, the libretti being readily available if they were not already known by the singers.

The appearance of 'wordless' piano arrangements of operas at this point may also reflect the increasing publication of scores of various types during the nineteenth century. Starting with the higher-status genres like symphonies and string chamber music, scores began to take over some of the earlier functions of arrangements, especially those of education and *Bildung*. In particular, the publication of scores gave listeners an overview of works that only piano reductions had previously afforded. This potentially freed piano arrangements of operas for other functions. However, complete scores of operas were slow to appear. Instead, editions hint at the authority of the original score without reproducing it in full, using phrases like 'nach der Original-Partitur' (following the original score) frequently on the title pages of piano and other arrangements of operas. In any case, piano-vocal scores still had the upper hand in terms of compactness and convenience. Full scores could be used to read through a work at the piano, by ad hoc piano reduction. But bulky scores, such as opera scores, were better suited to silent study. That the pragmatic use of opera arrangements as a substitute for scores continued into the nineteenth century is suggested by a report in the *Allgemeine Wiener Musik-Zeitung* in 1841:

Piano reductions are useful aids for Capellmeisters, orchestra directors, for singers to facilitate the rehearsal, or the overview as a supplement to a lesser knowledge of the score (they should, of course, never rise to the level of a surrogate for playing the score). Not everyone has the opportunity or talent to acquire the exact knowledge of all musical instruments in relation to their range, treatment, beneficial use, even

---

[33] Klitzing, *Don Giovanni unter Druck*, p. 235.

structure ... or the unconditional skill in transposing, and the instantaneous arrangement for the pianoforte, finally the certain sensualisation of the written tones in the mind, so that one hears them, as it were, with an inner ear.[34]

This reviewer alludes to an advanced music literacy skill – that of silent score reading – which, he recognises, not every amateur will possess. What the writer omits to mention is that performing and listening to these opera arrangements could help develop a related advanced musical skill, one that not only involves the sensualisation of music that is written, but also the creation of music that is not. A reviewer of an 1828 reprint of an anonymous 1807 piano-quartet arrangement of Beethoven's *Eroica* symphony suggests that arrangements could inspire creative listening. This reviewer piles up visual metaphors, suggesting that the onus fell on the listener to 'perform' the work, via imaginative reconstruction and remembrance:

The copy of a giant tableau; a colossal statue on a reduced scale; Caesar's portrait shrunk by the pantograph; an antique bust of Carraran marble made over as a plaster cast. – One is readily satisfied, however, with a half-accurate silhouette when one cannot have the original. Then fantasy begins its sweet play, and all the world certainly knows the beneficial effects of the powers of imagination and recollection.[35]

So the 'wordless' piano arrangements of the time can be understood with reference to the reviewer's idea that the listener essentially 'completes' the work in his or her imagination – as they might mentally fill out a silhouette – exercising a cognitive skill that is far from small-minded.

It might be tempting to consider these 'ohne Worte' arrangements of opera to be a phenomenon of the Romantic movement. Thinkers like E. T. A. Hoffmann espoused purely instrumental music as the most 'romantic' of the arts for its ability to convey drama and because 'its sole subject is the infinite'; that is, it could not and need not be pinned down to explicit meanings conveyed by verbal texts.[36] Certainly the 'ohne Worte' phenomenon of the early-nineteenth-century arrangements is linked to the changing conception of operas as musical works in this era, itself related to the newly privileged status of instrumental music – including the opera

---

[34] Anon., 'Ueber das Arrangieren', *Allgemeine Wiener Musik-Zeitung* 97 (14 August 1841), p. 405.
[35] Anon., *Allgemeiner musikalischer Anzeiger* 1/50 (12 December 1829), p. 199; trans. Wayne M. Senner, Robin Wallace, and William Meredith, *The Critical Reception of Beethoven's Compositions by His German Contemporaries*, 2 vols. (Lincoln, NE: University of Nebraska, 1999–2001), vol. 2 (2001), p. 41.
[36] E. T. A. Hoffmann, 'Recension. . . . Sinfonie . . . No. 5', *Allgemeine musikalische Zeitung* 12/40 (4 July 1810), col. 631.

orchestra. Thomas Christensen notes that the growing number of piano-vocal scores offered in the late eighteenth century was partly due to operas being increasingly conceived as something separable from their original manifestation as staged spectacles performed 'in opera'.[37] This was related to the elevated status of the opera orchestra as a vehicle of the dramatic content from at least Gluck onwards, and definitively with Berlioz.[38]

But it is also significant that these 'ohne Worte' arrangements appeared during a rapid internationalisation of publishing. On the one hand, German publishers tried to advertise arrangements of German music as national cultural products by using German on title pages, especially after the Congress of Vienna, where once French and Italian had often been seen ('senza Parole' and so on). On the other hand, German music publishers sought a more international market with their editions, so that opera piano reductions with no words (as indicated on the title page, or tacitly presumed) catered to a broad European audience, especially after the 1829 formation of the Leipzig cartel of music publishers against reprinting.[39] So the many editions of opera arrangements 'ohne Worte' arguably have more to do with meeting the burgeoning market appropriately than with Romantic idealism.

Souvenir, Fantasia, Paraphrase: The Arranger as Author?

The shifting engagement with operas as musical works at this point is clearest in the increasing diversity of types of piano arrangement of operas. A case in point is Czerny's vast output of arrangements. Fully 30 per cent of them (including 861 opus numbers) are piano arrangements of operas and other compositions.[40] In Diabelli's third catalogue, Czerny's name figures frequently, as both composer and arranger, whereas his work appears only a handful of times in the second catalogue. This new emphasis on arrangers, including 'house arrangers' like Diabelli himself, reflects a change in the nature and status of arrangement during Czerny's era. Early in this period, composers took an active part in the practice of arrangement, producing

---

[37] Christensen, 'Public Music in Private Spaces', pp. 69–71.
[38] On this subject see especially David Charlton, *French Opera 1730–1830: Meaning and Media* (Aldershot: Ashgate, 2000), pp. 1–32.
[39] Klitzing, *Don Giovanni unter Druck*, p. 235.
[40] Franz Pazdirek, *Universal-Handbuch der Musikliteratur aller Zeiten und Völker: Als Nachschlagewerk und Studienquelle der Welt-Musikliteratur eingerichtet und hrsg. von Pazdirek*, vol. 3 (Vienna: Pazdirek, 1904), pp. 661–86.

them in the process of learning the art of composition, and especially developing their thinking about genre. Mendelssohn and Schumann worked at arrangement in their apprentice years. Brahms coordinated the publication of piano arrangements with that of larger ensemble works, and Liszt developed his skills as a transcriber throughout his entire life, extending the techniques of his teacher Czerny and composers such as Mendelssohn and Hummel.[41] In this era, composers also started to produce pieces based much more loosely on other original compositions, so that they could no longer be classed as 'arrangements'; nor were they intended simply 'for the home'.

Czerny was one such composer. He was a well-known pedagogue, as well as a composer and performer, with a constellation of talents possessed by several arrangers of the time, but few to the same level. As a student and friend of Beethoven and teacher of famed virtuoso Liszt, he was well placed to produce piano arrangements of large-scale works for two and four hands, of a wide variety of types, and for a broad range of performers. Czerny reported that Beethoven 'was always completely satisfied' with his (Czerny's) transcriptions and indeed had asked him to amend a piano trio of the second symphony arranged by Ferdinand Ries.[42] Czerny's three-volume *School of Practical Composition* lists many of his arrangements in diverse genres, including masses, operas, symphonies, sonatas, and overtures. Works by more than twenty-seven composers are represented, ranging from historical works by Haydn, Mozart, and Handel to more recently published works of contemporary composers such as Beethoven, Rossini, and Mendelssohn (see Table 6.3 for a selection). A footnote to this list suggests that it is far from complete: 'many other arrangements exist by the talented author of this work [Czerny], of which even the titles have escaped his memory'.[43]

Vocal music is prevalent, and opera most prominent, among Czerny's arrangements. Many of his arrangements are of large-scale music. Czerny, like Liszt, considered the piano to be superior to all other instruments due to its 'fullness and richness of harmony' and for its capacity to accommodate performance of 'nearly all the forms and species of composition customary in music'.[44] He found that the piano player could 'perform grand orchestral pieces with very considerable effect'.[45]

---

[41] Kregor, 'Franz Liszt and the Vocabularies of Transcription', p. 1–2.

[42] Carl Czerny, *On the Proper Performance of all Beethoven's Works for the Piano*, ed. Paul Badura-Skoda (Vienna: Universal Edition, 1970), pp. 9 and 14. Evidence to corroborate Beethoven's reported opinion of Czerny's arrangements has not been found.

[43] Carl Czerny, *School of Practical Composition* vol. I (London: R. Cocks & Co., 1830), xiv.

[44] Czerny, *School of Practical Composition* vol. I, p. 3; Czerny, *Complete Theoretical and Practical Piano Forte School*, vol. III (London: R. Cocks & Co., 1839), p. 104.

[45] Czerny, *Complete Theoretical and Practical Piano Forte School*, vol. III, p. 104.

Table 6.3 A selection of Czerny's arrangements by publication date, showing the range of genres he covered in his career

Composer	Work	Genre	Original publication date	Transcription publication date[*]
Beethoven	*Adelaide*, Opus 46	Lied	1802	1829
	Eroica Symphony, Opus 55	Symphony	1804	c.1836
	Pastoral Symphony, Opus 68	Symphony	1808	1836
	Symphony No. 7, Opus 92	Symphony	1816	c.1831
	Trio No. 6, Opus 97	Piano Trio	1811	1838
George Frideric Handel	'For Unto Us a Child is Born' from *Messiah*	Oratorio	1741	1840
Jan Kalivoda	Symphony No. 1, Opus 7	Symphony	1827	1853
Felix Mendelssohn	Piano Concerto No. 2, Opus 40	Concerto	1837	1839
Mozart	Overture to *Le nozze di Figaro*	Opera	1786	1844
	Requiem	Mass	1790s	c.1830
Rossini	*Stabat Mater*	Sacred	1841	1844
	Overture to *Semiramide*	Opera	1823	1845
Spohr	Symphony No. 4, Opus 86	Symphony	1834	1835
	Symphony No. 6, Opus 116	Symphony	1839	c.1842

[*] The exact publication date of some transcriptions is unknown, as the scores do not always contain this information. The publisher's plate number provides an estimated publication date, but there may be a one- to three-year difference between presumed and actual publication dates.

The critics were divided on Czerny's arrangements. On the one hand, some found that they tried to remain too close to their originals, resulting in too much high-register playing for the primo in particular, and technical difficulties in general. So, for example, John Sullivan Dwight found that 'Czerny always brings in play the entire surface of the keyboard, from the lowest to the highest tones; hence there is an end to all alternation of colouring; a continual screaming discant tortures the nerve of hearing, besides falsely representing the orchestral effect'.[46] Other critics praised them as arrangements that retained the voice-leading and sonority of their originals as far as possible.[47]

However, by no means all of Czerny's arrangements are literal transcriptions. Although such transcriptions are among the longest of his arrangements, the bulk are works that take their inspiration from one or more operas, developing themes and motifs in a new form – variations,

---
[46] John Sullivan Dwight, *Dwight's Journal of Music* 4/6 (1853), p. 41.
[47] See Christensen, 'Four-Hand Piano Transcription', pp. 271–2.

rondolettos, potpourris, paraphrases, and so forth. What links these diverse compositions is their connection to opera – or rather Czerny's connection to opera. Chanyapong Thongsawang has carried out an extensive survey of Czerny's many opera paraphrases, connecting them to Czerny's love of improvisation as well as his passion for opera.[48] Of all composer-pianists of the era, Czerny produced this kind of work in the greatest numbers. In these paraphrases, far from slavishly transcribing operas to help disseminate them, or to link his name with greater stars, he was actively engaging with operas as a composer, 're-reading' them as a performer.

Michael Heinemann notes the great difference between paraphrasing a movement or part of a movement and arranging an entire work. The former allows the assertion of oneself as author much more prominently than the other kinds of arrangement, because it enjoins much less concern with representation of the original and much more emphasis on imagination or fantasy based on a few ideas from the original.[49] Such an assertion is implied by many of the fantasies in *Souvenir théâtral*, Op. 247, Czerny's most extensive series of opera paraphrases. The works in this opus often appear in sets of three – each fantasia being devoted to a specified act. Rather than moving through the main themes in an orderly fashion, Czerny seems to browse a given act like a bee in a bed of mixed flowers – pulling out choice themes for extended improvisatory development in each fantasia. Like the eighteenth-century fantasia, the works of *Souvenir théâtral* might be taken to expose the thoughts and feelings of the composer, here in response to the given opera.[50]

By way of example of this 'browsing', we can consider the third fantasia 'sur les motifs favoris' of Bellini's *La Sonnambula* in *Souvenir théâtral* (Example 6.2). The opening of the opera is condensed at the level of bar and phrase so that a fifty-four-bar introduction is reduced to twelve bars, after which the chorus is reproduced using a chordal right hand and repeated notes with sustained bass in the left. Czerny then creates his own high-register segue into the Allegro risoluto (now molto Allegro quasi Presto), then thickens the texture again with octaves to produce the chorus. What follows is similar in procedure: textures are

---

[48] Chanyapong Thongsawang, 'Opernparaphrasen für Klavier in der ersten Hälfte des 19. Jahrhunderts als Quellen für die Aufführungspraxis', PhD diss. (Universität für Musik und darstellende Kunst, Vienna, 2015), especially pp. 27–49.
[49] Michael Heinemann, 'Der Bearbeiter als Autor: Zu Franz Liszts Opernparaphrasen', in Hinrichsen and Pietschmann (eds.), *Jenseits der Bühne*, p. 89.
[50] See Annette Richards, *The Free Fantasia and the Musical Picturesque* (New York, NY: Cambridge University Press, 2000), pp. 134–5.

Example 6.2 Excerpt from Bellini's *La Sonnambula* showing 'browsing' from the score: (a) Czerny's *Fantaisie 3ième sur les motifs favoris de l'op[é]ra Sonnambula de Bellini* for solo piano, bars 1–32 (Vienna: Diabelli, 1833)

recreated for piano, cuts take us to the main moments, improvisation-like links are created, and keys are changed to navigate a new auditory pathway through the work. The result is for advanced performers, to be sure, and could be defined as a showpiece. But the performers will glean from Czerny's work some tips for creating their own piano reductions at sight from a score, using cuts and similar pianistic tricks; and both performer and listener will gain an overview (partly Czerny's) of the work.

210   Opera Arrangements in Czerny's Vienna

Example 6.2 (b) full orchestral score, bars 1–7 and 55–62

Example 6.2b (cont.)

A token of an event or experience: this meaning of the word souvenir dates from the late eighteenth century. It is relevant to the *Souvenir théâtral* and indeed the rest of Czerny's opera paraphrases and arrangements, which were closely related to actual productions. As Wehmeyer has shown, the history of Czerny's opera paraphrases and other opera arrangements is a history of the most popular events and experiences in Vienna's theatres in his day.[51] After commemorating the Rossini rage, Czerny turned more to French opera, including numerous arrangements from works by Meyerbeer, Auber, Boieldieu, and Harold. Following the

---

[51] Wehmeyer, *Carl Czerny und die Einzelhaft am Klavier*, pp. 40–53.

German rage for British libretti he wrote fantasias inspired by Scott's *Guy Mannering*; and during the wave of German nationalism he turned to Spohr, Weber, and Beethoven.

It is tempting to understand these arrangements, following Peter Szendy, as 'listenings' – allowing us to 'eavesdrop' on the way Czerny heard the works in question. Szendy finds that arrangers like Schumann and Liszt are 'remarkable listeners who sign and write down their listenings'.[52] In Szendy's understanding, if we listened to Liszt's *Fantasy on Themes from Mozart's Figaro and Don Giovanni* (*Fantasie über Themen aus Mozarts Figaro und Don Giovanni*, 1842) we would gain insight into how Liszt actually heard those Mozart operas. Regarding Liszt's opera paraphrases, Heinemann likewise places the emphasis on Liszt as author, observing the way arrangement allowed him to assert his own authorial voice: 'Only the confrontation with the work of a third party enables Liszt to formulate his own artistic statements; only in the mode of arrangement – through the mediation of a third party – does the constitution of an aesthetic subject occur, which in turn is inseparable from the empirical person'.[53]

But these arguments, which foreground the arranger as author, risk perpetrating the intentional fallacy (judging an artwork by the intent or purpose of its artist, generally agreed to be ultimately unknowable), and also raise the problem of treating listening as historically invariant. The 'listenings' that Liszt et al. offer us through their arrangements are not straightforwardly or certainly ways of conveying how they listened. They may also be ways of telling us what to listen for, or how we ought to listen to the works in question; their functions can be normative, clarifying, or corrective, and they certainly play a role in canon formation.[54] Arrangements with a 'corrective' function might be understood as resembling certain images by visual artists of the mid–to-late nineteenth century: by depicting silent, reverent listening, these images implicitly show us *how to* listen, rather than (or as well as) how the artists or their subjects listen.[55] Czerny's Bellini arrangements might take us closer to Czerny's own performance practices, or to the way Czerny wanted us to perform Bellini. They might also take us to his own 'hearing' of Bellini (Szendy would say so), or to the way Czerny wanted us to hear Bellini. Indeed, some of the arrangements of the mid-nineteenth century might be precisely geared to preparing listeners to listen attentively to 'Masterworks' in the concert hall.

---

[52] Peter Szendy, *Listen: A History of Our Ears*, trans. Charlotte Mandell, foreword by Jean-Luc Nancy (New York, NY: Fordham University Press, 2008), p. 39.
[53] Heinemann, 'Der Bearbeiter als Autor', pp. 88–9.   [54] Szendy, *Listen*, p. 43.
[55] See my *Cultivating String Quartets*, pp. 190–4.

In this sense, such arrangements align with and reinforce the emerging concept of the musical work in the nineteenth century.

These more instructive, pedagogical, or developmental understandings of arrangement seem especially germane to Czerny. In the making of his many and various arrangements, there is an implicit concern not just with furthering his own agency, but also with promoting the 'voices' of other performers, and developing budding performers. The promotion of other performers via arrangement was already integral to the culture of arrangements, showing that composers recognised that paraphrases were not merely derivative but, in a sense, 'authored' works in their own right. For example, Czerny produced a four-hand piano arrangement of Thalberg's *Fantasie* on Mozart's *Don Giovanni*, Op. 14 (Vienna: Haslinger, 1835), so that this 'public' showpiece based on the opera could be enjoyed at the piano in the home; and Giulio Regondi did the same, later in the century, this time for guitar.[56] Several of Czerny's works based on operas extend not only the popularity of particular works but also that of particular singers – especially Italian opera and Italian singers. So, for example, in 1822 Steiner and Haslinger released Czerny's Op. 25 for four hands at the piano, which was a four-hand version of a favourite cavatina from Rossini's *Corradino* (*Matilde di Shabran*), as sung by Giacomo David. And in 1829 Diabelli released Czerny's Op. 196 for solo piano, *Introduction, Variations and Rondo for piano forte on the popular cavatine by Giuseppe Nicolini (Or che son vicino a te) sung by Mad. [Giuditta] Pasta in Vienna at the performance of the opera Tancredi* (*Introduction, Variations et Rondo für piano forte über die beliebte Cavatine v. Giuseppe Nicolini [Or che son vicino a te] gesungen von Mad. Pasta in Wien bei Vorstellung der Oper: Tancred*). As Example 6.3 shows, in such arrangements, particular vocal ornaments are transcribed for the piano.

Czerny's opera arrangements and paraphrases can be seen as pedagogical and developmental in similar ways to Czerny's better-known performance treatises and etudes. These publications all share a general concern with not only how to listen, but also how and what to perform. His series *Le goût moderne* is one instance among many of Czerny's conviction that modern opera could be important for forming contemporary taste (Figure 6.5). His titles often refer to taste, popularity, and

---

[56] Giulio Regondi, *Fantasie über 'Don Giovanni' nach Sigismund Thalberg: Für Gitarre/Solo on Don Giovanni Partly from Thalberg's Piece: For Guitar*, ed. Stefan R. Hackl (Vienna: Doblinger, 2008).

Example 6.3 Czerny Op. 196 for solo piano: *Introduction, Variations et Rondo für piano forte über die beliebte Cavatine v. Giuseppe Nicolini (Or che son vicino a te) gesungen von Mad. Pasta in Wien bei Vorstellung der Oper: Tancred* (Vienna: Diabelli, 1829), showing end of Introduction, with the singer's ornamental embellishments; and Allegretto grazioso, bars 1–18

choice: Czerny was positioning himself as the guiding hand, steering his pupils to the 'honey' (the choicest themes from the best operas), and also creating multiple access routes and scaffolding his pupils' learning in the

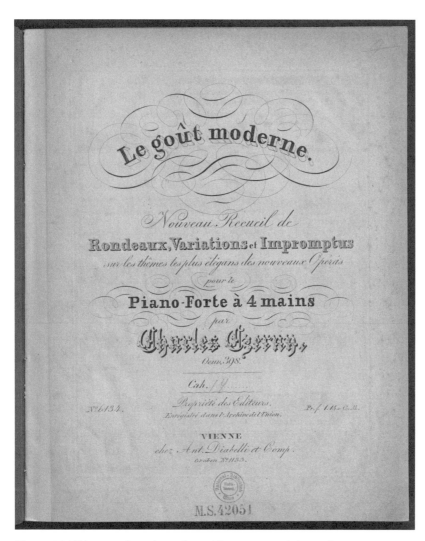

Figure 6.5 Title page, *Le goût moderne: Nouveau recueil de rondeaux, variations et impromptus sur les thêmes les plus élégants des nouveaux opéras,* for piano four hands, Op. 398 (a periodical publication from Diabelli, 1830s). Courtesy of Österreichische Nationalbibliothek Musiksammlung, shelf mark L18. Kaldeck 42051–4°/1

process. He frequently arranged a given opera in more than one piano version. The title page of Op. 196, for instance, bears the note that 'the same variations are also available for piano four-hands'. The following

Czerny piano works based on Bellini's *Norma* (1831) appeared with Haslinger and Diabelli in the years 1833–5:

Souvenir théâtral: Fantaisie 1ière sur les motifs favoris de l'opéra: Norma di Bellini: oeuvre 247 (also Fantasies Nos. 2 and 3). Diabelli & Co., 1833–4

Variations brillantes pour un piano-forte à 6 mains concertantes sur un thème de l'opéra Norma, de V. Bellini composées par Charles Czerny. Oeuvre 297. Diabelli, 1835

Thema aus der Oper: Norma von Bellini, mit Variation von C. Czerny. Haslinger, 1835

Impromptu über ein Motif aus der Oper: Norma, von Bellini. Componirt von C. Czerny. Haslinger, 1835

Rondoletto auf ein Thema aus der Oper: Norma, von Bellini. Haslinger, 1835

With the exception of Op. 297, each version of *Norma* listed here is for piano solo. Czerny also produced more than one type of arrangement in terms of instrumentation for particular works. His Op. 160, *Introduction, variations and polacca in the brilliant style for fortepiano on the favourite cavatina: (Tu vedrai la sventurata) sung by Mr [Giovanni Battista] Rubini in the opera: Il Pirata, by Mr Bellini* (*Introduction, variations et polacca dans le style brillant pour le piano-forte sur la cavatine favorite: [Tu vedrai la sventurata] chantée par Mr Rubini dans l'opéra: Il Pirata, de Mr Bellini*), appeared in versions for solo piano and for string quartet with four-hand piano (Diabelli, 1828).

This concern with accessibility extends to careful layout to facilitate page turns; tempo instructions; fingering; octave transposition; and numerous performance indications such as dynamics and articulation (see Example 6.3, for instance). The pieces in *Le goût moderne* might seem tricky until one realises that the more exacting primo part could be performed by a teacher or more experienced player, and so might help with training. Such is the case with quite a few of Czerny's four-hand piano arrangements, for instance the *Variations Brillant* on *Il crociato in Egitto* by Meyerbeer (1826), which contains more complexity in the right hand, including very high registers and the more 'brilliant' sections (Example 6.4). So among his paraphrases and arrangements of operas we find not only a clear intention to appeal to burgeoning dilettantes, but also a dedicated effort to develop those same pianists into advanced performers, capable of performing his more exacting paraphrases such as those in *Souvenir théâtral*; or, for example, another arrangement of Meyerbeer, from *Robert le diable* (1832; Example 6.5). Czerny asks the pianist to reproduce the noisy sound world that typified French opera

Example 6.4 Czerny's four-hand piano arrangement of the *Variations Brillant* on *Il crociato in Egitto* by Meyerbeer, Op. 125 (Vienna: Haslinger, 1826), bars 1–16

from this time (as it did Rossini's music), using tremolos, octaves, and accents.[57]

Arrangements consciously addressed to the learner are manifold. This trend continues after the heyday of Rossini. Czerny's arrangement of Bellini's *Norma* in *Bibliothek für die Jugend* makes an apt comparison to his more advanced arrangement of the same in *Souvenir théâtral*

---

[57] On this subject see Benjamin Walton, *Rossini in Restoration Paris: The Sound of Modern Life* (Cambridge: Cambridge University Press, 2007), especially pp. 148–9 and 172 (regarding Rossini and noisiness).

Example 6.4 (cont.)

(see Example 6.6). The advertisement for Haslinger's two series *Musicalische Jugend-Bibliotheque* and *Bibliothek für die Jugend* contains the line 'For the pianoforte with and without accompaniment and for four hands' ('für das Pianoforte mit und ohne Begleitung und zu 4 Händen'), suggesting a pedagogical purpose for the four-hand repertoire. Czerny's pianoforte treatise, too, hints at the intended performers of these arrangements. It indicates that, from his perspective at least, the average pianist of at least one year of training should be fully equipped to enjoy playing material of some complexity. His *Complete Theoretical & Technical School*, Op. 500 (1839) introduces embellishments, arpeggios,

Example 6.5 From Czerny's *Souvenir théâtral*, Fantaisie (No. 1) on Meyerbeer's *Robert le diable* (Vienna: Diabelli, 1832), bars 1–32

and crossing of hands in the last few chapters of the first volume.[58] His *Letters to a Young Lady, on the Art of Playing the Pianoforte* (1838; first published in Vienna *c.*1830) encouraged the student to undertake up to three hours of piano per day, including scales, technical exercises, previously learnt repertoire, and the study of new pieces.[59] This

---

[58] Published in Vienna as *Vollständige theoretisch-practische Pianoforte-Schule von dem ersten Anfange bis zur höchsten Ausbildung fortschreitend, und mit allen nöthigen, zu diesem Zwecke eigends componirten zahlreichen Beispielen, in 3 Theilen* (Diabelli & Comp., 1839).
[59] Czerny, *Briefe über den Unterricht auf dem Pianoforte*, p. 9.

Example 6.6 Opening of Czerny's arrangements of Bellini's *Norma* in: (a) *Bibliothek für die Jugend* (Vienna: Haslinger, c.1835), bars 1–21

significant time commitment would have encouraged the acquisition of a high level of skill, enabling the performance of his more difficult arrangements.

Bourgeoise Domesticity and Female Agency

One could argue that two principal types of arrangement emerged in the early-to-mid nineteenth century: various 'public' arrangement types, such as those of Clementi, Czerny, Hummel, and Liszt, primarily for performance by virtuosi; and various 'private' types, for private entertainment and

Example 6.6 (b) Souvenir théâtral (Vienna: Diabelli, 1833), bars 1–21

education. The public ones are usually signed and dedicated to the virtuoso performer-composers who made them; the private ones are often – but certainly not always – anonymous, and designed specifically for amateurs. This typology comes with the caveat that history is more complex than such a tidy split allows. At any point in the history charted in this book, various types of arrangement co-existed; contexts of performance varied on a spectrum between the truly private and the fully public; and performers of varying levels of skill moved between contexts.

What we can say is that anonymous arrangements, and those by arrangers whose names are unknown or lesser known today, have been much less privileged, especially when they are seen to have been mass-produced. Szendy, who discusses at length a concept of 'Romantic arrangements' based on those of Schumann and Liszt, has nothing to say about the many others from this era; and Christensen tends to dismiss them, noting 'the ubiquitous parlour genres one would expect: Waltzes, galops, marches, fantasies, variations … Potpourris of opera tunes and the like', but also 'a large number of transcriptions of more sober concert repertory', apparently of greater value.[60] The bulk of this repertoire seems to amount to easy works for a mass market, as Waissenberger would have it: 'Clearly this music proved to be ideally suited for domestic music-making practice, and the publishers knew how to appeal to the growing number of music-making dilettantes and to encourage them to buy easily playable music'.[61] Scholars typically have little time for more 'trivial' categories of arrangement – notably those based on opera.

But Czerny's numerous arrangements, in particular, mess up any tidy categorisation of arrangements into 'high' and 'low' art, and also confound the equation of industry and high productivity with low quality. In general, they promoted the agency of the listener, encouraging creativity. More specifically, they show Czerny to be an arranger who was concerned to develop pianists of various skill levels as agents within Viennese and European musical culture. To be sure, there are the more public-facing paraphrases, including those for piano and orchestra, clearly designed for high-level performers and concert settings; and fantasies like those in *Souvenir théâtral*, which, one might argue, foreground his authorship – and thus his own 'take' on a given opera. But Czerny, the leader among the substantial and largely male population of piano teachers, was promoting the careers of the substantial and largely female population of pianists in Vienna – sampled by Ziegler in his *Addressen-Buch* of 1823. Of course, Czerny himself did well out of the industry of arrangement, in terms of reputation and finances. This, with his teaching career, enabled him to move literally and figuratively from the periphery of Vienna to near the centre. In the process, though, he was pulling amateur pianists from the periphery of the home towards the new centre of musical life, the concert hall.

---

[60] Christensen, 'Four-Hand Piano Transcriptions', p. 257.
[61] Waissenberger, *Wien 1815–1848*, p. 261.

But wait! Was not the home the 'true' centre of life in this era? And were not women supposed to be at home, making the home, raising the children, and so enabling the public-sphere discourse of men, which would come about naturally from this haven of domestic bliss? This is the ideology of *Biedermeier* domesticity, which arose during this period and was consolidated in the later nineteenth century by writers such as Wilhelm Heinrich Riehl (notably in *Die Familie*, 1861), and confirmed by Jürgen Habermas.[62] As Solie points out, this was the time in which a new bourgeois culture was emerging more generally, with the home as the ideological wellspring of the public world.[63] A coherent system of values emerged, associated with domesticity and with the activities, including the music, found in the home. This ideology is transmitted and reproduced in paintings of bourgeois interiors of the time like Sebastian Gutzwiller's *Das Basler Familienkonzert* (1849; Figure 6.6) and descriptions of bourgeois living, such as the following retrospective account from Karl Kobold (more a product than vehicle of the ideology):

> Of course, in accordance with the musical spirit of the time, the piano of cherry wood was not missing, or the black alabaster timepiece, whose solemn tick reminded you of the impermanence of all earthly things. There was the dainty work-table, with work-basket of finest china, and there, too, was the big easy chair to rest in and spin dreams. From the walls laughed the portraits of handsome young men, with a soupçon of romance, and pretty girls' heads and beautiful women by Daffinger, Kriehuber, Reider, Teltscher. Black silhouettes looked out dreamily from cherry-wood frames, half-length oils breathed parental dignity, and above the canopy reigned also in oils the likeness of the worthy patriarch of the kingdom, Emperor Franz.[64]

This interior space was to be non-economic, non-political, and a place of original inner reflections and insights, gained, for example, while sitting in the comfy chair. It was a space graced and nurtured by women, from which (male) public-sphere discourse was thought to emerge. Although it is described in terms of relaxed happiness in such retrospective accounts and represented in pictures, there was a darker side to this cosy image: female confinement, isolation, and suppression in particular. A closed family circle is described, with a highly restricted sphere of operation for women: they look beautiful, play the piano (but not too well or too much),

---

[62] Habermas, *The Structural Transformation of the Public Sphere*, p. 45.
[63] Solie, 'Biedermeier Domesticity and the Schubert Circle', especially p. 130.
[64] Karl Kobold quoted in Charles Osborne, *Schubert and His Vienna* (London: Weidenfeld and Nicolson, 1985), p. 135 (my italics). Solie quotes a similar account, 'Biedermeier Domesticity and the Schubert Circle', pp. 128–9.

Figure 6.6 Sebastian Gutzwiller's *Basler Familienkonzert* (1849). Courtesy of Alamy Images

and raise the children to be moral citizens. Men engage in leisure activities as well; but when they are present in the home, they are there to moderate and govern; as, incidentally, does the watchful Emperor Franz, from his portrait or engraving. External forces are 'tamed' and 'neutralised'; even time is carefully contained and measured by the encased clock. And although there is a reverence for everyday products of industrial manufacture, including the piano, they are prettified, moderated, and scaled-down to suit women; women are present only insofar as they reinforce homemaking and the domestic economy.

Extrapolating from this construction of *Biedermeier* domesticity, *Biedermeier* music would ideally have specific characteristics and functions. It would reinforce women's roles as wives and mothers; demonstrate a reverence for industry, but on a modest, curtailed scale; and tame external forces to maintain a calm, happy, morally uplifting household. Ideally it would be 'absolute' music – pure, original, graceful, harmonising, and ennobling; but not Romantic music, in the sense of inspiring infinite longing, via overwhelming, uncontained aesthetic experiences like the sublime.[65] Its aesthetics were epitomised, rather, by the beautiful or the picturesque, as in Josef Kriehuber's landscapes or the portraits of Wilhelm August Rieder (himself shown in Figure 6.7, another bourgeoise interior, this time a Schubert soirée, discussed at the end of this chapter).

The piano-arrangement repertoire of this era both reinforced and departed from this ideology of *Biedermeier* domesticity. If the *Biedermeier* domestic oasis formed a comforting bulwark of fantasy against a frightening political atmosphere in this Age of Metternich, as Solie has it, then piano arrangements to an extent fostered this fantasy.[66] At least some arrangements, such as those found in the *Pfennig-Magazin*, provided easy music suited for female recreation and for demonstrating just the right amount of skill and industry (so, not too much). External forces, sublime and otherwise disturbingly noisy, might

Figure 6.7 Moritz von Schwind, Wilhelm August Rieder, and Anna Hönig (left, right, below), shown in a circle of Schubert friends at a 'Schubertiade'. Sketch by Moritz von Schwind (1868), from memory. Courtesy of Alamy Images

---

[65] See also Virgil Nemoianu's construction of *Biedermeier* in opposition to Romanticism, in *The Taming of Romanticism: European Literature and the Age of Biedermeier* (Cambridge, MA: Harvard University Press, 1984).
[66] Solie, 'Biedermeier Domesticity and the Schubert Circle', p. 129.

be 'tamed' – removed or 'domesticated', with a staged thunderclap becoming, for example, a tremolo bass. An Austrian writer of 1841 was well aware of the possible deficiencies of contemporary piano-vocal scores when it came to experiencing contemporary operatic works:

There are so many examples where the effect can only be obtained by the instruments for which it was written … Consider, too, the oboe solo in Lindpaintner's overture to Vampyr, the English horn solo in Rossini's William Tell, the frightening effect of the horns, tremolo violins, and violas with pizzicato basses in the second act finale of Weber's Der Freischütz[.][67]

In arrangements, operas were de-contextualised and de-politicised by removing the text, and, increasingly, by excerpting numbers and producing fantasias on themes. Further, many piano arrangements were created for performance by women (also potentially children, who might be taught by their mothers) or couples (duetting pairs) in the home, without need of others, reinforcing the models of the closed family grouping and female roles. And these arrangements were dedicated to the upright piano, *the* domestic instrument and potent symbol of industrialisation tamed and fitted for the home (simple and functional design in cherrywood; seat with tidy music storage).

But the same writer also acknowledged several important benefits of arrangements, including entertainment, and of making people 'more receptive to the beauties and the value of art'; which art can be 'masterpieces of our older as well as newer artistic heroes'.[68] For these purposes – entertainment, education, and canon formation – the writer found piano arrangements the best. Here he uses the metaphor of the silhouette compared with the fully realised painting:

Moreover, even these piano excerpts remain purely a silhouette of the tone painting itself, but the grandeur, sublimity, and beauty of it are less impaired, since the fortepiano, as the most extensive instrument, corresponds at least in part to the tonal range of all musical instruments that are common in our orchestra, and is thus also capable of transmitting more complicated tonal masses.[69]

Introducing grandeur, sublimity, and complexity into the bourgeoise home, the piano arrangement could subtly disrupt the idea of *Biedermeier* domesticity, perhaps especially with regard to the confined place it described for women. The Viennese fortepianos of the day were often wing-shaped rather than square and compact in design; could

---

[67] Anon., 'Ueber das Arrangieren', *Allgemeine Wiener Musik-Zeitung* 98 (17 August 1841), p. 411.
[68] Anon., 'Ueber das Arrangieren', *Allgemeine Wiener Musik-Zeitung* 97 (14 August 1841), p. 405.
[69] Ibid.

possess pedals for producing loud and exotic effects; and boasted at least triple stringing in the bass for added power. The female performer, if she undertook her three hours of practice per day, played Czerny's etudes, and worked diligently at new repertoire presented weekly in the *Pfennig-Magazin*, would soon be in possession of a fine technique and extensive repertoire. She might well upstage her male counterpart, playing the screaming high-register primo, or engage in risqué hand-crossing with her partner in a four-hand Czerny arrangement.

The Viennese salon, as we have seen, formed an important middle ground between the domestic drawing room and the public stage, in which such budding performers could extend themselves and gain formative experience in a supportive environment. The piano arrangement served to extend not only the performer's technique and repertoire but also the listener's powers of imagination, thanks to its silhouette-like powers of evocation. So piano arrangements might help women to escape the confines of the parlour, by helping them to upskill for performances in public. But even when this was not the upshot, piano arrangements at least promoted creative listening, and so equipped amateur performers and listeners for imaginative travel. Opera arrangements in general, and Viennese salons in particular, were helping to develop listening and performance practices vital to the formation of concert life around this time.

Women were key agents in this process. A final example brings together female agency, opera arrangements, the Viennese salon, and cultures of listening; and by pure coincidence it also returns to honey (Hönig). Figure 6.7 shows a 'Schubertiade' sketched by Romantic artist and Schubert friend Moritz von Schwind in 1868, from memory. This sketch is rather like an opera paraphrase, in that von Schwind has embellished on the theme of 'Schubert's artistic friends and sources of inspiration'. It is a retrospective composite bringing together people who were never actually present all at the same time.[70] Drawing attention to the illustrious male artist-friends of Schubert on the right, Maurice Brown finds:

If one considers what, as well as who, these people were, it is amusing to find that [Schwind] has placed not necessarily kindred minds, but kindred arts of interest

---

[70] Poet and friend of Schubert Johann Senn, for example, had been banished by the authorities before Schwind met Schubert, but is nonetheless shown here. See John M. Gingerich, '"Those of us who found our life in art": The Second-Generation Romanticism of the Schubert-Schober Circle, 1820–1825', in Christopher H. Gibbs and Morten Solvik (eds.), *Franz Schubert and His World* (Princeton, NJ: Princeton University Press, 2014), p. 68.

Example 6.7 Overture to *Alphonso und Estrella* for piano four hands, created for and dedicated to Anna Hönig by Franz Schubert, Op. 52 (Vienna: Sauer and Leidesdorf, 1826), bars 1–23[*]

[*] A scan, including title page, is available via ÖNB Digital: https://onb.digital/result/10030D6C.

Example 6.7 (cont.)

together. This hardly applies to the five ladies on the right of the piano: the only factor in common there is that all were wives of various Schubertians, but their group enshrines the grace and charm of the occasion.[71]

Solie takes exception: 'Surely Brown underestimates the representational importance of the presence of the women, not to mention the probability that their passionate attachment to the music was every bit as strong as their husbands' was.'[72] Indeed the five women are arguably the centre of attention here, as the focus of the composition, and not just for their charm and grace, but also for their attentive listening.

---

[71] Maurice J. E. Brown, 'Schwind's "Schubert-Abend bei Josef von Spaun"', in *Essays on Schubert* (London: Macmillan, 1966), p. 165. The details of the picture are elaborated in Otto Erich Deutsch, *Schubert: A Documentary Biography* (London: Dent, 1946), p. 784 (Plate 31).
[72] Solie, 'Biedermeier Domesticity and the Schubert Circle', p. 141.

These women's absorption in the music appears similar to the rapt attention of the Fröhlich sisters, who are central and prominent in Figure 4.1. Among the prominent women in Figure 6.7 is Anna ('Nettel') Hönig (1803–88; the third woman from the right), who was once engaged to von Schwind and later married one of Schubert's friends, officer Ferdinand Mayerhofer von Grünbühel. Schubert dedicated his four-hand piano arrangement of his *Alfonso und Estrella* to Hönig, who was an accomplished pianist, as can be seen from this score (Example 6.7). She frequently took part in the *Schubertiaden*.[73] Directly opposite Hönig, shown in profile in the lower left, is Eleonore Stohl, an outstanding Schubertian singer who was not born until 1832, after Schubert's death. She sang with pianist and Schubert friend Josef Gahy, and they played four-hand piano together. These women had most influence in private and semi-private music-making, but their example helped other women to navigate the reverse route to that of arrangements, from the home, through the salon, and onto the stage.

---

[73] The libretto is by poet and librettist Franz Adolph Friedrich Schober, shown seated behind Theresa Hönig (seated to the right of Anna Hönig), chatting to Justina von Bruchmann, sister of poet Franz von Bruchmann.

Bibliography

Adams, Sarah Jane. 'Quartets and Quintets for Mixed Groups of Winds and Strings: Mozart and His Contemporaries in Vienna, c. 1780–c. 1800.' PhD diss. (Cornell University, 1994).
Allgemeine musikalische Zeitung (1798–1882).
Allgemeine musikalische Zeitung mit besonderer Rücksicht auf den österreichischen Kaiserstaat (1817–1824).
Allgemeine Theaterzeitung und Unterhaltungsblatt für Freunde der Kunst, Literatur und des geselligen Lebens [formerly: *Wiener Theater-Zeitung*] (1806–60).
Allgemeiner musikalischer Anzeiger (1829–40).
Anderson, Emily (ed.), *The Letters of Mozart and His Family*, 3rd ed. (London: Macmillan, 1985).
Annalen der österreichischen Literatur (1802–12).
Anon. 'Über Wiener Theaterwesen'. *Berlinische Musikalische Zeitung* 13 (4 May 1793), p. 51.
Anon. 'Ueber das Arrangieren'. *Allgemeine Wiener Musik-Zeitung* 97–8 (14 and 17 August 1841), pp. 405 and 410–11.
Anon. 'Wien'. *Kurpfalzbaierisches Wochenblatt* 2/15 (11 April 1801), cols. 243–5.
Applegate, Celia. *Bach in Berlin: Nation and Culture in Mendelssohn's Revival of the St. Matthew Passion* (Ithaca, NY: Cornell University Press, 2005).
Bauer, Wilhelm A., Otto Erich Deutsch, Joseph Heinz Eibl, and Ulrich Konrad (eds.), *Mozart: Briefe und Aufzeichnungen; Gesamtausgabe*, 8 vols. (Kassel: Bärenreiter, 1962–2005).
Beck, Dagmar, Grita Herre, and Karl-Heinz Köhler (eds.), *Ludwig van Beethovens Konversationshefte*, 11 vols. (Leipzig: Deutscher Verlag für Musik, 1968–2001).
Beer, Axel. 'Die Oper daheim: Variationen als Rezeptionsform'. In Hans-Joachim Hinrichsen and Klaus Pietschmann (eds.), *Jenseits der Bühne: Bearbeitungs- und Rezeptionsformen der Oper im 19. und 20. Jahrhundert* (Kassel: Bärenreiter, 2011), pp. 37–47.
Beethoven, Ludwig van. *Wellingtons Sieg* [arranged for Turkish music ensemble] (Vienna: Steiner & Co., 1816).
Bernard, Paul P. *From the Enlightenment to the Police State: The Public Life of Johann Anton Pergen* (Chicago, IL: University of Illinois Press, 1991).
Biba, Otto. 'Public and Semi-Public Concerts: Outlines of a Typical "Biedermeier" Phenomenon in Viennese Music History'. In Robert Pichl, Clifford

A. Bernd, and Margarete Wagner (eds.), *The Other Vienna: The Culture of Biedermeier Austria* (Vienna: Lehner, 2002), pp. 257–70.

'Schubert's Position in Viennese Musical Life'. *19th Century Music* 3/2 (1979), pp. 106–13.

Bittrich, Burkhard. 'Österreichische Züge am Beispiel der Caroline Pichler'. In Karl Konrad Polheim (ed.), *Literatur aus Österreich, österreichische Literatur: Ein Bonner Symposion* (Bonn: Bouvier, 1981), pp. 167–89.

Bohlman, Philip V. 'Translating Herder Translating: Cultural Translation and the Making of Modernity'. In Jane F. Fulcher (ed.), *The Oxford Handbook of the New Cultural History of Music* (Oxford: Oxford University Press, 2011), pp. 501–22.

Botstein, Leon. 'The Patrons and Publics of the Quartets: Music, Culture, and Society in Beethoven's Vienna'. In Robert Winter and Robert L. Martin (eds.), *The Beethoven Quartet Companion* (Berkeley, CA: University of California Press, 1994), pp. 77–109.

Bourdieu, Pierre. *Distinction: A Social Critique of the Judgement of Taste*. Trans. Richard Nice (Cambridge, MA: Harvard University Press, 1984; original French ed., 1979).

Brandenburg, Sieghard (ed.), *Ludwig van Beethoven: Briefwechsel; Gesamtausgabe*, 8 vols. (Munich: Henle, 1996–8).

Brown, Maurice J. E. *Essays on Schubert* (London: Macmillan, 1966).

Budde, Gunilla-Friederike. 'Harriet und ihre Schwestern: Frauen und Zivilgesellschaft im 19. Jahrhundert'. In Ralph Jessen and Sven Reichardt (eds.), *Zivilgesellschaft als Geschichte: Studien zum 19. und 20. Jahrhundert* (Wiesbaden: VS Verlag für Sozialwissenschaften, 2004), pp. 327–43.

'Stellvertreterkriege: Politik mit Musik des deutschen und englischen Bürgertums im frühen 19. Jahrhundert'. *Zeitschrift für moderne europäische Geschichte* 5/1 (2007), pp. 95–118.

Bunzel, Anja, and Natasha Loges (eds.), *Musical Salon Culture in the Long Nineteenth Century* (Woodbridge: Boydell & Brewer, 2019).

Buurman, Erica. *The Viennese Ballroom in the Age of Beethoven* (Cambridge: Cambridge University Press, 2022).

Cambini, Giuseppe [Friedrich Rochlitz]. 'Ausführung der Instrumentalquartetten'. *Allgemeine musikalische Zeitung* 6/47 (22 August 1804), cols. 781–3.

Castelvecchi, Stefano. 'Sentimental and Anti-Sentimental in *Le nozze di Figaro*'. *Journal of the American Musicological Society* 53/1 (2000), pp. 1–24.

Castil-Blaze [François-Henri-Joseph Blaze]. *Dictionnaire de musique moderne*, vol. 1 (Paris: Au magasin de musique de la Lyre moderne, 1821).

Chaouli, Michel. *The Laboratory of Poetry: Chemistry and Poetics in the Work of Friedrich Schlegel* (Baltimore, MD: Johns Hopkins University Press, 2002).

Chapin, Keith. 'The Visual Traces of a Discourse of Ineffability: Late Eighteenth-Century German Published Writing on Music'. In Cliff Eisen and

Alan Davison (eds.), *Late Eighteenth-Century Music and Visual Culture* (Turnhout: Brepols, 2017), pp. 123–53.

Charlton, David. *French Opera 1730–1830: Meaning and Media* (Aldershot: Ashgate, 2000).

Christensen, Thomas. 'Four-Hand Piano Transcription and Geographies of Nineteenth-Century Musical Reception'. *Journal of the American Musicological Society* 52/2 (1999), pp. 255–98.

'Public Music in Private Spaces: Piano-Vocal Scores and the Domestication of Opera'. In Kate van Orden (ed.), *Music and the Cultures of Print*, Critical and Cultural Musicology (New York: Garland Publishing, 2000), pp. 67–93.

Clark, Michele Leigh. 'The Performance and Reception of Rossini's Operas in Vienna, 1822–1825'. PhD diss. (University of North Carolina at Chapel Hill, 2005).

Cox, Hugh Bertram, and C. L. E. Cox (eds.), *Leaves from the Journals of Sir George Smart* (London: Longmans, Green & Co., 1907).

Cypess, Rebecca. 'Ancient Poetry, Modern Music, and the *Wechselgesang der Mirjam und Debora*: The Meanings of Song in the Itzig Circle'. *Bach* 47/1 (2016), pp. 21–65.

Women and Musical Salons in the Enlightenment (Chicago, IL: University of Chicago Press, 2022).

Cypess, Rebecca, and Nancy Sinkoff (eds.), *Sara Levy's World: Gender, Judaism, and the Bach Tradition in Enlightenment Berlin* (Rochester, NY: University of Rochester Press, 2018).

Czerny, Carl. *Briefe über den Unterricht auf dem Pianoforte vom Anfange bis zur Ausbildung als Anhang zu jeder Clavierschule* (Vienna: Diabelli & Co., 1839).

Complete Theoretical and Practical Piano Forte School, vol. III (London: R. Cocks & Co., 1839).

On the Proper Performance of All Beethoven's Works for the Piano. Ed. Paul Badura-Skoda (Vienna: Universal Edition, 1970).

School of Practical Composition, vol. I (London: R. Cocks & Co., 1830).

Vollständige theoretisch-practische Pianoforte-Schule von dem ersten Anfange bis zur höchsten Ausbildung fortschreitend, und mit allen nöthigen, zu diesem Zwecke eigends componirten zahlreichen Beispielen, in 3 Theilen (Vienna: Diabelli & Comp., 1839).

Dahlhaus, Carl. *Nineteenth-Century Music* (Berkeley, CA: University of California Press, 1989).

Daub, Adrian. *Four-Handed Monsters: Four-Hand Piano Playing and Nineteenth-Century Culture* (Oxford: Oxford University Press, 2014).

Daviau, Donald G. 'Biedermeier: The Happy Face of the Vormärz Era'. In Robert Pichl, Clifford A. Bernd and Margarete Wagner (eds.), *The Other Vienna: The Culture of Biedermeier Austria* (Vienna: Lehner, 2002), pp. 11–27.

Davies, Stephen. 'Versions of Musical Works and Literary Translations'. In *Musical Understandings and Other Essays on the Philosophy of Music* (Oxford: Oxford University Press, 2011), pp. 177–87.

Davis, John A. 'Opera and Absolutism in Restoration Italy, 1815–1860'. *The Journal of Interdisciplinary History* 36/4 (2006), pp. 569–94.

Davison, Alan. 'Franz Liszt and the Development of 19th-Century Pianism: A Re-Reading of the Evidence'. *The Musical Times* 147/1896 (2006), pp. 33–43.

De Alwis, Lisa. 'Censorship and Magical Opera in Early Nineteenth-Century Vienna'. PhD diss. (University of Southern California, 2012).

De Certeau, Michel. *The Practice of Everyday Life*. Trans. S. Rendall, 3rd ed. (Berkeley, CA: University of California Press, 2011).

DeNora, Tia. 'Musical Patronage and Social Change in Beethoven's Vienna'. *American Journal of Sociology* 97/2 (1991), pp. 310–46.

Deutsch, Otto Erich. *Schubert: A Documentary Biography* (London: Dent, 1946).

Deutsch, Otto Erich (ed.), 'Leopold von Sonnleithners Erinnerungen an die Musiksalons des vormärzlichen Wiens'. *Österreichische Musikzeitschrift* 16/2–4 (1961), pp. 49–62, 97–110, and 145–57.

Domokos, Zsuzsanna. '"Orchestrationen des Pianoforte": Beethovens Symphonien in Transkriptionen von Franz Liszt und seinen Vorgängern'. *Studia Musicologica Academiae Scientiarum Hungaricae* 37/2–4 (1996), pp. 249–341.

Du Montet, Alexandrine Prévost de la Bouteitère de Saint-Mars. '1825, Vienne – Paris, 1826'. In *Souvenirs de la Baronne du Montet, 1785–1866*, 2nd ed. (Paris: Plon-Nourrit et Cie, 1904), pp. 263–96.

Dwight's Journal of Music (1852–81).

Eagleton, Terry. *Ideology: An Introduction*, rev. ed. (London: Verso, 2007).

Eibach, Joachim. 'Die Schubertiade: Bürgerlichkeit, Hausmusik und das Öffentliche im Privaten'. Themenportal Europäische Geschichte (2008), www.europa.clio-online.de/2008/Article=307.

Erickson, Raymond. 'Music in Biedermeier Vienna'. In Robert Pichl, Clifford A. Bernd, and Margarete Wagner (eds.), *The Other Vienna: The Culture of Biedermeier Austria* (Vienna: Lehner, 2002), pp. 227–41.

Schubert's Vienna (New Haven, CT: Yale University Press, 1997).

Esse, Melina. 'Rossini's Noisy Bodies'. *Cambridge Opera Journal* 21/1 (2009), pp. 27–64.

Everist, Mark. 'Reception Theories, Canonic Discourses, and Musical Value'. In Nicholas Cook and Mark Everist (eds.), *Rethinking Music* (Oxford: Oxford University Press, 1999), pp. 378–402.

Eybl, Martin. *Sammler*innen: Musikalische Öffentlichkeit und ständische Identität, Wien 1740–1810* (Bielefeld: Transcript, 2022).

Fellinger, Imogen. *Periodica Musicalia (1789–1830)* (Regensburg: Bosse, 1986).

Ferris, David. 'Public Performance and Private Understanding: Clara Wieck's Concerts in Berlin'. *Journal of the American Musicological Society* 56/2 (2003), pp. 351–408.

Fétis, François-Joseph. *Traité de l'accompagnement de la partition sur le piano ou l'orgue* (Paris: Pleyel et Cie, 1829).

Fillafer, Franz L. *Aufklärung habsburgisch: Staatsbildung, Wissenskultur und Geschichtspolitik in Zentraleuropa, 1750–1850* (Göttingen: Wallstein, 2021).

Fried, Michael. *Absorption and Theatricality: Painting and Beholder in the Age of Diderot* (Berkeley, CA: University of California Press, 1980).

Fuhrmann, Wolfgang. 'Gescheiterte Kanonisierungen: Drei Fallstudien zu Hasse, Paisiello und C. Ph. E. Bach'. In Klaus Pietschmann and Melanie Wald-Fuhrmann (eds.), *Der Kanon der Musik: Theorie und Geschichte; Ein Handbuch* (Munich: Text+Kritik, 2013), pp. 160–96.

 'The Intimate Art of Listening: Music in the Private Sphere during the Nineteenth Century'. In Christian Thorau and Hansjakob Ziemer (eds.), *The Oxford Handbook of Listening in the 19th and 20th Centuries* (Oxford: Oxford University Press, 2019), pp. 277–312.

Gingerich, John M. '"Those of us who found our life in art": The Second-Generation Romanticism of the Schubert-Schober Circle, 1820–1825' In Christopher H. Gibbs and Morten Solvik (eds.), *Franz Schubert and His World* (Princeton, NJ: Princeton University Press, 2014), pp. 67–113.

Goehr, Lydia. *The Imaginary Museum of Musical Works: An Essay in the Philosophy of Music*, rev. ed. (Oxford: Oxford University Press, 2007).

Goehring, Edmund. *Three Modes of Perception in Mozart: The Philosophical, Pastoral, and Comic in* Così fan tutte (Cambridge: Cambridge University Press, 2004).

Goldstein, R. J. 'Political Censorship of the Opera'. In *Political Censorship of the Arts and the Press in Nineteenth-Century Europe* (London: Palgrave Macmillan, 1989), pp. 155–74.

Good, Edwin M., and Cynthia Adams Hoover. 'Designing, Making, and Selling Pianos'. In James Parakilas (ed.), *Piano Roles: Three Hundred Years of Life with the Piano* (New Haven, CT: Yale University Press, 1999), pp. 31–71.

Goozé, Marjanne E. 'What Was the Berlin Jewish Salon Around 1800?' In Rebecca Cypess and Nancy Sinkoff (eds.), *Sara Levy's World: Gender, Judaism, and the Bach Tradition in Enlightenment Berlin* (Rochester, NY: University of Rochester Press, 2018), pp. 21–38.

Gradenwitz, Peter. *Literatur und Musik in geselligem Kreise: Geschmacksbildung, Gesprächsstoff und musikalische Unterhaltung in der bürgerlichen Salongesellschaft* (Stuttgart: Steiner, 1991).

Gramit, David. 'Selling the Serious: The Commodification of Music and Resistance to it in Germany (circa 1800)'. In William Weber (ed.), *The Musician as Entrepreneur, 1700–1914: Managers, Charlatans, and Idealists* (Bloomington, IN: Indiana University Press, 2004), pp. 81–101.

Green, Emily, and Catherine Mayes (eds.). *Consuming Music: Individuals, Institutions, Communities, 1730–1830* (Rochester, NY: University of Rochester Press, 2017).

Griesinger, Georg August. *Biographische Notizen über Joseph Haydn* (Leipzig: Breitkopf und Härtel, 1810).

Grodd, Uwe (ed.). *J. N. Hummel: Mozart's Six Grand Symphonies* (Wellington: Artaria Editions, 2015).

Grüß, Hans. 'Bearbeitung – Arrangement – Instrumentation als Form der Aneignung musikalischer Werke von Beethoven bis Schubert'. In Andreas Michel (ed.), *Ansichtssachen: Notate, Aufsätze, Collagen* (Altenburg: Kamprad, 1999), pp. 387–92.

Habermas, Jürgen. *The Structural Transformation of the Public Sphere: An Inquiry into a Category of Bourgeois Society*. Trans. Thomas Burger and Frederick Lawrence (Cambridge, MA: MIT Press, 1989).

Hansemann, Marlise. *Der Klavier-Auszug: von den Anfängen bis Weber* (Leipzig: Mayen, 1843).

Hanslick, Eduard. *Geschichte des Concertwesens in Wien* (Vienna: Braumüller, 1869).

Hanson, Alice M. *Die zensurierte Muse: Musikleben im Wiener Biedermeier* (Vienna: Böhlau, 1987).
  'Incomes and Outgoings in the Vienna of Beethoven and Schubert'. *Music & Letters* 64/3–4 (1983), pp. 173–82.
  Musical Life in Biedermeier Vienna (Cambridge: Cambridge University Press, 1985).
  'Vienna, City of Music'. In Raymond Erickson (ed.), *Schubert's Vienna* (New Haven, CT: Yale University Press, 1997), pp. 98–118.

Heindl, Waltraud. 'People, Class Structure, and Society'. In Raymond Erickson (ed.), *Schubert's Vienna* (New Haven, CT: Yale University Press, 1997), pp. 36–54.

Heinemann, Michael. 'Der Bearbeiter als Autor: Zu Franz Liszts Opernparaphrasen'. In Hans-Joachim Hinrichsen and Klaus Pietschmann (eds.), *Jenseits der Bühne: Bearbeitungs- und Rezeptionsformen der Oper im 19. und 20. Jahrhundert* (Kassel: Bärenreiter, 2011), pp. 88–92.

Hellyer, Roger. '"Fidelio" für neunstimmige Harmonie'. *Music & Letters* 53/3 (1972), pp. 242–53.

Heyden-Rynsch, Verena von der. *Europäische Salons: Höhepunkte einer versunkenen weiblichen Kultur* (Zurich: Artemis & Winkler, 1992).

Hinrichsen, Hans-Joachim, and Klaus Pietschmann (eds.), *Jenseits der Bühne: Bearbeitungs- und Rezeptionsformen der Oper im 19. und 20. Jahrhundert* (Kassel: Bärenreiter, 2011).

Hoffmann, E. T. A. 'Recension. ... Sinfonie ... No. 5'. *Allgemeine musikalische Zeitung* 12/40 (4 July 1810), cols. 630–42.

Hoffmann, Freia. *Instrument und Körper: Die musizierende Frau in der bürgerlichen Kultur* (Frankfurt am Main: Insel Verlag, 1991).
  'Klang und Geschlecht: Instrumentalpraxis von Frauen in der Ideologie des frühen Bürgertums'. *Neue Zeitschrift für Musik* 145/12 (1984), pp. 11–16.

Hogwood, Christopher. 'In Praise of Arrangements: the "Symphony Quintetto"'. In Otto Biba and David Wyn Jones (eds.), *Studies in Music History Presented to H. C. Robbins Landon on His Seventieth Birthday* (London: Thames and Hudson, 1996), pp. 82–104.

Holden, Amanda. *The New Penguin Opera Guide* (London: Penguin, 2001).

Hunter, Mary. *The Culture of Opera Buffa in Mozart's Vienna: A Poetics of Entertainment* (Princeton, NJ: Princeton University Press, 1999).

  '"To Play as if from the Soul of the Composer": The Idea of the Performer in Early Romantic Aesthetics'. *Journal of the American Musicological Society* 58/2 (2005), pp. 357–98.

Jahn, Michael. *Di tanti palpiti ... : Italiener in Wien*, Schriften zur Wiener Operngeschichte 3 (Vienna: Der Apfel, 2006).

Johnson, Claudia L. '"Giant HANDEL" and the Musical Sublime'. *Eighteenth-Century Studies* 19/4 (1986), pp. 515–33.

Jones, David Wyn. *Music in Vienna: 1700, 1800, 1900* (Woodbridge: Boydell & Brewer, 2016).

  The Symphony in Beethoven's Vienna (Cambridge: Cambridge University Press, 2006).

Jones, Lindsay. 'Music by the Ducat: Giuliani's Guitar and Vienna's Musical Markets, 1806–1819'. PhD diss. (University of Toronto, 2020), www.proquest.com/openview/31a49f74db3f24bd68d88f5310fb2d7b/1?pq-origsite=gscholar&cbl=18750&diss=y.

Kamatovic, Tamara. 'Censorship, Secrets, Correspondences, and Freedom: The Literary Public in the Viennese Biedermeier'. PhD diss. (University of Chicago, 2020).

Keefe, Simon P. *Mozart in Vienna: The Final Decade* (Cambridge: Cambridge University Press, 2017).

  Mozart's Piano Concertos: Dramatic Dialogue in the Age of Enlightenment (Woodbridge: Boydell & Brewer, 2001).

Kennerley, Philippa Jane. '"We always know when we are acting wrong": Performance and Theatricality in Jane Austen's Works'. MA thesis (University of Otago, 2013), https://ourarchive.otago.ac.nz/handle/10523/3961.

Kerman, Joseph. 'A Few Canonic Variations'. In Robert von Hallberg (ed.), *Canons* (Chicago, IL: University of Chicago Press, 1983), pp. 107–25.

Kier, Herfrid. 'Kiesewetters historische Hauskonzerte. Zur Geschichte der kirchenmusikalischen Restauration in Wien'. *Kirchenmusikalisches Jahrbuch* 52 (1968), pp. 95–119.

Kiesewetter, Raphael Georg. *Geschichte der europaeisch-abendlaendischen oder unsrer heutigen Musik* (Leipzig: Breitkopf & Härtel, 1834).

King, Margaret. 'Opera and the Imagined Nation: Weber's *Der Freischütz*, Schinkel's Neues Schauspielhaus and the Politics of German National Identity'. In Suzanne M. Lodato, Suzanne Aspden, and Walter Bernhart (eds.), *Word and Music Studies: Essays in Honor of Steven Paul Scher and on Cultural Identity and the Musical Stage* (Amsterdam: Rodopi, 2002), pp. 217–28.

Klitzing, Andrea. *Don Giovanni unter Druck: Die Verbreitung der Mozart-Oper als instrumentale Kammermusik im deutschsprachigen Raum bis 1850* (Göttingen: V & R Unipress, 2020).

'W. A. Mozart: Don Giovanni. Arrangements – Gedruckt im deutschsprachigen Raum bis 1850' (2020), www.vandenhoeck-ruprecht-verlage.com/media/pdf/c3/2f/03/TABELLE-V-R-W-A-MOZART-DON-GIOVANNI-ARRANGEMENTSJJ7FAJWC1dwHu.pdf.

Klorman, Edward. 'The First Professional String Quartet? Reexamining an Account Attributed to Giuseppe Maria Cambini'. *Notes, the Quarterly Journal of the Music Library Association* 71/4 (2015), pp. 629–43.

Mozart's Music of Friends: Social Interplay in the Chamber Works (Cambridge: Cambridge University Press, 2016).

Knaus, Kordula. 'Fantasie, Virtuosität und die Performanz musikalischer Inspiration: Pianistinnen und Pianisten in Wien um 1800'. In Patrick Boenke and Cornelia Szabó-Knotik (eds.), *Virtuosität*, Anklaenge: Wiener Jahrbuch für Musikwissenschaft (Vienna: Mille-Tre, 2013), pp. 57–73.

Koch, Heinrich Christoph. *Musikalisches Lexikon* (Frankfurt: August Hermann der Jüngere, 1802).

Koller, Walter, and Helmut Hell. *Aus der Werkstatt der Wiener Klassiker: Bearbeitungen Haydns, Mozarts und Beethovens* (Tutzing: Schneider, 1975).

Kord, Susanne. '"Und drinnen waltet die züchtige Hausfrau"? Caroline Pichler's Fictional Auto/Biographies'. *Women in German Yearbook* 8 (1992), pp. 141–58.

Kregor, Jonathan. 'Franz Liszt and the Vocabularies of Transcription, 1833–1865'. PhD diss. (Harvard University, 2007).

Liszt as Transcriber (New York, NY: Cambridge University Press, 2010).

Kroll, Mark. 'On a Pedestal and under the Microscope: The Arrangements of Beethoven Symphonies by Liszt and Hummel'. In M. Štefková (ed.), *Franz Liszt und seine Bedeutung in der europäischen Musikkultur* (Bratislava: Ustav hudobnej vedy SAV, 2012), pp. 123–44.

Kroll, Mark (ed.), *Mozart's* Haffner *and* Linz *Symphonies, Arranged for Pianoforte, Flute, Violin and Violoncello by J. N. Hummel*, Recent Researches in the Music of the 19th and Early 20th Centuries, vol. 29 (Madison, WI: A-R Editions, 2000).

Twelve Select Overtures, Arranged for Pianoforte, Flute, Violin and Violoncello by J. N. Hummel, Recent Researches in the Music of the 19th and Early 20th Centuries, vol. 35 (Middleton, WI: A-R Editions, 2003).

Ladenburger, Michael. 'Aus der Not eine Tugend? Beethovens Symphonien in Übertragungen für kleinere Besetzungen'. In *Von der Ersten bis zur*

Neunten: Beethovens Symphonien im Konzert und im Museum (Bonn: Beethoven-Haus, 2008), pp. 17–29.

Landon, H. C. Robbins and Dénes Bartha (eds.), *Joseph Haydn: Gesammelte Briefe und Aufzeichnungen* (Kassel: Bärenreiter, 1965).

Leopold, Silke. 'Von Pasteten und Don Giovanni's Requiem: Opernbearbeitungen'. In Silke Leopold (ed.), *Musikalische Metamorphosen: Formen und Geschichte der Bearbeitung* (Kassel: Bärenreiter, 2000), pp. 86–93.

Lindmaier, Hannah. 'Ortswechsel: Oper im Salon musizieren; Bearbeitungen als Teil der frühen *Fidelio*-Rezeption in Wien'. In Melanie Unseld and Julia Ackermann (eds.), *Beethoven.An.Denken: Das Theater an der Wien als Erinnerungsort* (Vienna: Böhlau, 2020), pp. 165–85.

Lindmayr-Brandl, Andrea. 'Music and Culture in Schubert's Vienna'. In Marjorie W. Hirsch and Lisa Feurzeig (eds.), *The Cambridge Companion to Schubert's 'Winterreise'* (Cambridge: Cambridge University Press, 2021), pp. 11–23.

Link, Dorothea. 'Vienna's Private Musical and Theatrical Life, 1783–92, as reported by Count Karl Zinzendorf'. *Journal of the Royal Musical Association* 122/2 (1997), pp. 205–57.

Liu, Chung-Mei. 'Die Rolle der Musik im Wiener Salon bis ca. 1830.' Master's thesis (University of Vienna, 2013).

Loesser, Arthur. *Men, Women and Pianos: A Social History* (New York, NY: Dover Publications, 1990).

Lott, Marie S. *The Social Worlds of Nineteenth-Century Chamber Music: Composers, Consumers, Communities* (Urbana-Champaign, IL: University of Illinois Press, 2015).

Mahling, Christoph-Hellmut. 'Zur Beurteilung der italienischen Oper in der deutschsprachigen Presse zwischen 1815 und 1825'. *Periodica Musica* 6 (1988), pp. 11–15.

Markx, Francien. *E. T. A. Hoffmann, Cosmopolitanism, and the Struggle for German Opera* (Leiden: Brill Rodopi, 2016).

Marshall, David. *The Surprising Effects of Sympathy: Marivaux, Diderot, Rousseau, and Mary Shelley* (Chicago, IL: University of Chicago Press, 1988).

Martin, Judith E. *Germaine de Staël in Germany: Gender and Literary Authority (1800–1850)* (Lanham, MD: Fairleigh Dickinson University Press, 2011).

Mathew, Nicholas, and Benjamin Walton (eds.), *The Invention of Beethoven and Rossini: Historiography, Analysis, Criticism* (Cambridge: Cambridge University Press, 2013).

McSherry, Hilary. '"Komm Hoffnung!" Hope, Opera and Diplomacy at the Congress of Vienna.' MA thesis (Dalhousie University, 2019).

Mettele, Gisela. 'Der private Raum als öffentlicher Ort: Geselligkeit im bürgerlichen Haus'. In Dieter Hein and Andreas Schultz (eds.), *Bürgerkultur im 19. Jahrhundert: Bildung, Kunst und Lebenswelt* (Munich: Beck, 1996), pp. 155–69.

Morrow, Mary S. *Concert Life in Haydn's Vienna: Aspects of a Developing Musical and Social Institution* (Stuyvesant, NY: Pendragon, 1989).

Moscheles, Charlotte. *Life of Moscheles, with Selections from His Diaries and Correspondence*, adapted from the original German by A. D. Coleridge, vol. 1 (London: Hurst and Blackett, 1873).

Mosel, Ignaz von. 'Uebersicht des gegenwärtigen Zustandes der Tonkunst in Wien'. *Vaterländische Blätter für den österreichischen Kaiserstaat* 1/6–7 (27 and 31 May 1808), pp. 39–44 and 49–54.

Mozart, W. A. *Le nozze di Figaro (Die Hochzeit des Figaro), Opera de W. A. Mozart arrangée en Quatuor à deux Violons, Alto & Violoncelle, Livere I u. II* (Bonn: Simrock, 1800).

Nemoianu, Virgil. *The Taming of Romanticism: European Literature and the Age of Biedermeier* (Cambridge, MA: Harvard University Press, 1984).

Newark, Cormac, and William Weber (eds.), *The Oxford Handbook of the Operatic Canon* (Oxford: Oxford University Press, 2020).

Novello, Vincent, and Mary Sabilla Hehl Novello. *A Mozart Pilgrimage: Being the Travel Diaries of Vincent and Mary Novello in the Year 1829* (London: Novello, 1955).

November, Nancy. *Beethoven's Symphonies Arranged for the Chamber: Sociability, Reception, and Canon Formation* (Cambridge: Cambridge University Press, 2021).

Beethoven's Theatrical Quartets: Opp. 59, 74 and 95 (Cambridge: Cambridge University Press, 2013).

Cultivating String Quartets in Beethoven's Vienna (Woodbridge: Boydell & Brewer, 2017).

'Die Streichquartette von Beethoven und Spohr: Ein Vergleich'. *Spohr Jahrbuch* 3 (2019), pp. 37–56.

'Louis Spohrs Salonmusik im Kontext'. *Spohr Jahrbuch* 5 (2021), pp. 9–30.

'Marketing Ploys, Monuments, and Music Paratexts: Reading the Title Pages of Early Mozart Editions'. In Cliff Eisen and Alan Davison (eds.), *Late Eighteenth-Century Music and Visual Culture* (Turnhout: Brepols, 2017), pp. 155–72.

'Performing, Arranging, and Rearranging the Eroica: Then and Now'. In Nancy November (ed.), *The Cambridge Companion to the* Eroica *Symphony* (Cambridge: Cambridge University Press, 2020), pp. 221–38.

'Picturing Nineteenth-Century String Quartet Listeners'. *Music in Art* 41/1–2 (2016), pp. 237–48.

'Theater Piece and Cabinetstück: Nineteenth-Century Visual Ideologies of the String Quartet'. *Music in Art* 29/1–2 (2004), pp. 134–50.

November, Nancy (ed.), *Chamber Arrangements of Beethoven's Symphonies. Part 1: Symphonies Nos. 1, 3, and 5 Arranged for Quartet Ensemble*, Recent Researches in Nineteenth-Century Music, vol. 75 (Middleton, WI: A-R Editions, 2019).

Chamber Arrangements of Beethoven's Symphonies, Part 2: Wellington's Victory and Symphonies Nos. 7 and 8 Arranged for String Quintet, Recent Researches in Nineteenth-Century Music, vol. 77 (Middleton, WI: A-R Editions, 2019).

Chamber Arrangements of Beethoven's Symphonies, Part 3: Symphonies Nos. 2, 4, and 6 Arranged for Large Ensembles, Recent Researches in Nineteenth-Century Music, vol. 78 (Middleton, WI: A-R Editions, 2020).

Osborne, Charles. *Schubert and His Vienna* (London: Weidenfeld and Nicolson, 1985).

Oswin, Matthew. 'Beethoven's "Kreutzer" Sonata: Nineteenth-Century Art of Arrangement – One Piece, Three Ways. MMus thesis (Victoria University of Wellington, 2013).

Parakilas, James. 'The Operatic Canon'. In Helen M. Greenwald (ed.), *The Oxford Handbook of Opera* (New York: Oxford University Press, 2014), pp. 862–80.

'The Power of Domestication in the Lives of Musical Canons'. *Repercussions* 4/1 (1995), pp. 5–25.

Pazdirek, Franz. *Universal-Handbuch der Musikliteratur aller Zeiten und Völker: Als Nachschlagewerk und Studienquelle der Welt-Musikliteratur eingerichtet und hrsg. von Pazdirek*, vol. 3 (Vienna: Pazdirek, 1904).

Peham, Helga. *Die Salonièren und die Salons in Wien: 200 Jahre Geschichte einer besonderen Institution* (Vienna: Styria Premium, 2013).

Perger, Richard von. *Geschichte der K. K. Gesellschaft der Musikfreunde in Wien,* vol. 1, *1812–1870* (Vienna: K. K. Gesellschaft der Musikfreunde in Wien, 1912).

Petrat, Nicolai. *Hausmusik des Biedermeier im Blickpunkt der zeitgenössischen musikalischen Fachpresse (1815–1848)* (Hamburg: Wagner, 1986).

'Musizierpraxis und Ideologie. Zur Hausmusik im 19. Jahrhundert'. *Das Orchester: Zeitschrift für Orchesterkultur und Rundfunk-Chorwesen* 38/5 (1990), pp. 494–500.

Pezzl, Johann. *Skizze von Wien*, vol. 1 (Vienna: Krauss, 1786).

Pichl, Robert, Clifford A. Bernd, and Margarete Wagner (eds.), *The Other Vienna: The Culture of Biedermeier Austria* (Vienna: Lehner, 2002).

Pichler, Anton (ed.), *Neuestes Sittengemählde von Wien* (Vienna: Pichler, 1801).

Pichler, Caroline. *Denkwürdigkeiten aus meinem Leben*, 4 vols. (Vienna: Pichler, 1844).

Piperno, Franco. 'Italian Opera and the Concept of "Canon" in the Late Eighteenth Century'. In Cormac Newark and William Weber (eds.), *The Oxford Handbook of the Operatic Canon* (Oxford: Oxford University Press, 2020), pp. 51–70.

Platoff, John. 'Mozart and His Rivals: Opera in Vienna in Mozart's Time'. *Current Musicology* 51 (1993), 105–11, Trinity College Digital Repository, https://digitalrepository.trincoll.edu/facpub/302.

Raynor, Henry. *Music and Society Since 1815* (London: Barrie and Jenkins, 1976).

Regondi, Giulio. *Fantasie über 'Don Giovanni' nach Sigismund Thalberg: Für Gitarre/Solo on Don Giovanni Partly from Thalberg's Piece: For Guitar*. Ed. Stefan R. Hackl (Vienna: Doblinger, 2008).

Reichardt, Johann Friedrich. *Vertraute Briefe geschrieben auf einer Reise nach Wien und den Oesterreichischen Staaten zu Ende des Jahres 1808 und zu Anfang 1809*, vol. 1 (Amsterdam: Kunst und Industrie-Comtoir, 1810).

Richards, Annette. *The Free Fantasia and the Musical Picturesque* (New York, NY: Cambridge University Press, 2000).

Rumph, Stephen. 'A Kingdom Not of This World: The Political Context of E. T. A. Hoffmann's Beethoven Criticism'. *19th-Century Music* 19/1 (1995), pp. 50–67.

Schneider, Herbert. 'L'arrangement d'opéras pour quatuor à cordes: Le cas de Guillaume Tell de Rossini'. In Joann Élert, Etienne Jardin, and Patrick Taïeb (eds.), *Quatre siècles d'édition musicale: Mélanges offerts à Jean Gribenski* (Brussels: Peter Lang, 2014), pp. 229–40.

Schönfeld, Johann Ferdinand von. *Jahrbuch der Tonkunst von Wien und Prag* (Vienna, 1796; repr. Munich: Katzbichler, 1976).

Schultz, Hartwig. *Salons der Romantik: Beiträge eines Wiepersdorfer Kolloquiums zu Theorie und Geschichte des Salons* (Berlin: De Gruyter, 1997).

Schwab, Heinrich W. 'Kammer-Salon-Konzertsaal: Zu den Aufführungsorten der Kammermusik, insbesondere im 19. Jahrhundert'. In Kristina Pfarr, Christoph-Helmut Mahling, and Karl Böhmer (eds.), *Aspekte der Kammermusik vom 18. Jahrhundert bis zur Gegenwart* (Mainz: Villa Musica, 1998), pp. 9–29.

Sealsfield, Charles [Karl Postl]. *Austria As It Is: or Sketches of Continental Courts, by an Eye-Witness* (London: Hurst and Chance, 1828).

Seibert, Peter. *Der literarische Salon: Literatur und Geselligkeit zwischen Aufklärung und Vormärz* (Stuttgart: Metzler, 1993).

Senici, Emanuele. '"An Atrocious Indifference": Rossini's Operas and the Politics of Musical Representation in Early-Nineteenth-Century Italy'. *Journal of Modern Italian Studies* 17/4 (2012), pp. 414–26.

  Music in the Present Tense: Rossini's Italian Operas in Their Time (Chicago, IL: University of Chicago Press, 2019).

Senner, Wayne M., Robinh Wallace, and William Meredith. *The Critical Reception of Beethoven's Compositions by His German Contemporaries*, 2 vols. (Lincoln, NE: University of Nebraska, 1999–2001).

Seyfried, Ignaz R. von. 'Louis van Beethoven: Troisième grande Sinfonie en *ut* mineur, (c-moll) Oeuvre 67; arrangée pour Pianoforte, avec accompagnement de Flûte, Violon, et Violoncelle, par *J. N. Hummel* . . . '. *Caecilia: Eine Zeitschrift für die musikalische Welt* 10/39 (1829), pp. 174–8.

Siegert, Christine. 'Autograph – Autorschaft – Bearbeitung. Überlegungen zu einer Dreiecksbeziehung'. In Ulrich Krämer, Armin Raab, Ullrich Scheideler, and Michael Struck (eds.), *Das Autograph – Fluch und Segen: Probleme und Chancen für die musikwissenschaftliche Edition; Bericht über die Tagung der Fachgruppe Freie Forschungsinstitute in der Gesellschaft für Musikforschung, 19.–21. April 2013*, Jahrbuch 2014 des Staatlichen Instituts für Musikforschung Preußischer Kulturbesitz (Mainz: Schott, 2015), pp. 99–112.

'Semantische Aspekte instrumentaler Opernbearbeitung'. In Hans-Joachim Hinrichsen and Klaus Pietschmann (eds.), *Jenseits der Bühne: Bearbeitungs- und Rezeptionsformen der Oper im 19. und 20. Jahrhundert* (Kassel: Bärenreiter, 2011), pp. 10–24.

Solie, Ruth A. 'Biedermeier Domesticity and the Schubert Circle: A Rereading'. In *Music in Other Words: Victorian Conversations*, California Studies in 19th-Century Music (Berkeley, CA: University of California Press, 2004), pp. 118–52.

Sonnleithner, Leopold von. 'Musikalische Skizzen aus "Alt-Wien"'. *Recensionen und Mittheilungen über Theater, Musik und bildende Kunst* 7/47 (1861), pp. 737–41 and 48, 753–7; 8/1 (1862), pp. 4–7; 8/12 (1862), pp. 177–80 and 8/24, pp. 369–75; and 9/20 (1863), pp. 305–25.

Sonnleitner, Johann. 'Vom Salon zum Kaffeehaus. Zur literarischen Öffentlichkeit im österreichischen Biedermeier'. In Robert Pichl, Clifford A. Bernd, and Margarete Wagner (eds.), *The Other Vienna: The Culture of Biedermeier Austria* (Vienna: Lehner, 2002), pp. 71–83.

Speight, Allen. 'Friedrich Schlegel'. In Edward N. Zalta (ed.), *The Stanford Encyclopedia of Philosophy* (2016), https://plato.stanford.edu/archives/win2016/entries/schlegel.

Spiel, Hilde. *Fanny von Arnstein: Daughter of the Enlightenment*. Introduced by Michael Wise (New York, NY: New Vessel Press, 2013).

Sponheuer, Bernd. *Musik als Kunst und Nicht-Kunst: Untersuchungen zur Dichotomie von "hoher" und "niederer" Musik im musikästhetischen Denken zwischen Kant und Hanslick*, Kieler Schriften zur Musikwissenschaft (Kassel: Bärenreiter, 1987).

Spontini, Gaspare. 'Le commencement de l'Ouverture de l'Opera: Fernand Cortez'. In *Anthologie musicale ou Recueil périodique pour le Forte-Piano/Musikalischer-Sammler für das Forte-Piano* (Vienna: Artaria & Co., n.d.).

Szendy, Peter. *Arrangements, dérangements: La transcription musicale aujourd'hui* (Paris: Ircam L'Harmattan, 2000).

Listen: A History of Our Ears. Trans. Charlotte Mandell, foreword by Jean-Luc Nancy (New York, NY: Fordham University Press, 2008).

Tanner, Matthew. 'Chemistry in Schlegel's Athenaeum Fragments'. *Forum for Modern Language Studies* 31/2 (1995), pp. 140–53.

Temperley, Nicholas, and Peter Wollny. 'Bach Revival'. *Grove Music Online* (2001), https://doi.org/10.1093/gmo/9781561592630.article.01708.

Thongsawang, Chanyapong. 'Opernparaphrasen für Klavier in der ersten Hälfte des 19. Jahrhunderts als Quellen für die Aufführungspraxis'. PhD diss. (University of Music and Performing Arts, Vienna, 2015).

Thormählen, Wiebke. 'Playing with Art: Musical Arrangements as Educational Tools in van Swieten's Vienna'. *Journal of Musicology* 27/3 (2010), pp. 342–76.

Thormählen, Wiebke, Jeanice Brooks, and Katrina Faulds. 'Music, Home and Heritage' project, www.rcm.ac.uk/research/projects/musichomeandheritage/.

Traeg, Johann. 'Nachricht an die Musikliebhaber'. *Wiener Zeitung* 16 (25 February 1784), pp. 395–6.

Triest, Johann Karl Friedrich. 'Bemerkungen über die Ausbildung der Tonkunst in Deutschland im achtzehnten Jahrhundert'. *Allgemeine musikalische Zeitung* 3/14 (starting on 11 March 1801), cols. 225–35; 15, cols. 241–9; 16, cols. 257–64; 17, cols. 273–86; 18, cols. 297–308; 19, cols. 321–31; 22, cols. 369–79; 23, cols. 389–401; 24, cols. 405–10; 25, cols. 421–32, and 26, cols. 437–45. Trans. Susan Gillespie as 'Remarks on the Development of the Art of Music in Germany in the Eighteenth Century', in Elaine Sisman (ed.), *Haydn and His World* (Princeton, NJ: Princeton University Press, 1997), pp. 321–94.

Vago, Alexandra A. 'Musical Life of Amateur Musicians in Vienna, ca. 1814–1825: A Translated Edition of Leopold von Sonnleithner's "Musikalische Skizzen aus 'Alt-Wien'" (1861–1863)'. MA thesis (Kent State University, 2001).

Van Dine, Kara L. 'Musical Arrangements and Questions of Genre: A Study of Liszt's Interpretive Approaches'. PhD diss. (University of North Texas, 2010).

Vellutini, Claudio. 'Italian Opera in *Vormärz* Vienna: Gaetano Donizetti, Bartolomeo Merelli and Habsburg Cultural Policies in the Mid-1830s'. In Axel Körner and Paulo M. Kühl (eds.), *Italian Opera in Global and Transnational Perspective: Reimagining Italianità in the Long Nineteenth Century* (Cambridge: Cambridge University Press, 2022), pp. 96–112.

Vick, Brian E. *The Congress of Vienna: Power and Politics after Napoleon* (Cambridge, MA: Harvard University Press, 2014).

Waidelich, Till Gerrit. 'Das Opern-Potpourri: Musikalisches Kaleidoskop, ars combinatoria oder musikimmanente Pornographie?'. In Hans-Joachim Hinrichsen and Klaus Pietschmann (eds.), *Jenseits der Bühne: Bearbeitungs- und Rezeptionsformen der Oper im 19. und 20. Jahrhundert* (Kassel: Bärenreiter, 2011), pp. 127–39.

Waissenberger, Robert. *Wien 1815–1848: Bürgersinn und Aufbegehren: die Zeit des Biedermeier und Vormärz* (Vienna: Überreuter, 1986).

Waldoff, Jessica. 'Sentiment and Sensibility in *La vera costanza*'. In W. Dean Sutcliffe (ed.), *Haydn Studies* (Cambridge: Cambridge University Press, 1998), pp. 70–119.

Walton, Benjamin. *Rossini in Restoration Paris: The Sound of Modern Life* (Cambridge: Cambridge University Press, 2007).

Warsop, Keith. 'Spohrs Potpourris'. *Spohr Journal* 33 (2006), pp. 15–21, www.spohr-society.org.uk/spohr_journal_33_2006_p15_warsop_spohrs_potpourris.pdf.

Weber, William. 'The Contemporaneity of Eighteenth-Century Musical Taste'. *The Musical Quarterly* 70/2 (1984), pp. 175–94.

The Great Transformation of Musical Taste: Concert Programming from Haydn to Brahms (Cambridge: Cambridge University Press, 2008).

'The History of Musical Canon'. In Nicholas Cook and Mark Everist (eds.), *Rethinking Music* (Oxford: Oxford University Press, 1999), pp. 336–55.

'The Muddle of the Middle Classes'. *19th-Century Music* 3/2 (1979), pp. 175–85.

Music and the Middle Class: The Social Structure of Concert Life in London, Paris and Vienna between 1830 and 1848, 2nd ed. (Aldershot: Ashgate, 2004).

'Redefining the Status of Opera: London and Leipzig, 1800–1848'. *The Journal of Interdisciplinary History* 36/3 (2006), pp. 507–32.

Webster, James. 'The Creation, Haydn's Late Vocal Music, and the Musical Sublime'. In Elaine Sisman (ed.), *Haydn and His World* (Princeton, NJ: Princeton University Press, 1997), pp. 57–102.

Haydn's 'Farewell' Symphony and the Idea of Classical Style: Through-Composition and Cyclic Integration in His Instrumental Music (Cambridge: Cambridge University Press, 1991).

'Haydn's Sacred Vocal Music and the Aesthetics of Salvation'. In W. Dean Sutcliffe (ed.), *Haydn Studies* (Cambridge: Cambridge University Press, 1998), pp. 36–69.

Webster, James, and Mary Hunter (eds.), *Opera Buffa in Mozart's Vienna* (Cambridge: Cambridge University Press, 1997).

Wehmeyer, Grete. *Carl Czerny und die Einzelhaft am Klavier, oder, Die Kunst der Fingerfertigkeit und die industrielle Arbeitsideologie* (Zurich: Atlantis, 1983).

'Czerny, Carl'. In Ludwig Finscher (ed.), *Die Musik in Geschichte und Gegenwart: allgemeine Enzyklopädie der Musik*, 2nd ed., Personenteil vol. 5 (Kassel: Bärenreiter, 2001).

Weinmann, Alexander (ed.), *Johann Traeg: Die Musikalienverzeichnisse von 1799 und 1804* (Vienna: Universal Edition, 1973).

Weliver, Phyllis. *Mary Gladstone and the Victorian Salon: Music, Literature, Liberalism* (Cambridge: Cambridge University Press, 2017).

Whistling, Carl Friedrich. *Handbuch der musikalischen Literatur oder allgemeines systematisch-geordnetes Verzeichniss der in Deutschland und in den angrenzenden Ländern gedruckten Musikalien auch musikalischen Schriften und Abbildungen mit Anzeige der Verleger und Preise*, vol. 1 (Leipzig: Hofmeister, 1844–5), https://babel.hathitrust.org/cgi/pt?id=umn.31951002245016j&view=1up&seq=5.

Wieland, Christoph Martin. *Musarion oder die Philosophie der Grazien (Musarion or the Philosophy of the Graces)* (Leipzig: Reich, 1768).

Wiener Theaterzeitung (1806–60).

Wiener Zeitschrift für Kunst, Literatur, Theater und Mode (1816–49).

Wiener Zeitung (1703–).

Wilhelmy-Dollinger, Petra. *Der Berliner Salon im 19. Jahrhundert: 1780–1914* (Berlin & New York: De Gruyter, 1989).

Williams, Simon. 'The Viennese Theater'. In Raymond Erickson (ed.), *Schubert's Vienna* (New Haven, CT: Yale University Press, 1997), pp. 214–45.

Woodmansee, Martha. *The Author, Art, and the Market: Rereading the History of Aesthetics* (New York, NY: Columbia University Press, 1994).

Yates, W. E. *Theatre in Vienna: A Critical History, 1776–1995* (Cambridge: Cambridge University Press, 1996).

Ziegler, Anton. *Addressen-Buch von Tonkünstlern, Dilettanten, Hof- Kammer- Theater- und Kirchen-Musikern, Vereinen, Lehr- und Pensions-Instituten, Bibliotheken zum Behufe der Tonkunst; k.k. privil. Kunst- und Musikalien-Handlungen, Instrumentenmachern, Geburts- und Sterbtagen vorzüglicher Tonkünstler &c. in Wien* (Vienna: Strauß, 1823).

Index

Page numbers in *italic* or **bold** refer to a figure or table, respectively. Page numbers in ***bold italic*** indicate a music example.

Alessandri, Felice, 13, **23**
Allgemeine musikalische Zeitung, 20, 65
amateurs *see* dilettantes
André, Johann Anton, 133
Anfossi, Pasquale, 13, **23**
Arnstein, Fanny von, 79, 80, 85–94
Arnstein, Nathan Adam von, 86, 94
arrangements
   authorisation of, 151
   canon formation and, 124–36
   completeness of, 66, 151–4, 166–9
   genres for, 26–36, 148–50
   mass production of opera, 195–200
   multilingual, 56
   pedagogical and developmental, 46–7, 118, 133, 164–5, **166**, 213–20
   popularity of opera, 15, 21–2, **23**, **24**, 24–6, **56**, **57**, 148
   potpourris, 81–2, 155–6
   price of, 30, 33, 160–4
   'public' versus 'private' types, 220–2
   in salon repertoire, 99–100
   transformative nature of performance, 91–2
   as 'translation', 1, 22–6, 60–72
   see also piano music; string-quartet arrangements
arrangers, 36–8, 153, 169–72, 205–20
   see also Czerny, Carl; Hummel, Johann Nepomuk; Kiesewetter, Raphael Georg; Pössinger, Franz Alexander; Triebensee, Joseph
Artaria & Comp. (publisher)
   editions 'mit text', 201
   Mozart arrangements, **34**, 34–5, ***61***, 62, 63, **66**, 66–8, ***67***
   multilingual arrangements, 56
   Rossini arrangements, 148, 151–2, 153
   Spontini arrangements, 125
Auber, Daniel, 197

audience engagement, 15
   see also listening; repetition
Austen, Jane, 178

Bach, Johann Sebastian, 111–12
Barbaia, Domenico, 142–3, 182
Beaumarchais, Pierre, 78
Beethoven, Ludwig van
   as arranger, 37
   canonic status, 123–5
   chamber music, 21, 37
   conversation book comments on censorship, 122
   Czerny's transcriptions, 206
   financial data from, 164
   on noise of invasion, 130
   opera and theatrical works, 17–18
   rehearsal of his quartets, 65
   works
      Egmont, 202
      Fidelio, 140
      variations based on Paisiello's *La molinara*, 15, 134–5
Bellini, Vincenzo, 197, 208–9, ***209***, 212, 216, 217–18, ***220***
Berlinische musikalische Zeitung, 19
Bermann, Moritz, 92
Bertuch, Carl, 90
Bianchi, Francesco, **23**
Biba, Otto, 42, 49, 95, 114–15
Biedermeier, use of term, 81, 180–1, 184, 185, 187–8
Biedermeier domesticity, 223–30
Bildung, 52, 78, 109–13
Blum, Carl, 132
Böcking, Wilhelm, 106
Böhm, Joseph, 114–15
Boieldieu, François-Adrien, **142**
Borgondio, Gentile, 142
Brown, Maurice, 227–9

247

Brunati, Gaetano, **14**
Budde, Gunilla, 95
Burgtheater, 12–13, 18, 89, 138

Campi, Antonia, 54
canon formation, 103–36
    'classic' music and, 113–20, 135–6
    female amateur pianists' role, 131–4, 164–5
    opera split from instrumental music, 131–6
    pedagogical canon, 108, 113, 133
    performing canon, 84, 108, 133
    politics and, 120–31
    professional performance and, 109–12
    salon as a centre for, 104–9
    scholarly canon, 108, 143–4
    shared experience via arrangements, 116–17
Cappi & Diabelli (publishers), 146, 157–65, **159**, **162**, **165**, **166**
Carpani, Giuseppe, 90
Casti, Giovanni Battista, **14**
Castil-Blaze (François-Henri-Joseph Blaze), 113, 119
Cavalieri, Caterina, 12
censorship, 121–2, 138–9
Certeau, Michel de, 47
chamber music, 21–2, 26–36
    see also arrangements and individual genres
Cherubini, Luigi, 15, 19, 33, 45
children, as performers, 46–7, 133, 164–5, **166**, 193
choral music, 106
Christensen, Thomas, 205, 222
Cimarosa, Domenico, 13, **23**, **28**, **29**
Clark, Michele Leigh, **134**, 134–5, 138, 140–1
Clary family, 193–4, **194**
class
    dilettantes, 47–9, 55
    equalising effect of chamber music, 45, 51
    genres and instruments, 43–7, 49
    in opera plots, 13–14, 78
    salons and, 79–80, 95–6, 115–16
classic music, 113–20, 135–6
comedy, 84–5
composers
    and arrangement, 20–2, 36–8, 151, 205–13
    and opera, 12–19
    popularity, 22–4, **23**, **139**, 139, 141, **142**, 197
    see also individual composers
concert life, 20–1
    see also salons
Congress of Vienna, 79, 80, 90, 92–4, 121, 157
copyright, 33
csakan music, 146, 150, 198

Cypess, Rebecca, 75, 89
Czerny, Carl
    as arranger, 185, **186**, 196, 205–20, **207**, *214*, **217**, *220*
    female pianists, dedication to, 133, 187
    Le goût moderne, 213–15, **215**, 216
    Pfennig-Magazin, 198–200, **199**
    Souvenir théâtral, 208–12, *209*, *219*, *220*
    as teacher, 193, 194, 222
    variations on *Zelmira*, 146

Da Ponte, Lorenzo, 13, **14**
Dahlhaus, Carl, 176
dances, based on opera themes, 156
Danzi, Franz, 132
Daviau, Donald, 120, 121, 179, 184
Dembscher, Ignaz Anton Aloys, 115
Diabelli, Anton (publisher; Cappi & Diabelli *later* Diabelli & Co.)
    csakan and guitar music, 146, *149*, 149, 150
    dance music, 156
    music sets and series, 157–65, **165**, **166**
        Euterpe, 134–5, 157–64, **159**, **162**, **163**
        Le goût moderne, 213–15, **215**, 216
        Philomele, 197
        Souvenir théâtral, 208–12, *209*, *219*, *220*
    pedagogical editions, 47, 133
    Rossini arrangements, **56**, 56, **57**, 134–5, 146, 148, *149*, 149, 150, 156, 157–60, **160**, **162**, 164–5, **165**
    third publishing catalogue, 196–7
Diderot, Denis, 178
dilettantes
    canon formation role, 131–4
    definition, 76
    gender and class, 47–50, 55
    musical preferences, 54–9
    performance skill and standards, 47–50, 60–72
    public music-making role, 190–5
    Viennese accounts of, 50–3
domesticity, *Biedermeier*, 223–30
Donizetti, Gaetano, 182, 197
duets
    flute or violin, 31, 32, 44–5
    piano, 69, 157–60, **160**, 213, 216–17, **217**
Dukaten Konzerte, 157
Duschek, Josepha, 53
Dwight, John Sullivan, 207

Eisner, Anton, 45
equality, chamber-music and, 45, 51
Euterpe series (Diabelli), 134–5, 157–64, **159**, **162**, **163**
Everist, Mark, 104

Fellinger, Imogen, 197
female participation
  as arrangers, 47–9
  Biedermeier domesticity and, 223–30
  canon formation, 131–4, 164–5
  genres and instruments played, **43**, 44, 47, 49–50, 198
  musical education of children, 46–7, 133, 164–5, **166**
  piano playing
    canon formation, 131–4, 164–5
    function and benefits, 46, 69–72, 98–102, 164–5
    Paradis' piano salons, 98–100
    popularity of, 49, 53, 190–5
    Reichardt's account of Fanny and Henriette von Arnstein, 91–2
    Ziegler's *Addressen-Buch*, 193–5
  as salon hosts, 52, 85–94, 95–102
  singing, 53–4, **54**, 99–100
Fétis, François-Joseph, 188
Fier, Jean Baptiste, **57**
Fioravanti, Valentino, 83, 84
flute music, 31, 32, 44–5, 148–9, 150, 198
folk music movement, 56–8
Fordo, Josephine, 172
foreign musicians, 50, 51, 55
four-hand piano arrangements, 69, 157–60, **160**, 213, 216–17, **217**
Francis I, Emperor, 80
French opera, 19, 125–31, 140, **141**, 197
Frischling, Franz, 107
Fröhlich sisters, 109–10, **110**, 112–13

Gallenberg, Wenzel Robert von, **142**
Gazzaniga, Giuseppe, 13, **23**
Gelinek, Joseph, 59, 81
gender, **43**, 43–7, 49–50, 115, 117, 194, 198
  see also female participation; male participation
genres
  for opera arrangements, 26–36, 148–50
  performer class and gender, **43**, 43–7, 115
  Rossini's blurring of, 174–5
Genzinger, Maria Anna von, 47–8
German language, 25–6, 94, 138–40, 147–8, 205
German nationalism, 59, 92–4, 138–40
German opera and Singspiele, 25–6, 56, 138–40, **141**
Gesellschaft der Musikfreunde, 91, 101, 106, 193
Giuliani, Mauro, **56**, **57**, 84, 149–50, 157, *159*
Gluck, Christoph Willibald, 93

Goldoni, Carlo, **14**
goût moderne, Le (Czerny, pub. Diabelli), 213–15, **215**, 216
Graf, Conrad, 189
Greiner, Franz Sales von, 41
Grétry, André, 37
Griesinger, Georg August, 16
Grillparzer, Franz, 122
Guglielmi, Pietro Alessandro, 13, **14**, **23**, **29**
guitar music, 50, 146, *149*, 149–50, 157, *159*, 213
Gutzwiller, Sebastian, 223, **224**
Gyrowetz, Adalbert, 56, **57**, 141, **142**

Haibel, Jakob, 56–8, **58**
Handel, George Frideric, 90–1, 118
Hanslick, Eduard, 36, 52–3, 76, 78, 84, 104, 105, 179–80, 190–3
Harmoniemusik (wind ensembles), 26–7, **29**, 30, 33, 44, 45–6, **58**
Harnisch, Johann, 45
harp music, 50
Haslinger, Tobias (publisher), 125, 133, 190, **191**
Hatwig, Otto, 107
Haydn, Joseph, 15–16, 21, 36–7, 47–8, 111
Heinemann, Michael, 208, 212
Hellmesberger, Georg, 110
Himmel, Friedrich Heinrich, **56**
Hochenadl, Josef, 73–4
Hochenadl, Katharina, 73–4, 82, 100–1, 109, 193
Hochenadl salons, 73–4, 82–5, 100–2, 107–8, 109, 110
Hofburgtheater, 12–13, 18, 89, 138
Hoffmann, E. T. A., 123, 204
Hofmeister, Adolf, 195–6
Hoftheater, K. K., 182–4, **183**, 185–6
Höllmayer, Anton, 45
Holz, Karl, 65
Hönig, Anna ('Nettel'), **225**, **228**, 230
Hummel, Johann Nepomuk, 59, 153, 157
Hunter, Mary, 15
Hutschenreiter, Adam, 111
Hutschenreiter, Johann, 130

instruments, **43**, 43–7, 49–50, 148–50, 194
  see also genres; piano developments
Isouard, Nicolo, **57**, **142**
Italian opera, 13–15, **14**, 19–20, 21, 24–5, 55–6, **56**, **57**, 138, 140–3, **141**, 182

Jahn, Michael, 141
Jansa, Leopold, 190, *192*

Jewish people, 85–7, 90–1, 94
Jones, David Wyn, 33
Joseph II, Emperor, 11, 12, 13, 25, 69, 85, 138
Journal für Quartetten Liebhaber, **139**, 139

Kärntnertortheater, 36, 45, 84, 111, 126, 137, 138, 140–3, **141**, **142**, 182
Kerman, Joseph, 118
Kiesewetter, Raphael Georg, 101, 109, 111–12, 121, 135
Kinsky, Josef, **142**
Klein, George, 45
Klitzing, Andrea, 94, 202–3
Kobold, Karl, 223
Koch, Heinrich Christoph, 31, 44, 67–8
Kord, Susan, 96
Kuffner, Christoph, 122
Kurzböck, Magdalene von, 90, 92

Lange, Aloisia (née Weber), 99
language, 25–6, 94, 138–40, 147–8, 205
Laucher, Antonia Juliana, 54
Laucher, Cäcilia, 54
Leidesdorf and Sauer (publishers), **152**, 152–3
Leidesdorf, Maximilian Joseph, 132
Liechtenstein, Prince Alois, 45
Lindmayr-Brandl, Andrea, 120
Link, Dorothea, 20, 25, 53, 77
listening, 105, 112–13, 204, 212–13, 227, 229
Liszt, Franz, 189, 212
Loesser, Arthur, 189–90
Lott, Marie, 41–2

male participation, **43**, 43–6, 52–3, **54**, 79, 194
Maria Theresa, Empress, 49, 80, 85
Martín y Soler, Vicente, 13, **14**, 22, **23**, **24**, 24, **28**, **29**
Martinez, Marianne von, 26, 51
Mayseder, Joseph, 84, 157, *158*, 170–2
Méhul, Étienne, **142**
Metternich System, 41, 120–3, 138–9, 179–81
Meyerbeer, Giacomo, 90, 133, **217**, *219*
Milder-Hauptmann, Pauline Anna, 54
military music, 45, 47, 150, 151–2
Militz, Maler, **130**, 131
mixed quintets (wind and strings), 32
Mollo, Tranquillo (publisher), 63, *64*, 69, *70*, *71*
Montet, Baroness de, 96
Moscheles, Ignaz, 84, 90, 122, 174, *175*
Mosel, Ignaz von, 46, 49–50, 51, 54–6, 90, 91–2, 109
Mozart, Constanze, 23–4
Mozart, Wolfgang Amadeus

and Fanny von Arnstein, 89
arrangements of his operas
  numbers and variety, 22–4, **23**, **24**, 25, 30, 33, **34**, 34–6, **35**, **43**, 43
  piano, 69, *70*, *71*, 132
  quintet, 25
  string-quartet, **28**, *60*, 60–9, *61*, *64*, *67*, 202
  wind ensemble, **29**, 45
  works based on operas, 82, 190, **191**, *192*
as arranger, 37, 52
his fortepiano, 97–8
and opera, 11, 12–13, 16–17, **17**, 19
popularity, **14**, 22–4, **23**, **24**, 30, **142**, 197
Vienna dubbed 'Klavierland' by, 195
works
  La clemenza di Tito, **29**, **35**, 45
  Così fan tutte, **29**, **35**, 45
  Don Giovanni, 26, 27, **28**, **29**, **35**, 38, 45, 63, *64*, 180, 202–3, 213
  Die Entführung aus dem Serail, 13, **28**, **29**, **35**, 69, *70*, *71*, 89
  Le nozze di Figaro, **14**, **24**, 24, 26, 27, **34**, 34–5, **35**, **43**, 43, *61*, 62, 63–5, 66–8, *67*, 78, 180, 190, *192*, 202
  Der Schauspieldirektor, **17**
  Die Zauberflöte, 1, 25–6, **28**, **29**, **35**, 46, *60*, 60–2, 82, 93–4, 140, **142**
Müller, Sophie, **110**
Müller, Wenzel, 85
Müllner, Josephine, 50
multilingual arrangements, 56
music series, 157–65, **165**, **166**, 197–9
  Euterpe (Diabelli), 134–5, 157–64, **159**, **162**, **163**
  goût moderne, Le (Czerny, pub. Diabelli), 213–15, **215**, 216
  Pfennig-Magazin (Czerny, pub. Haslinger), 198–200, **199**
  Philomele (Diabelli), 197
  Souvenir théâtral (Czerny, pub. Diabelli), 208–12, **209**, **219**, **220**
musikalische Biene, Die (Hoftheater), 182–4, **183**, 185–6
Musikalische Damen-Journal (Steiner & Comp.), 132–3

Napoleon, 126–7, 130
nationalism, 59, 92–4, 138–40
Naumann, Johann Gottlieb, 97
Nestroy, Johann, 111, 121
Neuling, Vinzenz, 111
Newark, Cormac, 119, 135

Nicolini, Ernesto, 83, 84
noisy music, 130, 144, 175–6, 216–17, 225–6

'ohne Worte' arrangements, 200–3
opera
   appeal, for composers, 18–19
   as classic repertoire, 113–15
   French, 19, 125–31, 140, **141**, 197
   German and Singspiele, 25–6, 56, 138–40, **141**
   Italian, 13–15, **14**, 19–20, 21, 24–5, 55–6, **56, 57**, 138, 140–3, **141**, 182
   plots, 13–14, 25, 57–8, 78, 173
   political significance, 92–4
   popularity in Vienna, 12–14, **14**, 140–3, **142**, 148
opera buffa, 13–15, **14**, 21, 24–5
orchestras, 20–1, 45
overtures, 35, 153

Paër, Ferdinando, 33, 54, 56, 84
Paisiello, Giovanni, 13, **14**, 15, 22, **23**, **24**, 24, 25, **28**, **29**, 135
Palomba, Giuseppe, **14**
Paradis, Maria Theresia von, 97, 98–102, 110–11
Parakilas, James, 103, 116–17, 118, 119–20, 131, 135
parlour music, 117–18
pedagogical arrangements, 46–7, 133, 164–5, **166**, 213–20
pedagogical canon, 108, 113, 133
Pereira-Arnstein, Henriette von, 86, 91–2, 95
performance standards, 47–50, 109–12
performers, role in realising arrangements, 60–72
performing canon, 84, 108, 133
Pergolesi, Giovanni Battista, 119
Petrosellini, Giuseppe, **14**
Pettenkoffer, Anton von, 107
Pezzl, Johann, 87
Pfennig-Magazin (Czerny, pub. Haslinger), 198–200, **199**
Philomele series (Diabelli), 197
piano developments, 97–8, 130, 188–90, 226–7
piano music
   capacity to reproduce orchestral music, *127*, 130, 188–90
   'complete' editions, 151
   diversity of opera arrangement types, 205–13
   diversity of skill level, *167*, 167–9, *170*
   female market for, 46–7, 132–3, 198
   four-hand arrangements, 69, 157–60, *160*, 213, 216–17, **217**
   mass production, 195–200

'ohne worte' arrangements, 200–3
Pichler's salons, 97–8
sets and series, 134–5, 157–64, **159**, *160*, **162**, **163**, **166**
Traeg's 1799 catalogue, 30–1
Traeg's 1804 supplement, 33
variations on opera themes, 15, 30, 58–9, 190
see also female participation; piano playing
piano-quartet arrangements, 32
piano-trio arrangements, 32
Pichler, Anton, 50–1
Pichler, Caroline (née von Greiner), 41, 80, 95–8
Pierperno, Franco, 119
Platoff, John, 13–14, **14**
plot types, opera, 13–14, 25, 57–8, 78, 173
political context, 41, 120–3, 138–9, 177–81, 182
Pössinger, Franz Alexander, 59, 150, 153–4, **154**
Postl, Karl Anton ('Charles Sealsfield'), 123, 131, 164, 179–80
potpourris, 81–2, 155–6
private and public music-making, 40–2, 51–3
   see also salons
professionalism, 109–12
publishers and publishing
   canon formation, 124–5
   female market for, 46–7, 132–3, 198
   genres for opera arrangements, 26–36, **28**, **29**, **43**, 43–4
   Hoftheater's *Die musikalische Biene*, 182–4, **183**, 185–6
   mass production, 195–200
   'ohne worte' arrangements, 200–3
   pedagogical arrangements, 46–7, 133, 164–5, **166**, 213–20
   popularity of opera arrangements, 21, 22–6, **23**, **24**, 33, 56–9, 79, 125, **134**, 134, 190, **191**
   Rossini arrangements, **134**, 134, 145–72
publishing catalogues
   Hofmeister's 1844, 195–6
   salon repertoire deduced from, 79
   Senefelder, Steiner, and Haslinger, 1830s and 1840s, 190, **191**
   Steiner and Haslinger's, 125
   Traeg's 1799, 1, 21, 22–6, **23**, **24**, 27–32, **28**, **29**, **43**, 43–4
   Traeg's 1804 supplementary, 33
Puffendorf, Baroness von, 51

quartet arrangements, 25
   see also piano-quartet arrangements; string-quartet arrangements
quintet arrangements, 25, 32, 44

Raimund, Ferdinand, 121
Randhartinger, Benedict, 172
Rathmayer, Mathias, 55
Regondi, Giulio, 213
rehearsal, or lack of, 65
Reichardt, Johann Friedrich, 89–90, 91–2
repetition, 15, 156, 157, 165, 174
review, public, 105, 116
Righini, Vincenzo, 13, **23**, **29**
Rochlitz, Friedrich, 65
Rohrer, Ignaz, 111
Romantic movement, 204–5
Rossini, Gioachino, 137–81
    arrangements of his operas, 145–72
        contents of, 151–4
        ensemble choices, 148–50
        in *Musikalische Damen-Journal*, 132–3
        types, aligned with criticisms, 173–6
        works based on operas, 155–72
    critical dissent about, 143–5, 173–6
    popularity, 137–43, **142**, 148, 173–81, 197
    theatricality of his operas, 176–81
    works
        Il barbiere di Seviglia, **147**, 147
        La gazza ladra, 144, 153–4
        L'italiana in Algeri, **56**, **57**, 150
        Otello, 158, **160**, 172
        Le siège de Corinthe, **167**, 167–9, ***170***
        Tancredi, **56**, **57**, 137, 141–2, **142**, ***149***, 149, 150, **154**, 154, 157, ***158***, ***159***, 173, 174, ***175***
        Zelmira, 143, 146, 150, 151–2
Rumph, Stephen, 123

Salieri, Antonio, 13, **14**, 22, **23**, **28**, **29**
Salonmusik, 76–7, 81–5
salons, 7, 75–80
    Fanny von Arnstein's, 79, 80, 85–94
    canon formation and, 104–9
    educational function, 98–100
    exclusivity or openness of, 51–2, 95–6, 116
    Josef Hochenadl's, 73–4, 82–5, 100–2, 107–8, 109, 110
    Raphael Kiesewetter's, 109, 111–12
    male leadership, 52, 79
    Maria Theresia von Paradis', 98–102, 110–11
    Parisian compared with Viennese, 78–9
    Caroline Pichler's, 95–8
    political and cultural significance, 74–5, 79–80, 92–4, 123–4
    repertoire, 25, 82–5, 97, 107–8, 110–12, **114**, 114–16
    Ignaz Rohrer's, 111
    Ignaz von Sonnleithner's, 106, **114**, 114–15, 128, 130
    as training for musical professionals, 109–12
Sarti, Giuseppe, 13, **14**, **24**, **28**, **29**
Sauer and Leidesdorf (publishers), **152**, 152–3
Schenk, Johann Baptist, **142**
Schikaneder, Emanuel, 57–8
Schlegel, Friedrich, 86, 88–9
Schleiss, Ferdinand, 45
Schmid, Julius, **110**, 112–13
Schmidt, Johann Phillipp Samuel, 126
Schmiedel, Johann, 111
Schneider, Jean Herbert, 153–4, 165
Schoberlechner, Franz, 153, ***167***, 167–9
scholarly canon, 108, 143–4
Schönfeld, Johann Ferdinand von, 20–1, 26, 47, 49, 51, 52, 91, 98, 99
Schörtzel, Franz Joseph Rosinack, **58**, 58
Schubert, Franz
    and chamber music, 21, 80
    home and salon music-making, 95, 106–7, 112
    and opera, 18, **228**
    Schubertiades, 79, 109–10, **110**, 112, **225**, 227
Schuppanzigh, Ignaz, 116
Schwind, Moritz von, **225**, 227–30
scores, 203–4
Sealsfield, Charles (Karl Anton Postl), 123, 131, 164, 179–80
semi-private music-making, 42, 51–3
semi-public music-making, 42
Senefelder, Steiner, and Haslinger (publishers), **190**, **191**
Senici, Emmanuele, 144, 145, 173–4, 176, 177
sextets, 32
singers and singing
    choral music, 106
    as female music-making, 53, 100
    influence on arrangements, 213, ***214***
    interpretation as arrangement, 172
    Mosel's list of, **54**, 54–5
    salon music-making, 98–100, 107
Singspiele (German opera form), 25–6, 56, 138–40, **141**
Smart, Sir George Thomas, 115, 116
Solie, Ruth, 184, 223, 229
Sollerer, Johann, 1, **2**
Sonnleithner, Ignaz von, 106, **114**, 114–15, 128, 130
Sonnleithner, Joseph Ferdinand, 91
Sonnleithner, Leopold von

as amateur musician, 106, 109
on Rossini's popularity, 137, 144
on salons, 75–6, 104–7
    Hochenadl's, 73, 77, 82–3, 108
    Kiesewetter's, 111–12
    Paradis', 98, 99–100
    Zizius', 117
Souvenir théâtral (Czerny, pub. Diabelli), 208–12, ***209***, ***219***, ***220***
Spazier, Johann Gottlieb Carl, 19
Spielmann, Franziska von, 91–2
Spina, Friedrich Joseph, 149, 150
Spohr, Dorette, 71
Spohr, Louis, 71, 81–2, 83, 97, 155
Spontini, Gasparo, 19, 78, 115, 125–31, ***127***, ***129***, ***130***, ***142***
Starke, Friedrich, **57**, 150, 151–2
Stein, Johann Andreas, 98
Steiner, Franz, 45
Steiner, Sigmund Anton, 124–5, 148
Stohl, Eleonore, 230
Storace, Stephen, **14**, **23**, **24**, **28**, **29**
Streicher, Johann Andreas, 91–2, 189
Streicher, Nannette, 97–8
string-quartet arrangements
    canon formation, 106, 115–16
    ideal for opera, 44, 195–6
    as male music-making, 44, 52–3
    Pössinger's, 59, 150, 153–4
    role of the performers, ***60***, 60–9, ***61***, ***64***
    Schneider's study of Rossini opera arrangements, 153–4, 165
    text, presence or absence, 202
    Traeg's 1799 catalogue, 27–8, **28**, 30, 32
    Traeg's 1804 supplement, 33
    Wranitzky's arrangement of *Fernand Cortez*, 126, ***129***
string-quintet arrangements, 32, 44
Stumpf, Johann Christian, 31
sublime, the, 63, 128–30
Süßmayr, Franz Xaver, 54
Swieten, Gottfried van, 52
Szendy, Peter, 212, 222

text, presence or absence, 200–3
Thalberg, Sigismund, 169, ***170***, 213
theatre and theatricality, 11, 77–8, 84–5, 97, 107–8, 137–43, 176–81
    Burgtheater, 12–13, 18, 89, 138
    Kärntnertortheater, 36, 45, 84, 111, 126, 137, 138, 140–3, ***141***, ***142***, 182

Theater auf der Wieden, 46, 57
    Volkstheater, 121
Thongsawang, Chanyapong, 208
title pages, language of, 94, 205
Tomaschek, Wenzel Johann, **57**
Traeg, Johann (publisher), 32–3
    1799 catalogue, 1, 21, 22–6, **23**, **24**, 27–32, **28**, **29**, **43**, 43–4
    1804 supplementary catalogue, 33
    Mozart opera arrangements, **35**, 35–6
Triebensee, Joseph, 45–6
Triest, Johann Karl Ferdinand, 16

Umlauf, Ignaz, 12–13

variations on opera themes, 15, 30, 58–9, 146, 156–7, 190
Vick, Brian, 78
Viennese currency, 161–4, **163**
violin music, 31, 44–5
vocal music *see* singers and singing
vocal text, 200–3
Vogl, Johann Michael, 126
Volkstheater, 121

Waissenberger, Robert, 184, 222
Waldoff, Jessica, 16
waltzes, based on opera themes, 156
Warsop, Keith, 82
Weber, Carl Maria von, 38, 56, 140, **142**, 189, 226
Weber, William, 108, 113, 119, 135
Webster, James, 16
Wehmeyer, Grete, 195, 211
Weigl, Joseph, 22, **23**, **28**, **29**, 30, 89, **142**
    Die Schweizer Familie, 36, 59, 78, 93, **142**
Whistling, Carl Friedrich, 196
Wiener musikalisches Pfennig-Magazin für das Piano-Forte allein (Czerny, pub. Haslinger), 198–200, **199**
Wiener Zeitung, 32, 146
Wilde, Josef, 156
Wilhelm Friedrich III, King, 127
wind ensembles (*Harmoniemusik*), 26–7, **29**, 30, 33, 44, 45–6, **58**
Winter, Peter, 19, 33, 36, 82
Wise, Michael, 87–8
women *see* female participation
Wranitzky, Anton, 126, ***129***
Wranitzky, Paul, 19, 37

Zerrissenheit, 121, 179
Ziegler, Anton, 49, 193–5, **194**
Zini, Francesco Saverio, **14**
Zinke, Friedrich, 45
Zinzendorf, Count, 41, 52, 53, 77
Zizius' salons, 117
Zmeskall, Nikolaus von, 115–16
Zois, Baroness, 51
Zulehner, Karl, 37–8

Printed by Printforce, United Kingdom